D1613357

University
for the
Creative Arts

Fort Pitt
Rochester
Kent   gatewayrochester@uca.ac.uk
ME1 1DZ   01634 888734

123127

Fashion
and
Politics

Fashion and Politics

Edited by Djurdja Bartlett

Yale University Press
New Haven and London

Contents

I.
Political Fashion,
Fashionable
Politics

Acknowledgements

The editor and the contributors are very grateful to Sophie Oliver, Art and Architecture Editor at Yale University Press, for her enthusiasm and encouragement in realising this project. We would like to extend our gratitude to Anjali Bulley at Yale for her support in finalising this book. Additionally, we would like to thank the copy-editor, Denny Hemming, for her care and attention, and Kathrin Jacobsen for her engaging design.

We would also like to thank the following individuals and institutions for their assistance, their permission to reproduce images, and generosity with regard to fees:

Alex Chatelain

Ana and Danko Steiner

Andrew Juries

Art Partner/ Tyler Mitchell

Artur Żmijewski / Galerie Peter Kilchmann, Zurich

Bahia Shehab

Central Saint Martins, UAL

Do Ho Suh / Lehmann Maupin, New York and Hong Kong

Getty Images

Iconic Images Ltd

Ivana Spinelli

Iziko Museums of South Africa

Kader Attia / Galleria Continua

Köken Ergun

London College of Fashion, UAL

Mary Boone Gallery, New York

Mella Jaarsma

Missoni

Musée de l'Histoire vivante, Paris

Osman Örsal

P R Consulting Paris / Raf Simons

Reuters

Rob Scott

Sharif Waked

Syd Shelton

The Nancy Spero and Leon Golub Foundation for the Arts / Hauser & Wirth

VETEMENTS

Victoria and Albert Museum / Elizabeth Wilson

Vogue Polska

Yoshua Okón / Mor Charpentier Gallery, Paris

Preface

Djurdja Bartlett

The world was stunned when, in March 2018, the whistleblower Christopher Wylie exposed the shady dealings of his former employer, the political consulting company Cambridge Analytica. It stood accused of inappropriately harvesting the Facebook profiles of more than 50 million people, in order to target them with political advertisements and so potentially influence the 2016 presidential elections in the United States, and the 2016 Brexit vote in the United Kingdom. *The Guardian*, followed by other leading political media, was crucial in offering Wylie a credible platform from which to elaborate on his work experiences, and address the wide societal consequences concerning the actions of Cambridge Analytica, in which, as an immensely talented data analyst and the company's Research Director, he played the most important role. The fashion media, however, not only acknowledged the political importance of his exposé, but also went into a frenzy describing Wylie's fashionable street-style looks. He was variably clad in a Raf Simons-lookalike jacket with photo collage patches, a T-shirt designed by New York streetwear brand Pleasures, a camouflage coach jacket from Canadian superstar The Weeknd's Merch Collection XO, a pair of Puma x Han Kjobenhavn trainers, and a neon-orange sweatshirt by Polish streetwear brand MISBHV, emblazoned with the name of the country's capital in Polish (fig. 1).[1]

A self-professed gay vegan, Canadian Wylie did not look like the typical whistleblower, customarily expected to deliver bombastic revelations in a neutral grey suit. Yet Wylie's sartorial choices have been closely related to his professional and academic interests. While working for Cambridge Analytica, Wylie started his PhD-related studies on fashion forecasting at the University of the Arts London. In academia, he planned to test his research hypothesis that sophisticated psychological profiles, based on harvested private and personal data, could be equally efficient in both fashion and political forecasting. He told *The Guardian* journalist Carole Cadwalladr that 'politics was like fashion'.[2] Referring to his meeting in 2013 with Steve Bannon, who would later become Donald Trump's chief strategist, Wylie clarified:

> *[Bannon] got it immediately. He believes ... that politics is downstream from culture, so to change politics you need to change culture. And fashion trends are a useful proxy for that. Trump is like a pair of Uggs, or Crocs, basically. So how do you get from people thinking 'Ugh. Totally ugly' to the moment when everyone is wearing them? That was the inflection point he was looking for.*[3]

FIG. 1
The whistleblower Christopher Wylie, sporting a sweatshirt by Polish streetwear brand MISBHV, March 2018
Photographer Dan Kitwood

9

For Wylie, grasping the significance of this ugly yet fashionable sartorial style was instrumental in imposing on the world its political equivalent: Donald Trump. Wylie further elaborated: 'People talk about how fashion reacted to politics. I don't actually agree with that. I think that fashion, music, and other visual media are very influential to politics and not the other way around.'[4] With his latest street-style fashion choices, his nose-ring, and his hair dyed variably grey, pink or green, Wylie has not only been far removed from a whistleblower's quiet normalcy; his clothes have also mapped a radical shift from the dark prince of fake news to a specific type of a fashion-conscious militant.

Indeed, political militancy has been performed in a range of sartorial guises. Bombarded by an endless stream of social media imagery, we are used to envisioning a contemporary militant as a person hiding behind a Guy Fawkes mask. Equally, we are prone to believe that all the feminists in the 1960s and 1970s had rejected fashion and femininity and were clad in a pair of baggy overalls and Dr Martens boots. The fashion designer Miuccia Prada, known for launching new fashion trends and wearing the most daring outfits from her collections, as well as for her membership of the Italian Communist Party in her youth, offers this interpretation: 'A clever woman can also be super-sexy, super-naked. She can be whatever she wants. I don't think there is a look for an intelligent, militant woman. She can wear anything she wants'.[5] Prada might be a contemporary trendsetter, but some of those militant women who preceded Mrs Prada were known to share a predilection for feather-embellished outfits in clashing colours. The scholar and writer Elizabeth Wilson lived and dressed in a way that merged her highly political agendas with her love of fashion at the beginning of the 1970s.

As a feminist, and one of the founders of the Gay Liberation Front, Wilson engaged in various political activities with the British Left, but this did not prevent her from wearing the latest fashions. As she describes in her autobiography, politics and fashion complemented each other in those politically and culturally turbulent times: 'In the Gay Liberation Front the hysterical peak of the hedonism of the late sixties and the moment of revolutionary fervour came together in an unrepeatable explosion'.[6] For her, it was not contradictory to wear clothes from the cult London boutique Biba while fighting for sexual freedom. When attending the first Gay Liberation Front ball at Kensington Town Hall in 1971, the first open, publicly-advertised gay event of its kind in the United Kingdom, Wilson donned an orange feather boa and a purple jersey dress, both bought at Biba, teamed with long purple boots from Anello & Davide, and an orange, black, purple and pink wool tank-top that she had hand-crocheted herself (fig. 2).[7]

Such sartorial statements show the close imbrication of fashion and politics. But the essays gathered in this book also acknowledge that there is no a simple answer to the question, 'Is fashion political?', and that fashion's engagement with the political may compromise political ideals and aims. Indeed, the book's contributors assess fashion's ambivalence within political, social and aesthetic moral systems.

Engaging in different disciplines – from philosophy to history, cultural anthropology, art history, visual culture, media studies, museology and curating – they attempt to establish a relevant discursive framework within which the relationship between fashion and politics can be addressed and explored. Consequently, they are able to draw into the conversation a diverse audience, from scholars to students, from fashion practitioners to the media and the general public. Structured around four key sections – Political Fashion/Fashionable Politics, Reform or Revolution, Bodies and Borders, and Resistance or Recuperation – this book moves away from the epistemological towards the performative. Instead of dealing with what fashion, style and dress mean and how they relate to each other, it investigates what these sartorial practices do in the visual realm of the political.

FIG. 2
Feather boa and purple
jersey dress from Biba, and
hand-crocheted tank-top, as
worn by Elizabeth Wilson to
the first Gay Liberation Front
ball at Kensington Town Hall,
London, 1971

In the first section, in the essay 'Can Fashion Be Defended?', Djurdja Bartlett contrasts Marx's strictly economic analysis of the commodity with the recent analyses that emphasise affective value in the commodity, thus enabling the investigation of contemporary transnational fashion as not only a complex economic enterprise, but also an emotionally charged phenomenon. Bartlett also discusses the well-established narrative of western modernity and its relationship with fashion, importantly investigated by, among others, Elizabeth Wilson, Christopher Breward and Caroline Evans.[8] Addressing a number of historical and contemporary case studies, Bartlett argues that modernity's, and fashion's, spread worldwide has nevertheless been tied up with the controversial advance of western capitalism, including the economic and cultural subjugation of less developed regions and brutal colonial conquests.

The second section, Reform or Revolution, opens with Barbara Vinken's philosophical essay, in which she revisits her highly original reading of western modernity, by focusing on the role of gender politics in the birth of fashion in the late eighteenth century. She maintains that fashion's disregard for the orders of class and gender continues to inform the perception of the phenomenon of fashion as 'an oriental tyranny' at the heart of western, masculine-led modernity. Focusing on the sartorial choices of the Chinese politician Wang Guangmei, who was shamed and imprisoned due to her alleged love of bourgeois-style fashions during the 1960s Cultural Revolution, Jin Li Lim's case study shows that fashion has mapped the uneven progress of modernity, and that, depending on the ideological framework, fashionable dress could be embraced or rejected. Driven by various political agendas, the late 1960s and early 1970s revolutionary fervour equally reverberated in the West, China and the United States. A smooth reform was not an option for the Chinese Red Guards, and it was even less so for the members of the Black Panther Party who invented their own revolutionary uniform, and activists in the late 1970s Rock Against Racism Movement. In her imaginative analysis, Carol Tulloch defines style activism as 'the embodied making of a political activist self', arguing that 'the styled body is a sincere identifier of the individual within an activist movement'.

Drawing on both historical and contemporary examples, Rhonda Garelick's essay 'Bombshell: Fashion in the Age of Terrorism' heads the third section, Bodies and Borders. Here, Garelick convincingly points to the uncomfortably close relationship between fashion, body, the culture of terror and commodified culture. She argues that discourses of fashion and terrorism equally deal with the possibilities of transgressing, overwhelming, or exploding the borders of the individual body and the body politic – either literally or figuratively. It is no coincidence that both Garelick and Gabi Scardi have chosen to accompany their respective essays with images by the Palestinian artist Sharif Waked, whose work at the same time highlights the vulnerability of individual and national borders and articulates our current culture of surveillance. Furthermore, reflecting on uniforms and their related rituals through the works of ten artists in her photo-essay, Scardi looks at the construction, representation and exercise of power, and its relationship to dress. Other contributors variably observe dress and fashion as performed, and politically relevant, practice at both individual and collective levels, showing that sartorial performance enables the cultural re-articulation of new and old hegemonies. Jane Tynan's essay on the historic and contemporary trajectory of the keffiyeh contextualises this scarf, originally worn by Palestinian peasants, within its vernacular culture, regional and world politics, and contemporary fashion.

The contributors in the last section, Resistance or Recuperation, address some of the contemporary burning issues in the practice and theory of dress. There is no doubt that modernity has, to a great extent, been a colonial project, and many museums throughout the world grapple with issues of race, class, tradition and modernity while revaluating their collections, facing similar challenges to those raised in Erica de Greef's photo essay on the process of decolonising the Iziko Museums in Cape Town, South Africa. But in the everyday, both personal and political, dress is revalued on a daily basis. Observing contemporary sartorial changes in the field of male-led institutional politics, Anthony Sullivan focuses on the recent sartorial styles of Europe's political Left, showing how its protagonists have shunned the male politicians' 'uniform', a conventional suit, and enacted their oppositional politics through oppositional styles of dress.

On the other hand, fashion's complicity with the global dispersion of commodity culture is unquestionable. Karl Marx and Friedrich Engels's statement – 'The bourgeoisie has through its exploitation of the world market given a cosmopolitan character to production and consumption in every country' – is even more valid today than in 1848 when the Communist Manifesto was published.[9] In his 1867 seminal work *Capital*, Marx had already detected the phenomenon of fast fashion, calling the ever-increasing seasonal changes 'the murderous, meaningless caprices of fashion',[10] and blaming them for the miserable life of textile workers, including children, on the factory floor and in their personal lives.[11] In his essay 'Thrown Away Like a Piece of Cloth', Serkan Delice investigates the exploitation of Syrian refugees in Turkish clothing production, which supplies fast fashion items to the global market. It seems that, in some parts of the world, not much has changed in the treatment of the poor and vulnerable, from Marx's time, through early twentieth-century workshop practices, and up to today. Delice argues for a new model that would comprise the interaction between textile workers and academia, so as to reconsider fashion 'in its entirety', including but no longer privileging the already well-established researches into its creative, aesthetic and immaterial aspects.

Yet, to return to the initial question. Can fashion, imperfect as it is, be defended? Bartlett maintains that, as an embodied everyday practice, fashion is endowed with the capacity to bring pleasure, to incite and transmit affect. Thus, in an era when politics is largely mistrusted, and increasingly divides people along lines of nation, class, race, sex and gender, fashion might effectively provide a means of challenging such dissension. As a globally dispersed, emotionally charged and highly visual practice in our image-saturated world, fashion may even go some way to repair old and new injustices, at the same time creating a bridge between politics and economics, so providing a platform for today's most urgent social and cultural conversations.

I

Political Fashion

Fashionable Politics

Can Fashion Be Defended?

Djurdja Bartlett

Fashionable objects are often dismissed as fetishistic commodities. And yet fashion is an embodied everyday practice, endowed with the capacity to bring pleasure, incite and transmit affect, as well as disturb authoritarian tendencies. These performative aspects of fashion are habitually ignored by the moral and gendered politics of consumption. While this essay does not question the role of fashion in capitalism, it does explore its performative power, both on a collective and individual level.

Fashion is a crucial element of modernity: its spread worldwide has been tied up with the controversial advance of western capitalism in all its expressions, including the economic and cultural subjugation of less developed regions and brutal colonial conquests. Yet, while accompanying the global march of capitalism, fashion has mapped the uneven progress of modernity, thus highlighting – and often resisting – the totalitarian, nationalistic and extreme religious spaces on the world map.

Thus fashion played a role in the national awakenings of mid-nineteenth-century Europe, and posed challenges to the authorities in interwar China, in socialist countries during the Cold War, and, more recently, in Iran and Poland. While such acts of performing national and individual identities are certainly complicit with commodity culture, they nevertheless show that sartorial performance enables the cultural re-articulation of new and old hegemonies. Precisely due to its universal, cosmopolitan appeal, fashion has facilitated, historically and today, new subjectivities as well as new looks. A critique of commodification does not take into account these complex social and personal relationships between the subject and her or his objects. In contrast to Marx's strictly economic analysis of the commodity, recent analyses suggest that affective value is always embedded in the commodity, ready to be activated and sustained by those who buy it. Contemporary transnational fashion is not only a complex economic enterprise, but also an emotionally charged phenomenon. The advanced spaces of digital transmission and exchange are inhabited by ghosts of the past, from the socialist to the colonial. Yet, endowed with political agency, and saturated with genuine pain, these spectres might help address old injustices, perhaps bringing change, not only in fashion but also in the wider world.

In this sense, the essay argues, through a range of historical and contemporary case studies, that fashion should not be dismissed but instead observed as an important social, cultural and political phenomenon. Its complicity with the global dispersion of commodity culture should not prevent us from investigating, and living, fashion as a site of shared pleasure which, in contrast to the divisive politics of the day, does not divide us along the lines of nation, race, sex and gender.

FIG. 3
Elisabeth von Österreich
Ungarn, Empress of Austria
and Queen of Hungary, 1867
Photographer Emil Rabending

Historically and today, fashion can be defended if we are to escape the interpretations that exclusively embed it in the framework of the commodification culture, as well as those that dismiss it as an ephemeral phenomenon.

The National

On 3 March 1864, the most distinguished French intellectuals and politicians attended a grand masked ball organised by the historian Jules Michelet in Paris. Although such balls are customary during Lent, this one, shrewdly mixing pleasure, dress and politics, was unique. Michelet and his wife Athénaïs, both fervent Republicans, asked their guests to mask themselves either as historical figures or nations, encouraging them to don the dress of the oppressed. Well known for exploring history by focusing on the people, and not solely its leaders or institutions, Michelet engaged the liberal-minded members of the French elite in political debates at his regular Thursday salon. On this special occasion, the guests gladly stretched their politics into the field of dress, and with France, indeed Europe, in social and political turmoil, inspiration was close by. In his diary Michelet wrote that 100 guests attended, and that the oppressed nations staged at the masquerade included Czech, Italian, Hungarian, Polish, Serbian, Venetian and Vlach.[1] The brothers Goncourt, who were among the attendees, prophetically observed that they 'seemed to watch dancing future revolutions in Europe'.[2]

For Michelet, this was not about entertainment. Bitterly regretting the failed 1848 bourgeois revolutions, the host and most of his guests took their liberal, antimonarchist beliefs seriously.[3] Under the masks of the oppressed nations, they dreamed of new political ruptures, resulting in successful bourgeois revolutions, not only in France, but also in a much wider geopolitical area, which, at the time, was under the control of the Austro-Hungarian, Russian and Ottoman empires.

Only three years after Michelet's ball, Elisabeth, Empress of Austria, known as Sissy, acknowledged as one of the most beautiful and stylish women of her era, performed her own political masquerade on the public stage. When she was crowned Queen of Hungary in 1867 she showed her presumed political sympathies towards the Hungarians with her choice of outfit, which was modelled on the Hungarian national gala costume: a white, richly embroidered dress with white lace apron, and black velvet bodice laced with heavy strings of pearls (fig. 3). The magnificence of the dress, which she commissioned from the Parisian House of Worth,[4] as well as its amalgamation of western elegance and domestic ethnic motifs, were meant to reassure Hungarians that they would be equal with Austria in the new dual monarchy. The highly fashion-literate Empress of Austria demonstrated impeccably that dress is about performing national as well as individual identities.

Dress and the new nation states

Such sartorial expertise was much needed. From the time of the 1848 revolutions, the Austro-Hungarian, Russian and Ottoman empires had been in turmoil, and dress played a crucial role in the processes of social and cultural modernisation, national awakening, dismantling of the three empires and establishing of the new European states following the end of the First World War. Whichever empire they lived under, various ethnicities wanted to free themselves from their oppressive rulers. They dreamed of establishing their own sovereign states, which would be organised around a concept of one nation. In order to put into practice the idea of the nation state, the emerging politics of national representation relied on common characteristics, such as language and history, but also needed strong visual statements to engage potential followers in the process of national awakening. In the second half of the nineteenth century, western fashion was vigorously rejected, and the search for new national dresses started in earnest.

Baró Hatvany Ferencné
(Pántlika szalon modelljében)

Gróf Széchenyi Hanna
(Holzer Simon modelljében)

Gróf Széchenyi Maja
(Paulette szalon modelljében)

Existing ethnic dress represented a myriad of cut, colour and adornment differences. Indeed, the geopolitics of dress demonstrates that there are no 'national dresses', but rather only local or regional dress. To confine them within political boundaries is an ideologised practice.[5] In order to unite all citizens of a new nation state under one banner, and to raise a new dress above all sartorial differences, ethnic quotations became geographically vague, amalgamating specific regional differences into an imaginary national dress.[6]

Once established, the concept of national dress, embellished with ethnic motifs, informed the concept of nationhood and national identity in Russia, Eastern Europe and Eastern Central Europe. Fashion magazines such as the Hungarian *Geranium* (*Muskátli*), founded in 1931, had an important role in promoting the nation state through the use of domestic ethnic motifs in dress and interiors, complementing Hungarian nationalist politics, itself very much mourning the country's lost territory and influence following the end of the First World War. Equally, the most prominent Hungarian designer in the interwar years, Klára Tüdős, fused a nationalist political agenda and elitist fashion in her Budapest haute couture salon Ribbon (Pantlika). She started her career as a costume designer for the Hungarian Royal Opera in Budapest, and, subsequently, her fashion relied on flamboyant interpretations of a glorious Hungarian past. The aesthetic culminated in 1938 at a gala event held at the Opera House, where, at the invitation of Magdolna Purgly de Jószáshely, the wife of the Hungarian Regent Miklós Horthy, the aristocratic female guests wore luxuriously embroidered evening outfits based on Hungarian gala dresses, all designed by Tüdős and other domestic salons (fig. 4).[7] Once more, circumstances outside fashion, in this case Horthy's right-wing politics, informed the perception and application of ethnic motifs.[8]

FIG. 4
'The Hungarian Opera Ball',
Theatre Life (*Színházi élet*),
no. 16, 1938

In the field of socialist fashion in the Soviet Union and the countries of the so-called Eastern bloc, the ethnic was also an ideologically informed quotation. As early as the 1920s, the Bolsheviks frowned on western fashion and its Art Deco opulence, and chose the ethnic as the least confrontational type of embellishment (fig. 5). Decorative but not fashionable, vernacular but purified to abstract lines, ethnic motifs were useful tools in the international promotion of the new socialist state as a modernist, yet visually unique project. Later, such timeless decoration perfectly suited Stalinist isolationism and its idea of uniqueness (fig. 6). Change became an ontological obstacle for the post-1920s system, organised around five-year plans and hierarchical levels of decision-making, as, in contrast to western fluidity and rapid change, the epic socialist master narrative expressed itself through the slow movement of time.[9]

Negotiating hegemonies

In contrast, from the late 1950s, socialist women's interest in fashionable dress took place in a parallel modernity, informed by a faster and more fragmented conception of time, and was performed through a range of minor practices such as home dressmaking, using the services of a dressmaker and purchases made on the black market, all discreetly approved by the consecutive regimes. Ephemeral, temporal, dispersed and rooted in the everyday, the practice of fashionable dress under socialism matched Michel de Certeau's definition of tactics. In contrast to strategies that seek to conquer visible and well-defined space, and master time and knowledge, in order to exercise their power, tactics are 'an art of the weak',

FIG. 5
Fashion drawing, *Art of Dressing (Iskusstvo odevatsiia)*, no. 8, 1928

FIG. 6
Ethnic motifs, *Soviet Woman (Sovetskaiia zhenschina)*, no. 4, 1946

their conception of space and time dispersed.[10] Fashion tactics introduced the political into socialist everyday life, a performing device enabling women to negotiate official strategies.

Fashionable dress universally signalled the arrival of modernity – and thus capitalism itself – from the mid-nineteenth century onward, yet its progress took place within the geographically uneven processes of industrial modernisation, colonial conquests, nation building, and media and market development. In this sense, Fredric Jameson's claim that there are not alternate and multiple modernities, such as 'a Latin-American kind, or an Indian kind or an African kind … [as] … this is to overlook the other fundamental meaning of modernity which is that of a worldwide capitalism itself',[11] is ultimately true, but too rigid. Fashion accompanies capitalism and its market economy on its global march, but its uneven advance highlights the totalitarian, nationalistic and extreme religious spaces on the global map, and threatens those powerful local players who prefer the status quo and fear change. While the global advance of western-informed modernity has been controversial in many ways, fashion has nonetheless functioned as a performative tool in opposing the autocratic and nationalistic regimes that have attempted to subjugate women through mandatory dress codes, or to discipline them by disapproving of fashion.

For example, in interwar China the fashionable *qipao* – a dress of simple cut with a high, side-closing collar, whose silhouette reflected contemporary western fashion (fig. 7) – became the ultimate nationalist sartorial statement when it was embraced by Soong May-ling, wife of the fervently nationalist Chiang Kai-shek. When, in 1934, Chiang Kai-shek launched the New Life Movement, a revival of traditional Confucian values, the *qipao*, with its revealing side slits and distinctly feminine textile patterns, was no longer ideologically acceptable. As the Movement's public face, Soong May-ling covered her refined *qipao* with a long military coat. And yet, in the booming mass culture of the mid-1930s, women's sartorial choices could not be ideologically imposed. For them, there was no way back to the traditional concept of submissive femininity. A long, curvy *qipao* was a self-assured statement, serving to show that women were becoming strong by engaging in sport, and glamorous by mimicking the stars of the latest films.

More recently, in Iran in 2018, some women opposed the hijab as compulsory dress by performing the staged ritual of removing their veils in public.[12] Perhaps even more challenging to the present regime and its ultra-conservative values is the visibility of western fashion brands on the streets of Tehran, where young women are openly dressed in the latest western fashions, their heads barely

FIG. 7
Qipao, *The Young Companion* (*Liangyou*), cover, no. 99, 1934

covered. If such acts of performing identity are complicit with commodity culture, and ultimately may not alter imbalances of power in gender relations, they show that fashion is capable of rearticulating hegemonies.[13] In very different cultural and geopolitical circumstances, women have negotiated their position, drawing on fashion's cosmopolitanism to disturb nationalist, conservative and religious narratives.

Fashion versus nationalism

These social categories still interact, and inform each other in ever new, but still uneven and contradictory ways. During the Cold War, the West was only too happy to criticise the boring style of socialist fashion. But this aesthetic has acquired new connotations in post-socialist times, and the previously dull has become a new cool, at least for some. The cover of the first issue of Polish *Vogue* (March 2018), shot by Juergen Teller outside Warsaw's Stalinist-era Palace of Culture and Science, caused mixed reactions within the country (fig. 8). Anja Rubik and Małgosia Bela – both of Polish origin and internationally well-known models – pose in minimalist Celine black coats by a mighty black Volga, the pride of the Soviet car industry. The likely inspiration for this image was a cover of the weekly magazine *Friendship* (*Przyjaźń*) from March 1960, in which the model is similarly depicted against the Palace of Culture, reclining on a black Volga. With her big hair, a conventional black-skirted suit, white gloves and white high-heeled shoes, she embodies socialist fashion chic at its best.

The iconography of the Polish *Vogue* cover shows Teller's rough and dark aesthetic, his willingness to challenge prevailing values and assumptions. In line with his other work, this cover is disturbing and provoking. One Polish commentator responded: 'Nothing there is ours, not the palace, not the car, not anything.'[14] Analysing the domestic reactions to this cover, Agata Pyzik and Michał Murawski observed 'a combination of hurt aesthetic feelings and wounded national pride', and stated that 'most Poles would rather have something along the lines of *Vanity Fair*: photoshopped, heavy on bling and celebrity', instead of such a strong visual reminder of their socialist past.[15]

Mario Testino's cover for the first issue of Russian *Vogue* (September 1998) and his accompanying editorial depict the latest western fashions against a backdrop of Moscow's stereotypical, tourist destinations.[16] It was meant for the New Russians, whom Condé Nast had detected as customers of the leading western fashion brands. Condé Nast made a different decision by choosing Juergen Teller to shoot its first Polish *Vogue* cover. The subject of Teller's cover is not the models, but the most controversial building in Warsaw, Stalin's 1955 'present' to the Polish nation. Inside the magazine, he has Rubik posing in a Versace evening dress against a pile of potatoes on a decayed parquet floor of the Palace. In another, she operates an industrial vacuum cleaner in its vast neoclassical hall, dressed in a long, equally special, Louis Vuitton gown. By interspersing his fashion editorial with portraits of

FIG. 8
First issue of Polish *Vogue*, cover, March 2018
Photographer Juergen Teller

CAN FASHION BE DEFENDED?

leading liberal or avant-garde public and cultural figures, Teller took an even more controversial stance in relation to the country's official, culturally and politically conservative values. The first was ex-president Lech Wałęsa, lauded and despised in equal measure in his homeland.

By preferring Teller's arty and unorthodox aesthetic, Condé Nast has shown that its targeted audience in Poland is not only interested in the 'cool' and expensive brands such as Celine, Gucci and Balenciaga, but is also artistic, educated and internationally minded. More significantly, Teller's imagery makes a political statement, as this section of society is largely on the other side of official ideology. Pyzik and Murawski acknowledge that the first issue of Polish *Vogue* is an attempt by its editors 'to demonstrate their rejection of the current regime's paranoid attitudes to history, sex and national identity' – referring to the ruling, right-wing Law and Justice Party, with its anti-communist and conservative agenda – yet lament that, without any 'leftwing representation in parliament ... the subversive political potential with which the Palace is imbued is so easily ironized, sexualized and commodified'.[17]

Indeed, such a representational intervention may not by itself bring political change. But why should a glossy magazine such as *Vogue* not be political? Is there not more to it than commerce? For fashion, says the art historian Boris Groys, 'is radically anti-utopian and anti-totalitarian: its constant shifts attest that the future is unpredictable and cannot escape historical change and that there exist no universal truths that might completely determine the future'.[18] The future may be ultimately unpredictable, perhaps, but the Marxist historian Eric Hobsbawm recognised that, in unstable times, fashion articulates a mood at large in culture and society more generally:

> Why brilliant fashion designers, a notoriously non-analytic breed, sometimes succeed in anticipating the shape of things to come better than professional predictors, is one of the most obscure questions in history, and, for the historian of culture, one of the most central. It is certainly crucial to anyone who wants to understand the impact of the age of cataclysms on the world of high culture, the elite arts, and, above all, the avant-garde.[19]

Fashion has – historically and today – a role to play in performing national identities, as well as individual identities in relation to political hegemonies. In order to explore Hobsbawm's 'obscure question' in more detail, it is necessary to look at fashion's relation to the commodity, which so often appears to restrict its political relevance.

The Commodified

In 2013, Franca Sozzani, the long-term editor-in-chief of Italian *Vogue*, stated in an interview: 'Here's what I think: fashion isn't really about clothes. It's about life. Go into the street, and you see it: everyone can afford fashion on some level, everyone can talk about it. So what else can we say? We can't always be writing about flowers and lace and aquamarine.'[20] Presenting her Autumn/Winter 2017–18

ready-to-wear collection in February 2017, Angela Missoni seemed to apply this approach by ending her show with the models wearing 'pussy' hats (fig. 9), the visual symbol of protest and female solidarity that first appeared a month earlier when hundreds of thousands of women filled the streets of cities across the United States and Europe in an unprecedented wave of rallies against US President Donald Trump, and his 2005 boasting statement about grabbing women's genitals.

In some ways it was a predictable fashion show, displaying Missoni's customary knits, love of colour and 1970s quirkiness. But at the end, surrounded by world-famous models and members of her family, all donning the 'pussy' hats, Missoni delivered a passionate speech:

> *I feel the need to recognize that in a time of uncertainty there is a bond*
> *that can keep us strong and safe, that unites those that respect all human*
> *rights. Let's show the world that the fashion world is united and fearless.*[21]

The show notes stated that Missoni 'communicates the femininity of our times, prepared to confront the conflicts and dilemmas of our contemporary society: the conditions, needs and rights of all women and all minorities'.[22] With some proceeds from the collection going to the American Civil Liberties Union and the UN Refugee Agency, the purpose of the hats had moved beyond a symbolic gesture.[23]

FIG. 9
Missoni, 'Pussy' hats,
Autumn/Winter 2017–18
Photographer Victor Boyko

At the very least, Missoni's pussy hats showed, once more, that fashion lives and breathes with its times. In September 2016, Christian Dior's artistic director Maria Grazia Chiuri pointed to this interaction between our cataclysmic world and the rarefied world of high fashion at her first show for the house, with T-shirts printed with the slogan 'We Should All Be Feminists'. The message was already well known as the title of a popular 2012 TED talk by the Nigerian author Chimamanda Ngozi Adichie, which she consequently turned into a book-length essay. Yet, the fashion world was taken by surprise with this political turn at the revered Parisian fashion house. Some questioned Chiuri's political stand, suggesting she was merely capitalising on a trend. In defence, Chiuri argued: 'You can be both. It's not a contradiction to be politically serious and take pleasure in fashion. Fashion can be about rebellion. It's always a conversation, always about curiosity, dynamism. And I need to understand my interlocutors.'[24]

If, by 'my interlocutors', she was referring to her customers, Chiuri's mission has been very successful, with Dior's fashion division posting £1.92bn in revenue for 2017.[25] Besides, regardless of their non-egalitarian price of £490, the T-shirts in question sold out.[26] Does Dior's expensive T-shirt, quite likely combined with an equally expensive designer bag and perfectly groomed hair, show that the owner is 'woke' or just showing off? Or does the three-figure price tag in fact suggest a shift in the politics of the social group that could afford high-end fashion: instead of choosing logoed outfits, they have opted for a T-shirt with a political slogan. Can fashion even have political, perhaps subversive potential or will its status as a commodity always compromise it? After all, fashion items cannot avoid the dominance of surplus value over exchange value or use value, whether their aesthetic is progressive or not. The things circulating in the field of fashion are often distrusted. Fashion is considered the pre-eminent commodity, tarnished with the label of the fetish.

In *Capital*, Karl Marx argues that the capitalist mode of production changed the status of the commodity from a mundane object, 'a trivial thing' as he calls it, into a fetishistic object: 'This I call the Fetishism which attaches itself to the products of labour, as soon as they are produced as commodities'.[27] Commodity fetishism is 'a definite social relation between men themselves which assumes here, for them, the "phantasmagoric" form of a relation between things'.[28] For Marx, a commodity on the market is robbed not only of the labour of its maker but also of any history, memory and emotion, indeed any personal relationship between subject and object. Describing Marx's life through the coat he wore to the British Library, the coat that went in and out of the pawnshop, Peter Stallybrass argues: 'To have one's own coat, to wear it on one's back, was to hold on to one's past and one's future. But it was also to hold on to a memory system that at a moment of crisis could be transformed back into money.'[29] He continues:

> The problem for Marx was thus not with fetishism as such but rather with
> a specific form of fetishism that took as its object not the animized object

of human labour and love but the evacuated nonobject that was the site of exchange. In the place of a coat, there was a transcendental value that erased both the making and wearing of the coat. Capital *was Marx's attempt to give back the coat to its owner.*[30]

Observing the extreme poverty of members of the working class while writing *Capital*, Marx fervently wanted them to have decent coats on their backs. Ontologically, Marx craved a world that was fast vanishing in the mid-nineteenth century, a world in which social relationships stayed natural and self-evident. In this sense, his phantasmagoria metaphor can be read as a lament that the world around him was becoming increasingly mediated.

As later interpreters of Marx's theories, such as Georg Simmel and Walter Benjamin, acknowledged, the connection between man and the products of his labour had been lost in the wake of the industrial era, but the emotions and feelings were transferred to the relationship between the consumer and the object. As early as 1889, Simmel focused on circulation, exchange and consumption, claiming that the subject's will, and not productive labour, is the source of an object's value.[31] Exploring urban life in nineteenth-century Paris, Benjamin recognised the varied histories informing the universe of commodities, from the history of production to those of circulation and consumption, as well as a history of collective fascination and desires.[32]

A critique of commodification does not take into account these complex relationships between the subject and her or his objects. As a result, fashionable objects are dismissed as fetishistic commodities, and pleasure is ignored by the moral and gendered politics of consumption. Discussing the erotics and aesthetic of consumption in *The Gender of Modernity*, Rita Felski claims:

> *To view modernity from the standpoint of consumption rather than production is to affect a shift in perspective which causes taken-for-granted phenomena to appear in new light. ... The belief that Western history has repressed erotic drives through a prevalent ethos of discipline and self-restraint is called into question by the central role of hedonistic desire and sexualized representation in the rise of modern consumerism.*[33]

But, Felski further emphasises, this approach has often been trivialised as, from the mid-nineteenth century, the consumer was frequently represented as a woman:

> *The feminization of modernity, however, is largely synonymous with its demonization. In the writings of many radical and conservative intellectuals from the mid-nineteenth century onward, the idea of the modern becomes aligned with the pessimistic vision of an unpredictable yet curiously passive femininity seduced by the glittering phantasmagoria of an emerging consumer culture.*[34]

And yet, precisely because consumer culture institutes fashion at the heart of the modern, it is possible to analyse its potential transgressive and political traits. Indeed, fashion and pleasure grew increasingly transgressive in the second half of the nineteenth century, with the working classes blurring social boundaries by enjoying dance venues, music halls, circuses and fashion, and so asserting themselves in a different, rather than perceived, role in society.[35] Within the emerging proletarian cultures, fashion had developed as one of working women's subcultures, combining traditional working cultures, such as making your own clothes, with the emerging mass media, which helped to spread a vivid interest in fashion.

FIG. 10
'Parisian Working Women'
('Les Ouvrières de Paris'), *VU*,
cover, no. 247, 1932

Fashion and female citizenship

By turning the masses of newly employed women into consumers of fashionable goods and readers of mass media, the proletarianisation of the commodity drive also turned them into modern subjects. If left-leaning thinkers and their socialist and communist media dismissed or ignored working women's interest in fashion, due to its complicity with capitalism and its exploitative nature, they eventually started to introduce fashion advice in their media outlets, hoping that it could lead towards engaging women as supporters of their policies, and as potential voters. After all, fashion was one of the social vehicles towards female citizenship, just as the suffragette movement was a political vehicle. Discussing the position of women in the 1920s Weimar Republic, Kathleen Canning claims that new female subjectivities, in part created by the extension of citizenship rights in 1920, were also crafted and performed through women's engagement with printed mass media, popular novels and films, which ultimately turned women into new citizens. She emphasises that these practices are 'worthy of critical reflection, both with respect to the history of women and the history of Weimar's modernity and viability as a site of new democratic publics'.[36]

In the 1920s and 1930s, liberal bourgeois magazines such as the French *VU* and German *UHU* tried to bridge the difference between middle-class and working-class women by depicting a female white-collar worker at work and in her everyday life. In *VU*, the photographers Germaine Krull and André Kertész introduced a new type of Parisienne onto the city map, both in its working-class faubourgs and glittering boulevards. They visit her at her modest dwellings and observe her shopping, while cramming their photographic depictions with commodities (fig. 10).[37] To integrate a lower-middle-class woman in urban modernity they had no option other than through existing metropolitan rituals, inserting her on the street, in the park, in the department store. Their Parisienne might not yet fully belong to that smart, highly urbanised environment, but, due to her increased desire for fashion and urban entertainment, she is no longer straightforwardly a member of the poor part of the city into which she was born.

Similarly, the German photographers Yva and Karl Schenker present a young lower-middle-class female employee in a number of photo stories in the magazine *UHU*. These are characterised by numerous vivid details, as she powders her nose by her typewriter, eats her lunch at her desk, takes notes from her boss, uses the office's communal spaces such as the cloakroom and bathroom, and prepares herself for an evening out after work.[38] Such details contribute to the apparently realistic presentation not only of her existence but moreover of her assigned role in the smooth-running capitalist system, while swiftly translating class difference into an amusing photo document.

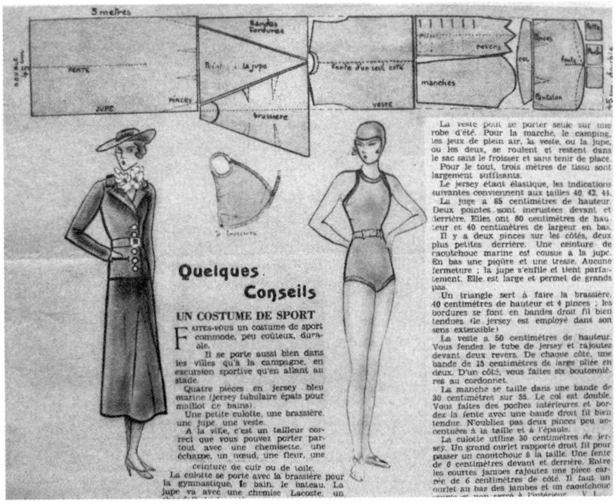

Nevertheless, her interest in fashion turned her into a modern woman, and consequently a modern subject, the most available option in the highly gendered culture of the day. Indeed, as observed by Groys, the early twentieth-century project of the New Man – and, one could add, the New Woman – became a commercially mediated one:

FIG. 11
Fashion drawing, 'Some Tips' ('Quelques Conseils'), *Views* (*Regards*), French communist weekly magazine, no. 70, 1935

> The rise of modern design is profoundly linked to the project of redesigning the old man into the New Man. This project, which emerged at the beginning of the twentieth century and is often dismissed today as utopian, has never really been abandoned de facto. In a modified, commercialized form, this project continues to have an effect, and its initial utopian potential has been updated repeatedly.[39]

The austere concept of gender in the socialist and communist media of the 1920s opposed the idea of woman as a consumer. While their journals presented a destitute proletarian mother, as well as a dedicated housewife, the New Woman was a problematic concept. Interested in fashion, make-up, shopping and having fun, she belonged to the exploitative capitalist world and was perceived as artificial. More broadly, the communist and socialist press strongly opposed fashion as a bearer of class difference. Attacks on fashion were frequent. In 1929, a prominent Austrian socialist and pioneer in fighting for women's rights, Marianne Pollak, raged against fashion in an article titled 'The Devil's Dresses' in the popular socialist women's weekly *The Discontented* (*Die Unzufriedene*).[40] Moreover, the socialist and communist media insisted on the strict division of the classes. In its 1930 article 'Women, the Stone Issues', the Austrian socialist picture magazine

The Cuckoo (*Der Kuckuck*) juxtaposes a photograph of a rich, perfectly groomed, luxuriously dressed woman, bedecked in jewellery dripping with precious stones, with one of an unadorned female bricklayer labouring in her modest work clothes. The article claims that while the former enjoys a leisurely lifestyle in her villa, the latter develops the so-called Red Death (tuberculosis).[41]

Ultimately the ideological position of the communist and socialist press was too rigid: it did not reflect the everyday reality of the social strata their party journals wanted to reach – the reality of an evermore diversifying urban society, in which the working classes increasingly interacted with bourgeois culture, and identified with its popular expressions. Recognising this, the left-wing media started to introduce women's pages, albeit conceptualised according to conventional notions of womanhood. Patriarchy informed the socialist and communist parties' policies, and their media reflected that.[42] Hesitantly, by publishing fashion advice, these magazines gradually acknowledged the new times, in which a working-class woman desired fashion, and might even manage to become modestly fashionable. From the end of the 1920s, journals such as the French communist weekly *Views* (*Regards*) offered basic drawings of simple outfits (fig. 11).[43]

Fear of the image

In the socialist and communist media, the modest drawing became the preferred visual device in presenting fashion. The unwillingness to use fashion photographs is based on the deduction that their seductive appeal veiled the reality of capitalist production. Considered commercial, excessive and too visual, the fashion photograph was associated with ideological corruption. This anxiety can be traced to Marx's concept of commodity fetishism and mediated relations, what Nancy Armstrong has argued 'might be called the first theoretical articulation of iconophobia'.[44] But urban working women grew increasingly visual, due to the richly illustrated printed media that they avidly consumed and, especially, due to the medium of film, which not only brought the world to them on screen, but also took them out into the world, via the film theatre.

A specific form of pleasure, and a specific type of knowledge, was inscribed in the cinema. Sabine Hake argues that the cinema, 'in its formative years … embraced a utopian potential: to be the place for the feminine and a place for women'.[45] As pointed out by film historian Miriam Hansen, classic Hollywood films 'succeeded as an international modernist idiom on a mass basis' due to 'the way they opened up hitherto unperceived modes of sensory perception and experience, and their ability to suggest a different organization of the daily world'.[46] Theorising 1920s Weimar modernity, Patrice Petro suggests what these kinds of experiences and new structures might be, claiming that 'modernity was experienced differently by women in the 1920s … women were indeed situated differently to men with respect to the images and to structures of looking', identifying 'women's closeness to the image against the male spectator's more objective, detached, and hence more mediated gaze'.[47] More specifically, Lesley Stern observes:

> ...the way in which the moving image (of the thing) has a capacity
> to move the spectator, to generate affect. ... the movement of the
> image simultaneously renders that presence potentially unstable and
> ephemeral. This is not to say that only in the cinema are things charged
> with affect, nor that they are necessarily more affective in the cinema,
> but, rather, that the movement of the image invests the delineation
> of things with a particular affectivity.[48]

This capacity to *move* is what worried the critics about the effects of the new entertainment industry on working women. In his essay 'The Little Shopgirls Go to the Movies', originally published in the German liberal newspaper *Frankfurter Zeitung* in 1927, the cultural and film historian Siegfried Kracauer defies their film preferences: 'Sensational film plots and life usually correspond to each other because the Little Miss Typists model themselves after the examples they see on the screen'.[49] Adhering to the contemporary Frankfurt School's understanding of the dangers of the mass culture for the lower classes, Kracauer further questions the shopgirls' predilection for melodrama and happy endings, or, indeed, sad endings. He claims that the former cheer their 'silly little hearts', while the latter provoke them to cry their eyes out. Pitying them and, at the same time, disapproving of their behaviour, Kracauer observes that 'clandestinely, the little shopgirls wipe their eyes and powder their noses before the lights go up'.[50]

It might have been true, but those emotions were transgressive, as the new medium of film facilitated the emergence of new female subjectivities and new self-representations. Immersing themselves in the images, they unfailingly spotted the latest model of hat, a new hairstyle, skilfully applied make-up, and a cut of dress that they themselves, or some inexpensive seamstress, could easily make. Hollywood films and their stars, as well as fast-developing domestic film industries, stretching from France to Russia, Germany, Central Europe and China, helped women to forge new cosmopolitan identities, whether they happened to be secretaries, cashiers, teachers, nannies, typists, cooks, maids, telephone operators or hairdressers. Indeed, the cinema promoted a democratisation of taste. In fashion, well-heeled women had Paris, while working-class women had Hollywood. From that point on, the elite did not have an exclusive monopoly on fashion trends and looks.

The politics of fast fashion
While not necessary promoting solidarity between the different social strata, fashion as a commodity has, then, been instrumental in transgressing social barriers. In his 1852 polemical essay 'The Eighteenth Brumaire of Louis Bonaparte', Marx uses the term lumpenproletariat for those existing at the margins of the established social order. Desperately disappointed with the 1848 failed French

bourgeois revolution, Marx calls Louis-Napoleon Bonaparte 'chief of the Lumpenproletariat', 'an old crafty roué', who 'conceives the historical life of the nations and their performances of state as comedy in the most vulgar sense, as a masquerade where the grand costumes, words and postures merely serve to mask the pettiest knavery'.[51] Marx is even more disparaging towards Bonaparte's political supporters, the lumpenproletariat, sarcastically depicting them as 'decayed roués with dubious means of subsistence and of dubious origin … ruined and adventurous offshoots of the bourgeoisie … in short, the whole indefinite, disintegrated mass, thrown hither and thither, which the French term *la bohème*'.[52]

'Lumpen' means 'rags' in German, and indeed the term lumpenproletariat has been customarily used to describe the poorest, *déclassé* social strata. On the other hand, quite likely, Marx used it as a metaphor for the people who not only disrespected the social norms, but also dressed in a way that would sartorially flaunt their disrespect. Theirs was a shady, demi-monde world, a world in which the separation of classes and of sexes was perverted. Singling out the socially ambiguous figures of the dandy and the coquette in that disparate social strata, Barbara Vinken argues that the Second Empire of Napoleon III was the birthplace of fashion in modernity, precisely due to fashion's disregard for the orders of class and gender:

> What the demi-monde *primarily destroys – and this is no less tolerable for Marx than it is for sociology – is the opposition of being and appearance, of* Sein *and* Schein. *The field in which demi-monde did and still does it is fashion. … As much as it may be condemned for its indifference to ethical and political purposes, fashion remains a disruption of the political and, as such, cannot be other than political.*[53]

Might we also conceive of the fast fashion of today as a political problem? As an exceptional rise in consumption is accompanied by equally significant rises in the profits of the fast fashion companies, the economic and social issues around this sector could increasingly turn into political ones. Environmentalists and advocates of sustainable fashion rightly challenge the business model of Primark – simultaneously the cheapest and financially most successful fast fashion brand – and others.[54] Yet the arguments about unethical production, usually followed by disdain for the throwaway practices of its consumers, do not answer the critical questions: Who buys fast fashion, and why do they buy it? Are the poor, relatively poor, or those who just do not earn enough, and thus live at the edge of our apparently affluent societies, the lumpenproletariat of our age? And if so, do they show a similar disrespect for the social rules of today, including the available knowledge of the merits of sustainable fashion, instead embellishing themselves in today's 'rags' of fast fashion?

The anthropologist Igor Kopytoff's analysis of the social life of things as they are commoditised might be relevant to understanding why those who buy fast fashion do so with disregard for its unethical production. He argues that, just like people, things have biographies: economic, technical, social and cultural.[55] Along these lines, the items in the field of fast fashion possess their own, socially low-rated, biographies. Moreover, Kopytoff emphasises: 'One can draw an analogy between the way societies construct individuals and the way they construct things'.[56] If so, constructing the biographies of disposable things, society may well be constructing corresponding biographies for their owners, those who do not earn enough to afford clothes with higher economic and cultural status. Millions of cheap items chased by millions of people in the endless circle of fast fashion are signs that contemporary societies fail many of their citizens.

The contemporary world of transnational fashion only makes this socially unhealthy relationship between things and people more apparent. As observed by Bruno Latour, 'things do not exist without being full of people, and the more modern and complicated they are, the more people swarm through them'.[57] Indeed, sartorially, there is hardly anything more modern than fast fashion, or more complicated, with its rapid relocations of production to ever more far-flung places, and its complex, digitally monitored global distribution. In this sense, fast fashion is the latest and technologically most sophisticated version of transnational fashion. At the same time, it reveals a tense encounter between worldwide hardship and desires for fashion that cannot be fulfilled in a sustainable manner as long as the system itself does not radically change.

The Transnational

However, fashion has always been transnational. Only ethnic dress, fashion's Other, strictly limited to a small geographical area, could claim authenticity.[58] Otherwise, in the field of fashion, authenticity is an artificial idea. In general, cultures have always been hybridities, the products of migration, exchange and cross-fertilisation, even before the advent of the colonial era. But everything has changed with the digital age, which has made the flow of global capital even speedier, more fluid, and immaterial. So, what is transnational fashion now? Undoubtedly a big business, but also an emotionally charged phenomenon. These apparently new spaces of exchanges and performances are inhabited, often unhappily, by the ghosts of times past, from the socialist to the colonial. The repressed returns in many, and often unexpected, sartorial expressions.

What is the role of affective economies in these processes? The digital media experts Joanne Garde-Hansen and Kristyn Gorton allow for a complex scenario by suggesting that affective value is always latent in the commodity:

> *Contra Marx, this value already resides in signs and commodities, waiting to be activated, developed and sustained by the consumer … While affect does indeed circulate in an economy, it is also built in to the commodity or sign from its inception, and is inseparable from its use value.*[59]

Socialist sartorial spectres

The huge success, both domestic and international, of the Russian designer Gosha Rubchinskiy shows how the affective economy functions in the fashion industry.[60] Addressing the disaffected youth in his home country, both with his affordable, sports-related fashion items and on social media, he has managed to engage this social strata in a global market. His worldly fashionability has been greatly helped since 2012 by the financial backing of the cool Japanese fashion company Comme des Garçons, but Rubchinskiy's strongest appeal has been to those who felt neglected before he reached them. His exclusively Russian models defy prevailing Russian concepts of masculinity, even when wearing tracksuits, as they are not men but boys, adolescents in search of their own social and sexual identity (fig. 12). Aesthetically he draws on the subversive elements of the early post-Soviet times, hoping, it seems, that his work will contribute to a new national narrative. Commenting on his Autumn/Winter 2017–18 show, sponsored by Adidas and held in Kaliningrad, Rubchinskiy emphasised: 'I chose to have boys from around Russia ... To me, it's like a portrait of Russia, an image of the youth generation of today'.[61] However, the often-used Russian name for these urban, androgynous boys is *gopnik*, a pejorative term describing 'bad' boys from the suburbs, squatting on the street corners in their counterfeit tracksuits.[62] As in Soviet times, these young men do not fit the official Russian ideal of youth, and live, often unemployed and underappreciated, at the margins of society. But precisely by staying true to this demographic, Rubchinskiy has managed to show the West a different

FIG. 12
Gosha Rubchinskiy, Collection for Autumn/Winter 2017–18

face of his homeland. Steve Slater, *i-D*'s fashion critic, has written: 'Mainstream media coverage of modern Russia largely centres on the excess of oligarchs and supermodels. Placing his lens over his reality, Gosha has opened the world's eye to a Muscovite underbelly we would not have encountered otherwise.'[63]

While he is patriotically Russian, Rubchinskiy's narrative is nevertheless universal in its appeal to the young and disenfranchised, as witnessed in his Spring/Summer 2018 collection, created in collaboration with Burberry.[64] When, in the mid-2000s in Britain, so-called 'chavs' started to don Burberry's trademark checked sports hats and scarves, the revered English fashion house was worried, fearing that they would fatally damage its prestige.[65] Now, however, Rubchinskiy's 'coolness' and the loyalty of his worldwide customer base make disenchanted young men a newly appealing association.[66] Certainly a shrewd business decision, but there might be more to it. Significantly, this collaboration brought together a well-established British company with an upper-class clientele, one that has historically suffered from counterfeits, and a young Russian who has built his meteoric global career by drawing on his country's counterfeit culture of the late 1980s and early 1990s. In 2016, Rubchinskiy reminisced: 'We knew about it, the brands, the logos – we just couldn't get it'.[67] The power of his clothes lies precisely in that desperate longing for fashion, which is embedded in his designs and, consequently, 'activated, developed and sustained' by his customers.

FIGS 13 & 14
VETEMENTS, Collection for
Spring/Summer 2016
Photographer Kay-Paris
Fernandes

Born in Moscow in 1984, Rubchinskiy grew up during the Perestroika years and then in post-Soviet Russia. While politically it was a messy period, the arrival of neo-liberal capitalism allowed for a burst of creativity and energy, and opened communication channels with the West. The free market arrived in Russia inscribed with logos – from Champion and Lacoste to Adidas, Nike, Levi's and others – reaffirming a longstanding Soviet obsession with western branded goods, which, at that point, would have mostly been available as cheap fakes. This socialist repressed has eventually returned in combination with Burberry's posh check patterns.

Of the same generation as Rubchinskiy, Georgian-born Demna Gvasalia, chief designer of both the fashion company Vetements and the Parisian fashion house Balenciaga, has excelled in translating the Soviet ugly into a new western beautiful, while simultaneously challenging notions of beauty, ugliness, banality, stereotypes and cultural appropriation.[68] Quotation is a legitimate practice in fashion, and western fashion trends combine the new with selective elements of previous trends. In Ulrich Lehmann's words: 'In order to become the new, fashion always cites the old, not simply the ancient or classical, but their reflection within its own sartorial past'.[69] However, cheap-looking, Russian-style tracksuits, dresses with loud flower patterns, polyester and fake leather are crude novelties in the sophisticated world of western fashion: originally they were cheap copies of western fashion trends that eventually turned into familiar sartorial codes in Russia. If western fashion's usual quotations from its own past are purely time-bound, these contemporary quotes of Soviet sartorial codes stretch the quotations space-wise, drawing on geographical sources that had previously never been present in the field of western fashion.

In contrast with Rubchinskiy's fascination with androgynous youth, Gvasalia draws on different adolescent memories.[70] Vetements swings between the Soviet romantic and highly sexualised Perestroika aesthetics. The rose-printed plastic tablecloths made into aprons and dresses on the Vetements Spring/Summer 2016 catwalk were an ode to Gvasalia's grandmother and exuded sweet memories of a simple domestic life during the Soviet period (fig. 13). On the other hand, dresses from the same collection executed in Soviet-inspired flower-patterned fabrics or shiny, cheap-looking velvets were accompanied by thigh-high boots. These two styles embodied two very different concepts of Soviet womanhood, accompanied by their respective notions of femininity and sexuality. While Pretty Woman – modestly feminine – was still a socialist ideal, the liberalisation processes triggered by Perestroika allowed for the phenomena of prostitution and pornography to appear in the domestic media.[71] And indeed, these Russian Pretty Women dressed like their western counterparts: sexy clothes, platform shoes, lurid colours. In Russia, this new style was considered glamorous (fig. 14).

Gvasalia brought even more of that crude sexualised aesthetic into his Spring/ Summer 2017 collection for Balenciaga.[72] The use of latex and Spandex, clothes clinging to the body in tight leggings or boots stretching up the whole leg, and colour clashes of orange, blue, red and purple, vividly refer to the high-class Russian prostitute of the late 1980s. Made from low quality fabrics and badly executed, her dress was aesthetically dubious but highly visible. Announcing a new relationship between a highly sexualised femininity and the world of commodities, she mingled with westerners in the shady surroundings of Intourist hotels, only to be magically transported to the rarefied world of contemporary Parisian fashion.

There are many other instances of 'Sovietness' in Vetements's aesthetic and Gvasalia's approach to design. For instance, his fondness for uniforms, which acts as a reminder of the lack of diversity in a period of his youth. His refashioning of existing clothes or work with recycled outfits, resembling a socialist DIY technique, and his visual references that mix radical punk, dark Gothic, army camouflage and the simply bland, bring to mind the deep-seated socialist hunger for difference. But why does the world like this aesthetic?

Jacques Derrida's *Spectres of Marx*[73] might be advantageous in tracing some tricky wanderings of the communist sartorial spectres in contemporary western fashion. Derrida reminisces on Marx's permanent immigrant status, both real and symbolic, and its consequences for the world of today:

> *Marx has not yet been received. … Marx remains an immigrant chez nous, a glorious, sacred, accursed but still a clandestine immigrant as he was all his life. He belongs to a time of disjunction, to that 'time out of joint' in which is inaugurated, laboriously, painfully, tragically, a new thinking of borders, a new experience of the house, the home, and the economy. Between earth and sky. One should not rush to make of the clandestine immigrant an illegal alien or, what always risks coming down to the same thing, to domesticate him. To neutralise him through naturalisation. To assimilate him so as to stop frightening oneself with him. He is not part of the family, but one should not send him back, once again, him too, to the border.*[74]

Marx had indeed been a poor and unwelcome immigrant. While writing *Capital*, he lived with his large family in one room in London's Soho. Marx's poverty was such that, when he pawned his coat so that he could buy writing paper, he could not go to the British Library to conduct his research.[75] Certainly, Marx's well-worn coat, going back to his Liverpool days, as he described it, was just a useful and practical outfit. By contrast, Vetements's expensive clothes are commodities that, due to their seductive appeal, fulfill Marx's concept of commodity fetishism. Yet, could Vetements's aesthetic relate to Marx's authentic experience of poverty and immigration?

The brand's Spring/Summer 2019 show in Paris was staged on a runway set up like a white table at a wedding reception, under a bridge over the Périphérique on the far edges of the 19th arrondissement, an area in which Middle Eastern and African migrants live in encampments along the road.[76] Why there, and why at that point? According to the designer, the presentation was a meditation on 'family and war and

violence', referring to the civil war of the 1990s in Georgia, which forced Gvasalia's family to flee their home town of Sukhumi:

> I feel everybody today talks about war, refugees. And I am like, yes, I know exactly what that means. It's weird. This is about my life, but also it's about everything you see on CNN, as well. ... It was like dressing a documentary of my life ... I dedicated this collection to Georgia, the Georgia where my brother Guram and I grew up together in the '90s, and the war that happened where we lived. I tried to face this angst and fear and pain in this show. I didn't want to remember before, I didn't want to go that far.[77]

A model in a black leather trenchcoat and an S&M mask embodied the horrors of the war (fig. 15). Apart from that outfit and thematic T-shirts with swear words in Russian and Georgian, embodying Gvasalia's angst, the clothes from this collection drew on the established Vetements's wardrobe: black leather jackets, oversized sweatshirts, ripped jeans, pleated flowery dresses and dramatic Gothic-and-Georgian-influenced black velvet and lace outfits. The *New York Times* fashion critic Vanessa Friedman wrote: 'If the clothes looked substantively familiar that's because they were. Not in their details (the Russian swear words) but in the way they referenced styles past as a primal scream'.[78]

Fashion has customarily been reproached for misinterpreting social inequalities, from poverty to the contemporary refugee crises, by either dressing them up, or displacing them onto another era. Along these lines, and indeed offering some convincing examples, the fashion theorist Llewellyn Negrin argues:

> In all of these cases, the threat posed by the dark underside of capitalist materialism is allayed by symbolically appropriating and aestheticizing it. Pauperist style references the 'repressed', but in a manner which renders it 'harmless' by stripping it of its disturbing elements. Through its conversion into an aesthetic style, poverty becomes less confronting to the more affluent.[79]

Thus, serving the existing social and economic order, fashion pretends to participate in the traumas of the Other, keeping instead a safe distance in order not to alienate its well-off customers. But what if the Other is suddenly one of us, yet still suffers his genuine pain? Is fashion permanently tarnished by its commercial nature, or could it be a carrier of authentic emotions? Consequently, could fashion expose social, political and cultural issues, both historical and contemporary, and their accompanying, still raw traumas? What if commodities like Vetements clothes realise their commodified, fetishised destiny but as objects soaked with painful memories, just as Marx's own coat had been for him? The trauma caused by the collapse of the Soviet Union that affected Rubchinskiy, as well as the personal trauma that Gvasalia brings to western commercial fashion, are their unique cultural capital. They transform genuine desperation and fervent hope into clothes that the pampered West desires, as if some authentic human craving is sewn into the seams of their outfits.

FIG. 15
VETEMENTS, Collection for Spring/Summer 2019

Fashion has increasingly become less polished, reflecting the troubled times in which we live. The advance of poor-looking yet expensive fashions might be read as the superficial attitude of the fashionable in their search for the new. But, as the consumers become more socially conscious and the times ever more testing, the capitalist market might need to offer new types of products which marry an expensive commodity with a potential to carry a credible personal narrative. Moreover, drawing on Derrida's interpretation of Marx's *Capital*, both Rubchinskiy's and Gvasalia's clothes could be perceived as spectres, the return of the repressed in the specific context of the writer Svetlana Alexievich's second-hand time that haunts contemporary Russia – and, it seems, the western world.[80] Metaphorically, their clothes might be seen as that fatal communist spectre, already announced by Marx and Engels in the first sentence of their Communist Manifesto of 1848. The two most eminent socialist thinkers and political activists would never have expected this, but the spectre of communism has returned to haunt Europe dressed in ugly Soviet-style clothes. As emphasised by Derrida in his *Spectres of Marx*:

> At a time when a new world disorder is attempting to install its neo-capitalism and neo-liberalism, no disavowal has managed to rid itself of all of Marx's ghosts. Hegemony still organizes the repression and thus the confirmation of a haunting. Haunting belongs to the structure of every hegemony.[81]

In her analysis of cultural trauma in relation to 1990s western fashion, Caroline Evans argues that fashion might be the right medium to operate a kind of 'return of the repressed', that it could be 'a symptom to articulate cultural trauma', and, moreover, that 'fashion might be able to put a finger on contemporary concerns in ways that more coherent narratives could not achieve'.[82]

Indeed, this might be possible. Gvasalia had been engaging with serious social issues before his highly personal Spring/Summer 2018 collection. Titled 'Archetypes', Vetements's Autumn/Winter 2017–18 collection played with a number of 'stereotypical' looks, from 'Milanesa' and 'Granny' to 'Tourist', 'Vagabond', 'Commando', 'Trash Metal', 'Punk', 'Bro', 'Broker' and many others. On this occasion, each fashion journalist, editor, buyer or celebrity was sent an invitation in the form of a fake ID, bearing her or his name but someone else's image, age and nationality. The fashion journalist Suzy Menkes perceptively observed: 'Those little cards that served as invitations were, according to Demna, "reproductions of ID from different countries, of nationalities – it was just fun because we like to play around with the invitations." But, of course, identity lies at the heart of the current turmoil about immigration'.[83] A seasoned immigrant, Gvasalia, whose life trajectory covers Georgia, Russia, Germany, Belgium, France and Switzerland, reversed the mirror in which an immigrant is an eternal Other.

With his 2017 Balenciaga Resort Collection, Gvasalia moved away from austere socialist uniformity to metropolitan uniformity, found in the underbelly of the city, the poor but multicultural and multiracial 10th arrondissement in Paris.

otography Danko Steiner
ling Ana Steiner

Don't touch me! Don't question me!
Stay with me

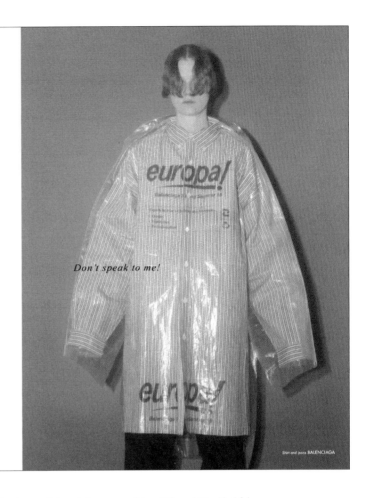

Don't speak to me!

The looks evoked the long striped dresses of traditional North African women carrying oversized bags, or young black women proudly flaunting their sexuality in tight black mini dresses. By drawing on European archetypes and subcultures, his multicultural Parisian neighbourhood, and indeed by printing 'Europa!' on his T-shirts and shirts, Gvasalia shows his newly gained power, not only as a world-renowned designer but also as an immigrant who, after difficulties and tragedies, has become a modern cosmopolitan (fig. 16). As claimed by the anthropologist Bruce Robbins, 'instead of an ideal of detachment, actually existing cosmopolitanism is a reality of (re)attachment, multiple attachments, or attachment at a distance'.[84] Of course, with his highly visible jobs, his earnings and the praise of the world media, Gvasalia is privileged. Yet, his greatest achievement might be the culturally messy space that he inhabits, in which 'cosmopolitanism is not a circle created by culture diffused from a center, but instead [in which] ... centres are everywhere and circumferences nowhere'.[85] It is equally significant that Gvasalia has carved that space for himself, and many others who share these values, in the world of fashion.

FIG. 16
'Balenciaga's Collection
for Spring/Summer 2018',
Re-Edition, Issue 9, Spring/
Summer 2018
Photographer Danko Steiner;
fashion director Ana Steiner

Colonial sartorial spectres

In today's highly politicised world, there are other spectres that haunt fashion. Among them, the colonial examples are the most prominent. Burdened with nostalgia, they have been present for a long time, either by evoking leisure clothes, once worn by the white colonisers, or by imagining ethnic dresses of the previously colonised peoples. However, the new colonial spectres, fuelled recently by the grassroots movement Black Lives Matter, are revenants of a different kind. By boldly mixing aesthetics and politics, they introduce blackness as a highly charged political project in the canon of western fashion.

The cover of American *Vogue* for September 2018, shot by the young black photographer Tyler Mitchell, shows Beyoncé wearing a loose, long-sleeved and high-necked Gucci white summer dress revealing only her legs. She sits on a low stool in front of a crisp white sheet. On her head, there is an extravagant flower arrangement, but her face is serious. The former editor-at-large, André Leon Talley, offers an interpretation of this image:

> As captivated as we are by our subject, we are equally drawn to the expanse behind her. With that immaculate sheet, Mitchell suggests the laundress, the bygone station of so many black women, in their own confident beauty, delivering white linens to the white master's big white house. We witness an homage to the ancestry of slavery that Beyoncé explores within the magazine. I see the influence of Kara Walker, Alice Walker and Zora Neale Hurston, along with the unnamed armies of black mothers and maids working for whites to keep food on their own tables. In all its elegance, the sheet symbolizes so many black women who struggled until they became towers of their community, of their family - but rarely of the world.[86]

Indeed, visible in the editorial – and prominent in *Vogue*'s 'behind the scenes' video – are large sheets of various colours flying in the breeze on a clothesline.[87] On the alternative cover of that issue, Beyoncé is stretching such a sheet above her head, while wearing an Alexander McQueen long evening gown. The usual highly polished glamour is not there. The photograph transmits only Beyoncé's natural beauty, with her hair styled in braids. The images shot in the interiors of a dilapidated English country house additionally avoid any sense of the opulence associated with such sumptuous clothes. Sitting barefoot in a lavish, long Dior gown, Beyoncé's legs are stretched wide on the mansion's stairs, in a pose too careless for a 'proper' lady. Maybe, long ago, the previous mistress of this house wore such a couture wardrobe. Self-confident in her beauty and her place in the world, Beyoncé does not seem to care. Putting nostalgic colonial spectres to rest, the whole editorial, and specifically this portrait, point towards the power of a new, politicised black imagery to disturb and, ultimately, disregard conventional western standards of beauty and race.

Mitchell emphasises this point in his interview with *Vogue*: 'For so long, black people have been considered things. We've been thingified physically, sexually, emotionally. With my work I'm looking to revitalize and elevate the black body.'[88] There is obviously both an ideological and an artistic contract between the photographer and his subject, as Beyoncé also emphasises that the aesthetic of this fashion shoot is infused with politics. While it is her fourth *Vogue* cover, it is clearly the most important to her:

> When I first started, 21 years ago, I was told that it was hard for me to get onto covers of magazines because black people did not sell. Clearly that has been proven a myth. Not only is an African American on the cover of the most important month for Vogue, this is the first ever Vogue cover shot by an African American photographer.[89]

The growing number of fashion editorials attempting to channel a black aesthetic could be seen as fashion appropriating and commoditising the visually attractive elements of black culture, while uprooting them from their historical and cultural context. But the increasing presence of black and brown models on the catwalk and in magazines, along with the 2017 appointment of the first black editor of British *Vogue*, Edward Enninful, and the 2018 promotion of Virgil Abloh to creative director of menswear at Louis Vuitton, suggest that the fashion industry is undergoing serious changes in terms of its representation of people of colour.

Beyoncé's sartorial choices show her trajectory from a fashion template, often still framed within standards of white beauty,[90] to an activist who uses fashion to articulate her political beliefs and consciously embrace the specifics of her body: 'I stripped away the wigs and hair extensions and used little makeup for this shoot. … my arms, shoulders, breasts, and thighs are fuller. I have a little mommy pouch, and I'm in no rush to get rid of it.'[91]

Of Beyoncé's performance during the 2016 Super Bowl, in which she and the all-female dance troupe raised their fists in a Black Panther-style salute, their Afro hair flying (fig. 17), Daphne Brooks has written: '[it was] an affirmation of swaggering black pleasure and joy in the face of black life under duress'.[92] Cautiously warning that 'we should not confuse the urgency of grassroots agitation with culture industry performances', Brooks nevertheless goes on to emphasise: 'But the Beyoncé conundrum time and again shows how popular music culture – and especially black women's popular culture – can awaken, acknowledge and articulate the pleasures and distastes of those in the margins'.[93]

The art historian Richard Powell finds black sartorial styles 'invariably linked to the subject's sense of self – an awareness that through self-adornment, self-composure, and self-imagining upsets the representational paradigm and creates something pictorially exceptional'.[94] Indeed, black culture has developed its unique, highly ornate and highly expressive, sartorial styles, often performed at the margins of conventional respectability. Pain, anger, passion and the desire to belong mix in these vigorous dress codes. For example, Monica Miller describes black dandyism as a 'ubiquitous, popular performance full of ambivalence' that 'teach[es] one about the myriad contexts in which black identity formation takes

FIG. 17
Beyoncé performing at
the Pepsi Super Bowl,
Santa Clara, California,
February 2016
Photographer Robert Beck

place' and 'visualize[s] the limitations that black people must negotiate and recombine as part of the act of self-definition'.[95]

Almost none of these exuberant and distinctive black styles, with their potential for multiple representations of selfhood, have been, until recently, present in contemporary fashion. One significant exception is the July 2008 issue of Italian *Vogue*, featuring exclusively black models and topics related to black culture. At that time its editor-in-chief Franca Sozzani said she was inspired by Barack Obama's presidential campaign. Her regular collaborator, the renowned American photographer Stephen Meisel, fully embraced the idea of an all-black issue, and promptly engaged a number of black models, from Naomi Campbell and

Tyra Banks to Jourdan Dunn, Liya Kebede, Alek Wek, Pat Cleveland and Sessilee Lopez. In an interview, Meisel expressed his feelings: 'I thought, it's ridiculous, this discrimination ... It's so crazy to live in such a narrow, narrow place. Age, weight, sexuality, race – every kind of prejudice'.[96]

Meticulously preparing for this shoot, Meisel drew on each and every visual stereotype of black culture, from its tendency towards over-decoration and negotiations with dominant culture in its lady-like embodiments to its vernacular gangsta chic and relationship to the canon of western art. In the latter case, Meisel's narrative relies on Manet's *Olympia*, whose black maid here becomes the central focus. Half-naked and leisurely stretched on a large bed, on which are scattered various delicacies, Naomi Campbell looks self-confident and very much aware of her beauty. In another photograph, clad in black lace underwear, Campbell is 'served' as yet another delicacy on the richly decorated table teeming with exquisite food. In a further portrait, she reclines on an antique table loaded with jewellery, naked except for a pair of the above-the-knee, fetishistic black boots and an expensive necklace.

Such poses could be interpreted as Meisel presenting Naomi Campbell as a racialised object, as unfortunate relics of an imperial past. But it could be equally claimed that the concept of an over-sexualised black female has not been truly abandoned, and that it still haunts the western imagination. In this context, this explicitly sexual presentation of the black body could emphasise a residual white fear of a corrupting black sexuality. Similarly, if Manet's *Olympia* was reproached in the artist's time because she, and his painting style, exceeded the bounds of bourgeois propriety, Meisel's shoot must be recognised for its presentation of exclusively black models, who themselves have not belonged to the bourgeois traditions of the leading fashion magazines.

In her 1995 essay 'In Our Glory: Photography and Black Life', bell hooks stresses the importance of visual representations for black people, arguing that the display of family photographs on walls was, for them, an important way to engage in visual discourses of self-representation. She names such displays 'pictorial genealogies' and states that 'they provided a necessary narrative, a way for us to enter history without words'.[97] Included in the fashion canon, prominent images of black people and culture become not only a legitimate part of fashion history, but also potentially a way to create new, modern genealogies. Tyler Mitchell suggests as much about his work, which also includes shoots for other Condé Nast publications and a number of advertising campaigns for prominent fashion and sports companies: 'I think what my pictures are doing are not necessarily making you want to buy more through exclusivity or selling this high lifestyle, but somehow resonating with those kids who are like, "We didn't see ourselves here before".'[98] 'Power Play', the title of the editorial that Mitchell photographed for January 2019 issue of British *Vogue* symbolically points to the changing dynamic of power in the field of fashion. Moreover, this editorial features the model Adut Akech Bior of South Sudanese origin, adding yet another layer to the shifting relation to the issue of race in the leading fashion media. Akech had to flee her home country, and before settling

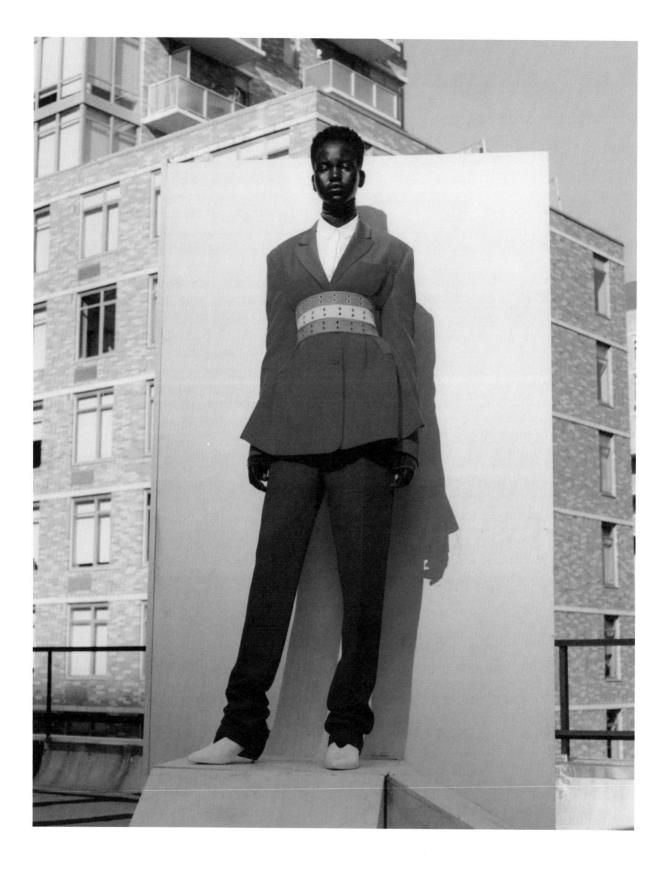

with her family in Australia, spent her childhood in a refugee camp in Kenya, only to turn into a prominent international model in the last couple of years (fig. 18).

Deciding to put Oprah Winfrey on the cover of the August 2018 issue of British *Vogue*, a shoot he styled himself, Edward Enninful stated in his 'Editor's Letter': 'Of course, I wanted to do her as an empress. She is so magnificent, so awe-inspiring, and she really went to the idea'.[99] It is compelling to imagine Winfrey styled as an empress not because she is a powerful media mogul but because she started life as a deprived and abused black child.[100] As observed by Richard Powell:

> Despite a sobering legacy of scorn and subjugation, peoples of African descent have psychologically 'clothed' themselves in fancier attire than others customarily allowed them, enacting personas that inspire awe and provide assurances about their place among life's movers and shakers.[101]

In this sense, the new, politically informed colonial spectres, splashed on the pages of leading fashion magazines, show that the historically unfulfilled emotions and expectations of the underrepresented in this field, and in the wider world, have recently been addressed.

Indeed, at the level of representation, fashion may go some way to repair these injustices, at the same time joining politics and economics as a sphere relevant to today's most urgent social and cultural conversations. Precisely because it is a visual phenomenon, fashion can subvert dominant constructions and presentations of identity – whether ethnic, class, race, sex or gender – a function that takes on even greater significance in the image-saturated digital realm.

Makeover culture: influencing emotions

There are many visual phenomena in the digital world that are directed towards the emotions and desires of specific social strata, insufficiently addressed by the beauty industry and mainstream media. As much is witnessed by the huge popularity enjoyed by Kim Kardashian, her sisters and their mother. In her essay 'Affective Economies', Sara Ahmed separates emotion from interiority and follows its effects in public discourse:

> In such affective economies, emotions do things, and they align individuals with communities – or bodily space with social space – through the very intensity of their attachments. Rather than seeing emotions as psychological dispositions, we need to consider how they work, in concrete and particular ways, to mediate the relationship between the psychic and the social, and between the individual and the collective.[102]

Affect is highly implicated in the social media-informed processes of improving one's looks. As Kardashian told Lynn Hirschberg in the November 2010 issue of the fashion magazine *W*:

> 'You know', she said, 'it used to be mostly men who were interested in me. But now with the website and the show, it's almost all women.

FIG. 18
'Power Play', British *Vogue*, January 2019
Photographer Tyler Mitchell; model Adut Akech Bior

They like that I'm close to my sisters, that I have flaws, that I have cellulite.'
Kardashian laughed. 'They like that I'm real', she said. 'As real as they are.'[103]
This issue of *W* was dedicated to the arts, and Kim Kardashian's profile is
accompanied by a naked cover image with the slogan 'It's all about me. I mean
you. I mean me', an artwork by Barbara Kruger, who herself once worked at
a Condé Nast magazine (fig. 19). With this work, Kruger continues to question
and promote various issues of power, control and affect. In her famous 1987
slogan 'I shop therefore I am', Kruger had challenged the male world of advertising
and its assumption that women only needed material objects to be happy and,
consequently, that men could control them by those means. At the same time,
feminist philosophers challenged the historical masculinisation of thought
as initially stated in Descartes's maxim 'I think therefore I am'. For example,
Susan Bordo argues that:

> *... its key term is detachment: from the emotional life, from the*
> *particularities of time and place, from personal quirks, prejudices, and*
> *interests, and most centrally, from the object itself. ... In this process,*
> *the characterization of both the scientific mind and its modes of access*
> *to knowledge as masculine is indeed significant. Masculine here connotes,*
> *as it so often does, autonomy, separation, and distance. ... The Cartesian*
> *reconstruction of the world is a defiant gesture of independence from*
> *the female cosmos ...[104]*

Bordo further states that, from that time on, 'there seemed no organic unity,
but only "I" and "she"– an unpredictable and seemingly arbitrary "she", whose
actions could not be understood in any of the old, sympathetic ways. "She" is
"other"; and "otherness" itself becomes dreadful – particularly the otherness
of the female ...'.[105] Throughout her work, Kruger has drawn on linguistic shifts
between 'I' and 'you', referring to changing patterns in sex relations. Kardashian's
W cover is equally gender-specific, but while Kruger inserted her slogan 'I shop
therefore I am' onto the photograph of a man's hand, here she has printed the
slogan 'It's all about me. I mean you. I mean me' across Kardashian's body,
addressing her prevalently female audience. 'I' and 'you' are both women,
and – moreover – are involved in an almost symbiotic relationship.

In her *W* profile, Kardashian claims, seemingly half-ironically, that her
audience believes that she is real, just like them. The relationship between
Kardashian and her female public is presented as something like a friendship, based
on sharing 'secrets' about makeover culture. Meredith Jones writes: 'Makeover
culture dictates that bodies, selves and environments must be in constant states
of renovation, restoration, maintenance and improvement'.[106] Kim and other female
members of the Kardashian family are 'exemplar makeover culture citizens and their
professionalism is based on being able to market those talents'.[107] By sharing her
highly performative activities on social media, Kim Kardashian engages her audience
in this process. While these women, due to lack of time and financial constraints,

FIG. 19
Barbara Kruger artwork
featuring Kim Kardashian, *W*
magazine, cover, Art Issue,
November 2010

might not be able to achieve her extraordinary figure, they nevertheless feel involved. The perpetually remade body and the affect related to the activities of physical self-improvement are 'more about becoming than being ... [they both are] a form of expressive learning and participation'.[108]

Their social media platforms enable the Kardashians to accumulate economic capital, but their audiences may also be developing their own social capital, as they 'negotiate' whether and how to use social media platforms and apps.[109] Kruger's message points not only to Kim Kardashian's exhibitionism but also to her audience's desire to exhibit and expose themselves. From an activist point of view, this also has currency today, as Nicholas Mirzoeff suggests when he writes of the selfie: 'From the new feminisms to the idea of the 99 percent, people are reimagining how they belong and what that looks like'.[110]

Engaging images: post-war ideologies and fashion

Even before the digital era, images possessed the emotional power to engage people. After the Second World War, those on the Left especially detested the new society of apparent abundance, behind which social and economic inequalities only grew. Performed in austere uniform-style dress, the long-dreamed of socialist utopia finally, it seemed, became a reality in faraway countries such as Cuba and China. Following Fidel Castro's death in November 2016, the British political journalist Andrew Marr argued, in an article entitled 'The Invention of Marxism's Mr Cool':

> *Imagine if Castro had preferred to remain clean-shaven, and eschewed scratchy military fatigues for comfortably cut grey suits brought in from Moscow with, perhaps, a handsome porkpie hat. Had he looked, in short, like a sweatier version of Erich Honecker, I don't think the world would be making such a fuss of him now.*[111]

ABOVE
FIG. 20
Che Guevara and Fidel Castro, Havana, Cuba, 1961
Photographer Alberto Korda

OPPOSITE
FIG. 21
Model Veruschka as Chairman Mao,
French *Vogue*, guest editor Salvador Dalí, December 1971
Photographer Alex Chatelain

Although, soon after taking power, Castro had exchanged his radical revolutionary ideals for Soviet-style socialism in order to secure military and financial help from the Soviet Union, his clothes continued to support his image as the leading world revolutionary. This image was cleverly manufactured, informed by his own understanding of how he should look, and aided by fellow Cuban photographer Alberto Korda, who in the 1960s depicted both Castro and Che Guevara as defiant freedom fighters (fig. 20). When Che Guevara was captured and killed in 1967, his executors understood well the power of his carefully curated revolutionary look. They attempted to rob him of his seductive visual authority by releasing an image of his half-naked body on a dreary cement catafalque. It did not work. Che remained a young, glamorous revolutionary in the minds of left-leaning youth all over the world. Sporting his unkempt beard, long hair, red-starred beret, green fatigues and his mud-covered military boots, he was an exemplary romantic hero on the walls of student bedsits in the West.

The uniform, as well as the ideology, of another well-known political leader, Mao Zedong, had an even more peculiar trajectory. From the early 1950s up to the mid-1970s, Mao made the Chinese people wear his favourite outfit: plain trousers and a tunic with a mandarin collar and two pockets on the chest, which in the West became known as the Mao suit.[112] Connected to the Cultural Revolution, which Mao instigated in the mid-1960s, this outfit carried a proletarian message in the West, promising a new social utopia. As, to western eyes, Mao's suit seemed gender- and class-neutral,[113] it perfectly fitted the decade's resistance to established cultural and political values. Consequently, this austere Chinese uniform became a transgressive and joyful item of dress, joining Che's beret in the wardrobe of young revolutionaries to be. Made of cotton and easy to produce due to its simple cut, the Mao jacket was cheap, whether imported or produced locally, and was sold in alternative clothes shops and department stores alike.[114] The years 1966–8 marked its peak, on the backs of rebellious Parisian students.[115] As observed by Valerie Steele and John Major in *China Chic: East Meets West*:

> *When Paris was filled with ardent Maoists, the workers' uniform was associated with leftist, anti-colonial politics. The romanticization of the Orient continued, in other words, but along with the old fantasy about opulent Cathay, there was a new Western fantasy about the workers' paradise.*[116]

In 1971, Salvador Dalí presented his surrealist interpretation of Mao in the Christmas issue of French *Vogue*, which he guest-edited.[117] As observed at the time by the *International Herald Tribune*'s fashion editor, Hebe Dorsey: 'the magazine has no fashion to speak of. Instead it is a surrealist montage of a number of fascinating if totally unrelated subjects'.[118] Among them was a portrait of the model Veruschka masquerading as Mao, shot by fashion photographer Alex Chatelain (fig. 21). In contrast to Joan Rivière's 1929 thesis on the socio-sexual role-play of 'womanliness' as masquerade, performed by women who consciously or otherwise preferred not to threaten the clear separation of the sexes,[119] Veruschka co-opts the male look. But not even a receding hairline or baggy Mao suit can conceal her femininity and extraordinary beauty. This fashion image symbolically destabilises male power, specifically Mao's omnipotence. Yet, photographed on a misty riverbank with a pensive expression on her face, Veruschka resembles Mao as self-styled philosopher and poet on the banks of the Yangtze River. Dalí was interested precisely in that vision of Mao. Far from the revolutionary hero adored by the uncritical Left, for Dalí Mao was a poet and the spiritual leader of a mysterious country, perfectly suiting his own, anti-Marxist political stand and surrealist artistic vision.

Whether considered an evil empire or a utopia evolving in real life, communism and socialism historically intrigued the West, as in Norman Parkinson's Soviet editorial for British *Vogue* in 1976 (fig. 22). On such occasions, the horrors of Stalin's politics were depoliticised, and ultimately exchanged for exotic imagery from the other side of the Iron Curtain. Equally, the western infatuation with Mao's suit

FIG. 22
Model Jerry Hall, waving the communist flag behind the Iron Curtain, British *Vogue*, December 1975/January 1976
Photographer
Norman Parkinson

and politics shows that a genuine search for a new utopia can latch on to highly ideologised, delusional thinking. Could such political naivety take place today, in a world that is connected as never before, in which information can technically be reported as it happens? Probably not. The visual authority commanded by Castro, Che Guevara and Mao documented a hierarchical political and societal order. Outside its place of origin, it mostly engaged only specific, left-leaning social groups.

Femininity and the political uprisings of the 2010s
In the digital world, politics is communicated and performed in a different way. The video artist and digital media scholar Hito Steyerl suggests how: 'Any image is a shared ground for action and passion, a zone of traffic between things and intensities'.[120] The hierarchical system still exists, but it has increasingly been disturbed by the horizontal organisation of movements such as Occupy and the Arab Spring, which did not produce any revolutionary leaders in the mould of Castro or Mao.

A number of images documenting the 2010s political uprisings have nevertheless shown the power that clothes can exercise in the fight for freedom and the struggle against autocratic regimes. While Che commanded his revolutionary message on posters plastered on the walls of student bedsits in the West, the image of the Turkish academic Ceyda Sungur, pepper-sprayed by police during a demonstration in Istanbul in May 2013, went viral (fig. 23). The protest started over proposals to redevelop the local Gezi Park. In her red summer dress, with a white shopping bag over one shoulder, Sungur looked as though she was just passing by when a policeman in riot gear attacked her.[121] Now known worldwide as the 'Woman in the Red Dress', she became a visual symbol not only of the Gezi Park protest, but also of a much wider dissent against injustice, cruelty and state power: a revolutionary heroine who did not look like one, looking instead like many other women walking the streets all over the world in similar summer dresses. The image depicting the policeman attacking Sungur, taken by the photographer Osman Örsal, was soon reinterpreted in murals, posters and memes.

Another revolutionary symbol derived from a protest event in Cairo's Tahrir Square in December 2011, during which an anonymous young woman was publicly assaulted by members of the Egyptian military (fig. 25). In the image that went viral, two soldiers are dragging her along the ground by her arms, which are raised above her head. She is wearing blue jeans and trainers but, half-divested of her abaya during the attack, is naked from the waist up apart from her blue bra.[122] Again it was an item of clothing – her bright blue bra – that caught the attention of other demonstrators and the world media. The day after the assault, thousands of people protested against police violence on the streets of Cairo, holding print-outs of the scene. The attack, as well as the blue bra itself, were further used in murals, posters and graffiti (fig. 24).[123] As observed by Mona Abaza, 'the blue bra became "a central icon for expressing dissent".'[124]

FIG. 23
Turkish academic, Ceyda
Sungur, pepper-sprayed by
police during a demonstration
in Istanbul, May 2013
Photographer Osman Örsal

These two brightly coloured feminine pieces of clothing singled these two women out from the crowd. They themselves picked them from their wardrobes, unaware that their sartorial choices would eventually turn them into unwilling performance artists and bring femininity into the centre of intense revolutionary activities. The revolutions are widely felt to have failed, but these two apparently frivolous items captured the world's attention, demonstrating that 'images and representative strategies have become both an integral part of a highly mediatized struggle and one of the main platforms through which [revolutionary] action is elicited and self-organized.'[125] Calling them 'poor images', Hito Steyerl writes that such images are defined by velocity, intensity and spread. Precisely because of that, as Steyerl further claims:

> They express all the contradictions of the contemporary crowd: its
> opportunism, narcissism, desire for autonomy and creation, its inability

*to focus or make up its mind, its constant readiness for transgression
and simultaneous submission [and] present a snapshot of the affective
condition of the crowd, its neurosis, paranoia, and fear, as well as its
craving for intensity, fun, and distraction.*[126]

Fashion is equally characterised by contradiction, velocity, intensity, spread, fun
and affect, which only intensifies the interdependent relationship between politics
and fashion in the digital age. And to address the key question: Can fashion be
defended? What, if any, is its political agency? 'There can be no pristine space of
resistance', writes Dorinne Kondo. 'Subversion and contestation are never beyond
discourse and power [and] consequently, there can never be a purely contestatory
image'.[127] As imperfect as it is, fashion is a globally dispersed, highly visual and
emotionally charged practice. Precisely because of its worldwide presence, fashion
can articulate and potentially subvert constructions and presentations of identity,
disturb totalitarian tendencies and visualise political dissent. In an era when politics
is largely mistrusted, and increasingly divides people along lines of nation, class,
race, sex and gender, fashion might effectively address old and new injustices, not
only those of fashion but also of the wider world.

FIG. 24
Bahia Shehab, 'No to Stripping
the People', graffiti, Cairo,
December 2011
The footprint reads 'Long
live a peaceful revolution'

FIG. 25
The stripping and beating
of a veiled woman during
a demonstration in Cairo's
Tahrir Square, 17 December
2011

Acknowledgements
The research for this article has been greatly assisted
by an Arts and Humanities Research Council Fellowship
grant. I would also like to thank Dr Sophie Oliver for her
thoughtful comments.

II

Reform or

Revolution

Fashion: An Oriental Tyranny in the Heart of the West?

Barbara Vinken

From Jean-Jacques Rousseau to Friedrich Nietzsche, from Thorstein Veblen to Simone de Beauvoir, philosophers who have written on fashion have stigmatised it as the Other of the West: as Oriental.[1] According to the antimonarchical, Republican ideology of the Modern, the empire of fashion is constructed as an 'Inner Orient' that is to be discarded. The tropes that constitute the Inner Orient stem from a well-known topic in the history of ideas, the 'Oriental Renaissance'.[2] In the ideology of modernity, the effeminate and idolatrous, decadent and ruinous cult of fashion has to be eradicated for progress to march on. An egalitarian male Republic – thus the political agenda against fashion – can be realised only once the stumbling block of fashion is out of the way.[3]

In the following essay, I do not support the attitude against the Inner Orient, since fashion is not only an essential ingredient of public life as well as private self-esteem, but a subtle politics against this mysogenist, anti-Semitic politics of the Modern. Its oriental appearance is a mark of civil freedom rather than of individual subjection. To denounce fashion is part of a dark heritage of modernity.

Consequently, I shall neither address any oriental influences on fashion, nor shall I discuss the fashion of orientalism. I use the concept of the Inner Orient in order to modify the thesis of Edward Said's *Orientalism* (1978), a book intended to revise and reset public opinion towards the Orient, but limited in the analysis of its many implications.[4] The West, Said argued, projects all things threatening – effeminacy, emasculation, inertia, tyranny, decadence – onto some outer Other called the Orient in order to consolidate its own identity. I argue instead that the West installs, within its Reformed Protestant or Republican discourses, an 'Inner Orient', which portends in its very heart a menacing Orient that undoes from within all things properly western: natural sexuality, to begin with, and consequently patriarchy, self-determination, self-control, progress and, thus, any meaningful sense of history. The concept of the Inner Orient became current in the nineteenth century, when the Catholic Church was stigmatised as oriental by German Protestants and French (and also some Italian) Republicans alike: as perverse, sterile, decadent, addictive, monstrous, effeminate, idolatrous.[5] A striking example of this discourse formation is Emile Zola's trilogy *Trois Villes* (1893–8), in which a

FIG. 26
Court suit, French, 1774–93
(detail)

61

Babylonian Lourdes (the most successful place of apparition of the Virgin Mary) and a decadent Rome (seat of the Popes) are overcome by a secular, vitalistic Republican Paris as the New Jerusalem.[6]

Anti-fashion discourse that casts fashion as an oriental colony in the heart of the West (exemplarily in Paris) evolved with the Enlightenment.[7] In the discussion that follows, I shall investigate the modernist, Republican rejection of fashion. The dominant Republican, virtuous, progressive discourses stigmatised fashion as the devastating, corrupting, effeminate Oriental Other. The authors of this monotonous narrative, crafted by Jean-Jacques Rousseau, remodelled effectively by Friedrich Nietzsche and Emile Zola, and starring theoreticians like Thorstein Veblen, Adolf Loos, Werner Sombart, Simone de Beauvoir and Pierre Bourdieu, have unanimously predicted, hoped for, and expected fashion's end. In their opinion, fashion had to be overcome on the way to a brighter, healthier future. For all these philosophers and writers the twilight of fashion – a side issue of Nietzsche's *Twilight of the Idols* (1889)– was necessary in order for a free, democratic, enlightened and egalitarian Republic to thrive. The political and aesthetic norm that modernists in general and Republicans in particular strove for is manifest in ideas from 'the straight man' and 'plain speech' to maxims like 'form follows function', 'ornament is a crime' and 'less is more'. It is diametrically opposed to their views on fashion, which they regarded as oriental, decadent, tyrannical and effeminate – in short, a perverse threat to all things Republican and modern.[8] According to this dominant philosophical discourse, the empire of fashion threatens to ruin Republican achievements such as, first and foremost, male virtue, followed by equality of the sexes and rational choice, the narratives of progress. Interestingly, that anti-fashion stance even includes the avant-garde notion of aesthetics.

As a cyclical return in the guise of 'the new', fashion was something to be overcome and remodelled as progress. Dominated by fetishism, fashion supposedly led to addictive consumerism, reducing free men to their basic instincts and turning women into commodities via marriage and the sex market, subject to the alienating rules of reification. Fashion is denounced in Republican discourse – a discourse to be analysed instead of taken for granted by the brave and the free – as that which will convert women into slaves. It is feared that men, in turn, will be turned into the slaves of fashion's ravishing, artificial idols. The authors on whom I shall focus in the following discussion all resisted fashion's seduction with the stern retort 'Reform', for the good of the Republic of free men to come.

In 1761, Rousseau presented pre-revolutionary Paris as a fascinating, though corrupt, new Babel. The symbol of its corruption was fashion. In Rousseau's view, fashion was a queering force, since it undid everything, notably that most natural of things, the division of the sexes.[9] 'Unable to make themselves into men, women make us into women', Rousseau wrote.[10] Fashion, which for Rousseau was synonymous with Parisian luxury, was a symptom of feudal decadence. Disfiguration, not perfectibility, was its driving force. Perverting the natural order of sex and class,

Artificer Fashion turned aristocratic ladies into whores: 'Thus, they cease to be women out of fear of being confounded with other women; preferring their rank to their sex they imitate whores so as not to be imitated.'[11] Fashion turns women into men and, most disturbing of all, effeminated men. At the end of the day, fashion was felt to undermine all *vir*-tue, or male qualities, the basis of Republican concern. Rousseau, one of the fathers of the Republic to come, not only charted a new social contract but also devised a new relationship between the sexes, which turned out to be the very condition of the new political order: the cleansing, or purging, of the feminine from the public sphere. The *res publica* is presented as a *res masculina*; a pure, virtuous masculinity that guaranteed the incorruptibility, military potential, health and order of the modern state.

The aristocratic salon society of pre-revolutionary Paris was constructed by Rousseau as the exact opposite of this Republican, all-male space of natural gender identity: Rousseau described it as an oriental harem headed not by a sultan, but, much worse, by a lady: 'And every woman in Paris gathers in her apartment a harem of men, more womanish than she.'[12] The effeminate ruled in erotic idolatrous cults, dominating Paris; they reduced men to eunuchs, to playboys performing at the mistresses' command. Under the spell of fashion, Paris, as perceived by Rousseau, was an artificial, namely an oriental, space opposed to the natural, austere, patriarchal home of the pure Republic of Geneva. Paris was the opposite of Rousseau's political ideal, the anti-space of Cato's virtuous Roman Republic. Parisian Eros ruled tyrannically through fashion; it ruined *virtus*, or manhood, indeed everything straight and proper. For the sake of the virtuous Republic to come, fashion, Rousseau suggested, had to be abolished. The concept of the *res publica* as a space that is cleansed of the feminine – and *a fortiori* of all things effeminate and effeminating, like fashion – gained credence with the French Revolution and has dominated the European idea of the state far into our century – if not until now.

Nietzsche, in his collection of aphorisms *Human, All Too Human: A Book for Free Spirits* (1878), put the ideal modern Republican garment – the suit Rousseau might have dreamt of – right before our eyes. Fragment 215 on 'Fashion and Modernity' is a fervent apology for the male suit and a stark condemnation of all things fashionable, in the overwhelming sense of feminine fashion. Nietzsche brilliantly illustrated and endorsed the ideology of the male suit as the cornerstone of modernist political and aesthetic ideals. In this short fragment, he takes a decisive break, the Great French Revolution of 1789, as the basis for a historic *a priori* in the order of clothes. John Carl Flügel's 'Great Male Renunciation' in fashion is, for Nietzsche, the positive hallmark of the timely modern politics of fashion.[13]

FIG. 27
Court suit, French,
1774–93

The modern male suit is the direct opposite of the feudal attire of the aristocrat, to whom clothes were everything. The new bourgeois man has nothing of the male courtier about him. He shows through his attire that he has more important things on his mind than clothes. Here, it is elementary to remember that before the French Revolution, it was aristocratic men who were the beautiful sex. They dressed with at least as much ostentation as aristocratic women (see figs 26, 27). The aristocracy as a whole dressed lavishly, while neither men nor women of the Third Estate, the 'commoners' of the *ancien régime*, sported silk, lace, velvet, feathers or colours. After the Revolution, it was not clothes that separated the three estates, but the sexes. Fashion became synonymous with the feminine or, rather, the effeminate. Only women distinguished themselves through their clothes; they indulged in adornment and displayed a beautiful body. In their fashionable women, one might say, the bourgeoisie displayed the castration of the aristocracy.[14]

The suit was for Nietzsche the essence of fashion in modernity, as it eliminated everything fashionable. Re-assessing social values, Nietzsche radically re-defined fashion: its true character was not change, but solid constancy. It was not about vanity, or the desire to stand out in an empty, superficial way.[15] For Nietzsche, fashion should not distinguish but equalise. The male suit – wool cloth, muted dark colours, loose cut, with no play between fabric and body, carefully constructed, with no revealing or clinging – in Nietzsche's account clothes the civil, intellectual body politic of modern society (see fig. 28). To dress 'modern' now means – to reformulate Nietzsche only slightly – to manage a rather paradoxical situation: to communicate through your clothes that you couldn't care less about what you are wearing. The mature European, ideally an independent intellectual male, distinguishes himself as *Geistesmensch* – a man of intellectual worth – not through his appearance, or frivolous frills, but through his vision and achievements. It is his character and individuality, his thoughts, that are at stake, not his body or beauty. It is an indifference to anything commonly understood as fashionable that distinguishes a person of worth.

The worn out, misogynistic opposition of flesh (female) and intellect (male), of an effeminate attitude and sober manhood, dominated Nietzsche's aphorism. If the male suit sublimated the body, female fashion shaped the seductive flesh. It is here that the Orient – the anachronistic, Eros-dominated Other of European sublimation and intellectual hypocrisy – sneaks into Nietzsche's essay. If fashion, as Nietzsche meditates rather than demonstrates, has its unifying, modern form in the suit, female fashion is bound to be exotically anachronistic and eclectic: 'There [in female fashion], one has mustered the inventiveness of older feudal cultures and

FIG. 28
Gentleman's morning suit, London, 1910
Manufacturer Brass and Pike

the whole orbit, the Spanish, the Turks and Old Greeks combined, in order to put the beautiful flesh on stage.'[16] Incapable of creating a meaningful form to shape modernity and its Republican body politic, female fashion borrows indiscriminately from everywhere. Since what it aims for is nothing but the *mise en scène* of beautiful flesh, it borrows from cultures unfit for sublimation, not yet reformed and not yet redeemed by modernity. Fashion masquerades in the clothes of the Court (the effeminate, tyrannical *ancien régime*), of Spanish influence (Andalusian), of Turkish styling (derived from the Ottoman Empire), of the orientalised Greeks (in particular, Cleopatra and the Egyptian horror of all things feminine). A mannerist arabesque, a potpourri, the dire return of a past one had hoped to leave behind: female fashion is fashioned by Nietzsche as the antithesis of all modern, Republican, virtuous striving.

Although women *had* left behind the idea of national and regional identity, as expressed by local costume, they still wanted to distinguish themselves through their clothes: as members of a class, and as individuals:

> European women are as yet far less mature, and for this reason
> the fluctuations with them are much greater. They also will not have
> the national costume, and hate to be recognised by their dress as
> German, French, or Russian. They are, however, very desirous of creating
> an impression as individuals. Then, too, their dress must leave no one in
> doubt that they belong to one of the more reputable classes of society
> (to 'good' or 'high' or 'great' society), and on this score their pretensions
> are all the greater if they belong scarcely or not at all to that class.[17]

In contrast, the male suit – Nietzsche's clear sight postulates – was the norm of modernity, to which all clothes should conform. There are far-reaching consequences to be drawn from this position. Women and idle young men (according to Nietzsche both unable and unwilling to distinguish themselves through their achievements) must compensate for intellectual emptiness by lavishing their efforts on their outer appearance. Stranded in another time, they have not yet arrived in modernity. But hope for the twilight of fashion should not be entirely abandoned: once the ladies' men and also the ladies themselves have finally been educated to become modern Europeans, there will be no further false fashioning. It will have simply vanished.

In 1883, Zola portrayed fashion, linked to mass consumption and the turbo capitalism of the Second Empire, as a full-blown Inner Orient. His novel *Au Bonheur des dames* (The Ladies' Paradise) depicts the Paris of Napoleon III as a ruinous, decadent, hysterical tyranny, a new Babylon in fact. A few traces of virtue are left, but they are rare. *Au Bonheur des dames* fictionalises one of the first department stores in Paris – Le Bon Marché, a true monument of capitalist ambition – as the return of the Old Babylonian cults, of flesh-consuming idolatrous deities like Baal and Moloch, combined with the cult of Cybele.[18] The department store is Zola's cathedral of the capitalist empire. Collectively, they are presented by Zola as women's worlds, brothels appropriately called 'Notre-Dame' or, close enough,

'Au Bonheur des Dames'. Modern consumerism becomes a Catholic-oriental, decadent cult of temple prostitution.

In Zola's fictitious store, a luxurious bazaar called The Paradise, women are dancing around the Golden Calf (smashed by Moses) and indulge in orgies of shameless vice. Their shopping is the modern version of temple prostitution. After a day of sales, the department store looks as if the shoppers had undressed on the spot, stripping off their clothes in an attack of neurotic desire.[19] Ravished, they bathe in the caresses of the public offers of the sales and are themselves offered to the public, pale with desire: 'The clients – raped, violated, plundered – went away, half-naked [...] they felt a faint shame as though having made love in a fishy motel.'[20] The department store becomes the central protagonist, a cannibalistic Baal; the store owner is portrayed as a vampire, who drinks the blood of women and sells their flesh 'like a Jew' – the most pertinent figure of the Inner Orient whose enduring memory was personified by Shylock in the nineteenth century – by the pound. The temples of modern consumption now enshrine the cult of female flesh; intoxicated by an overwhelming desire to consume, women worship at material altars. Femininity and money have become interchangeable. Universalised prostitution, in the form of the great whore Babylon, is capitalism's underlying metaphor and the moral of Zola's novel.

Zola criticises modern consumer culture, and its desire for ever more fashionable clothes, against the backdrop of Babylonian sacrificial cults. He models the cataracts of silk, the waterfalls of georgette, and the pool that they form – beside which women dream of an artificially fashioned, perfected femininity – on the source of the mythic Greek Adonis River, described by Ernest Renan in his *Mission de Phénicie* of 1864. Opposite the source of the river, Renan tells us, there was a temple dedicated to Venus, a place, it was thought, of temple prostitution. The department store, the spectacle of feminine self-fashioning in Zola's novel, is thus like an ancient temple of Venus – at once cathedral, brothel and bazaar. The source of the Adonis springs up from within this brothel, to mirror female narcissism.[21] At this primordial Greek starting point, sex and gold have become exchangeable; beneath an oriental mantel, femininity has become a commodity, and commodity the idea of the feminine.

Thus, a 'dialectic of enlightenment' (Max Horkheimer and Theodor W. Adorno's much later philosophical thesis of 1947) has come true and is fulfilled as the threat of fashion. According to nineteenth-century narratives like Zola's novels, modernity, with the global triumph of capitalism in its imperial form at hand, forgot its enlightening civilising mission; at its very heart – Paris, 'capital of the 19th century' as Walter Benjamin described it – the Orient triumphs. It was not France that conquered the colonies; the colonies took over France. The colonies were not reformed in the rational spirit of the Enlightenment; rather, Empire shone forth in the glaring light of the resurfacing oriental idolatry. The virtuous Republic vanished without a trace and had to be founded again by a new reformed saint, Denise (the heroine of Zola's novel), appropriately named after the patron saint of Paris, Saint Denis. But this dire salvation from effeminate capitalistic devouring by a thoroughly reformed female protagonist who has left all things effeminate behind, only leads to an all-paternalistic marriage with a great provider as husband. To quote Milton: 'all passion spent'.[22] The end.

At the end of the nineteenth century, Thorstein Veblen, whose immigrant parents came from a thoroughly reformed Norway, wrote an update of the harshest and most influential condemnations of fashion.[23] According to *The Theory of the Leisure Class* (1899), fashion had once again, and in the most pointed, revealing manner, become a feudal, oriental anachronism that must be left behind on the way to an emancipated, self-determined and democratic future. Clearly, Veblen was on a mission here with a historically, sociologically, analytically strengthened argument against what he cast as tyrannical, idolatrous, barbaric fashion. He positioned the 'leisure class' of the moneyed aristocracy – his fervour is most critical in this title of his – in parallel with the aristocracy of the French *ancien régime*. The American society described by Veblen is far from being an egalitarian Republican society of free men. In spite of the fact that this leisure class owes its riches to the capitalist principle that money makes money, this caste remains for Veblen a feudal relic. Like the older aristocracy, these people do not work but spend ostentatiously, so representing their wealth in the public eye. For the leisure class, on which fashion and its developments in Veblen's eyes depend, fashion is a form of serfdom inflicted on their women and their servants.[24] While the men of this class exhibit the labour, the exploitation and subjugation, of their servants – an activity that keeps them well-dressed in snow-white, carefully ironed shirts and polished patent leather shoes – they remain nonetheless the masters of a labour they do not perform, their bodies unconstrained. Their wives and their servants have to expose their subjection: in the liveries of servants, frocks of priests and corsets of wives their bondage is evident. Subjugated to their masters, their flesh is marked with the insignia of domination; as property, serfs and slaves are deprived of free movement. In the very heart of modernity, Veblen's argument continues, the mechanisms of subjugation are the same as in a monarchy, which knows subjects, but no free men. Even worse, these vassals are like 'primitive savages', who appear as the radical Other of any enlightened, rational modernity. The captain of industry, who parades his trophy wife on Fifth Avenue, acts like the North American Indian Kwakiutl chief, who carries his trophies in a triumph.[25]

Veblen described 'conspicuous consumption', the motor of modern capitalism, as a wild, barbaric, uncivilised, decadent practice dominated by reification and fetishism. This barbaric underside of modernity, which tyrannically enslaves and forces the subjugated to wear the stigmata of serfdom on their flesh like the slaves of the ancient world, like the serfs of the feudal age, and now like the wives of capitalist patriarchy, is illustrated by Veblen with an extreme emblem of oriental custom: the bound feet of aristocratic Chinese ladies. Veblen collects enemies, and these enemies of the projected Republic of equal, free and self-determined people are a strange mix: the Catholic Church, the feudal Middle Ages, the perverse, tyrannical oriental leisure class, including ancient slavery and pre-modern savages – in short, all those who resist reform and reformation.

Here, the bound feet are of emblematic significance, in that they tie together both barbaric origin and decadence.[26] Things were not much better in Veblen's contemporary United States. The female bound feet were to Chinese men what female corsets and high heels were to American men: crippling, barbaric stigmata that bring distinction. Men looked at their wives not for erotic thrills, but in order to distinguish themselves through their wives' reification and commodification. In a patriarchal society, women's function consists in demonstrating the credibility of the household through conspicuous consumption.[27] By no means superfluous, as it seems at first sight, this is the most utilitarian thing to do. The faster a fashion changes, the more ostentatious it is, the more a man of means can show his means by means of his wife. Demonstrating his power, she leads a life of luxury and leisure in the public eye (see fig. 29).[28] As the first servant of the house, she is part of his mobile goods, like a Maserati, or a luxury yacht. As reified status symbol, she usually even enjoys, as Simone de Beauvoir would later put it, her self-reification and alienation: 'If she has accepted her mission as a sexual object, she loves to adorn herself.'[29]

In spite of, and beside all these modes of tight subjugation in dire need of reform, there remained a bizarre phenomenon for Veblen and his disciples: the strange desire of some men, whom Veblen dismissed as effeminate, to wear, like fashionable women, uncomfortable, unmanly clothes.[30] He feared that not only women, priests and servants, but also homosexual men (the usual suspects) would never become the emancipated, self-determined subjects the free Republic of men depended upon.

After the turn of the century, the modernist architect Adolf Loos decried female fashion as the most 'disgraceful chapter in the history of civilization'.[31] Like Nietzsche, a fan of the male suit as the ideal garment of Republican freedom, Loos saw female fashion as a violation of almost every rule of modern aesthetic ideology. Overtly ornamental, he called fashion simply a crime. As a forerunner of the *Neue Sachlichkeit* (New Objectivity) movement, Loos was a decisive authority in formulating a new, and finally modern, aesthetic ideal that could be reconciled with the political ideal. For him, again, female fashion enslaved men and women alike. No free society, no equality, no virtue seemed possible for as long as women had to adorn themselves, and reduce themselves to the merchandise of a marriage or the sex market. Shamelessly, fashion seemed to appeal to the beast in man. Where Veblen saw socio-political reasons to do away with fashion, Loos receded to (in fact, late romantic) natural grounds, based on which the decadent culture of his time no longer allowed a 'healthy' sexuality. Otherwise (and seriously) – according to Loos – all humans would simply go naked. We find here the oldest of links, dating

FIG 29
Dinner dress, French, 1875–8
Designer Mon. Vignon

from Milton's *Paradise Lost*, of fashion to sin and, after the Fall, to a perverted sexuality. Loos's conclusion, however, as to what to do about the aesthetic and moral misery of modern sexual politics, is quite remarkable: without the right to self-determined work, woman is condemned to remain a creature of pleasure.[32] As long as women cannot compete *with* men but instead have to compete *for* men, attempts to reform fashion according to adequate aesthetic principles are doomed. As long as distinction is the motor of male fashion, female fashion must depend on changing sexual tastes: from masochism to paedophilia, from the dominatrix to the child woman. With women dressed up as decoys, female fashion has to meet the eye at any cost. Within patriarchal capitalism, Loos and Veblen agree, women are subjected, serving prestige, serving lust.[33] As feudal relics, they are like all servants, high and low (whether priests subjected to God, the king servant of the realm, or soldiers serving the country), clad 'in gold, velvet and silk', or stigmatised with bows, frills and feathers.[34] She, an individual, can only embark on her voyage into modernity once she has left behind, and erased, the oriental signature of the ornamental arabesque that is the aesthetic mark of fashion.[35] She has to learn the ABC of modernity that men have already learned by heart: 'form follows function', 'less is more' and, thus, 'ornament is something that must be overcome'.[36] When talking about female emancipation, Loos gets almost lyrical: only with her dress reformed does woman have a chance to be more than a feather in a man's cap: only then can she emancipate herself from servile beguiling and become a self-determined subject in a free society.

In contrast to Loos, jumping to such conclusions, it was the sociologist Werner Sombart who, at about the same time, in 1913, restated the basic oriental metaphor that continued to inform philosophical discourses on fashion: that of the harem as the perversion of free, natural sexuality, with its dialectics of master and slave, yet also with its reification and alienation of women as objects of lust.[37] However, in spite of his rather one-dimensional overall thesis, Sombart came up with a historical twist: capitalism, modern consumer society, cannot thrive in a patriarchy; it depends on free love. The luxury industry, and thus also fashion, boomed because in Europe love happened mostly outside marriage and free of institutional fetters. What drove the industry was neither vanity nor pride, but the cult of all things feminine, the total triumph of the *femmellette*. The 'paramours', who reigned well into the nineteenth century, forged the taste of their lovers and made them spend lavishly on their behalf. Without free love, there would be no thriving luxury industry. In the end, above and beyond its battle with institutional restraint, free love for Sombart existed as part of an oriental way of life, as the after-image of an effeminate monarchy, in a tamed, enclosed, even foreclosed fashion. It could not, rather than should not, corrupt free, enlightened subjects, and it would not effeminate the true, upright man, only a decadent monarch. The Inner Orient lay in the past for Sombart; it had lost its threat, it was nothing but a trace left behind in the progress of free men. Quite fittingly, almost emblematically, Sombart described Louveciennes, the love-nest that Louis XV had built for his *maîtresse en titre*, Madame du Barry, as a Turkish phantasy in which the king, subjected to the whims of the mistress of the realm, reigned as a 'marionette sultan'.[38]

The discourse of modernity – the hope for free men and women, for the upright man and for straightforward, plain speech – persists. Pierre Bourdieu, leading sociologist of the mid-to-late twentieth century, did not embark upon the perilous topic of fashion, a women's topic after all, without the expertise of a co-author, Yvette Delsaut. Our social practice, Bourdieu and Delsaut argued, shows the same misconception and the same superstition that the West ascribes to the decadent Orient, to the no less idolatrous Catholic Church and to barbaric savages (Veblen's choice). For Bourdieu, fashion was the foremost example of this misconception. Delsaut and Bourdieu's illustration of fetishisation is the *griffe*, the brand, which guarantees the (exorbitant) price.[39] The *griffe*, for them, is not the guarantee of value, of an artistic and aesthetic 'know how'. Rather, they saw it as the mark of a fetish. The brand, not the dress, carries the magic.[40] Its attraction is produced through the voodoo cults on the market. It is like a miraculous 'transubstantiation', Bourdieu and Delsaut argued, invoking once more the Catholic Church as the Inner Orient of modernism, an association with fetishism and superstition.[41] Again, fashion appears as a dance around a Golden Calf, this time that of late capitalism.

This latest version of idolatry critique, which has in Bourdieu its ablest propagator, badly needs to be dispelled by a different kind of analysis, an analysis aware of aesthetic aspects and political implications beyond the positivist limitation and restriction of mere social research. As a weird, incommensurable queering force, fashion needs to be read as a politics against the politics of plain speech, as a politics against the vicissitudes of functionalism, against Rousseau's phantom of virtuous, free all-maleness. In the last instance, fashion is indeed, and should finally be understood, as a politics against this politics of the Modern and the phantasm of the free, self-determined, self-controlled subject. Fortunately, with fashion, we have never come fully round to this humanistic, male phantom of politics. And this may be the best a future history has to say about us.

Wang Guangmei's Crimes of Fashion: The Politics of Dress in China's Cultural Revolution

Jin Li Lim

The Great Proletarian Cultural Revolution (1966–76) was the wayward child of Chinese Communist Party (CCP) Chairman Mao Zedong's revolutionary ambition and his political insecurities.[1] Mao believed that although the People's Republic of China had undergone a socialist transformation since its birth in 1949, it was still necessary to eradicate all that remained of the bourgeoisie.[2] Yet, since Mao also believed that 'he was the revolution' (and his Thought was its touchstone), progress required the eradication of his, and the revolution's, opponents.[3] The Cultural Revolution was launched to eliminate Mao's 'real or imagined enemies', to purge the party-state of bourgeois-ness, and to fulfil the communist utopia. To do this, Mao called the masses to direct action – indeed, to 'bombard the headquarters'.[4]

For many young Chinese, the call to rescue the Revolution from CCP 'capitalist roaders' had deep resonances.[5] At once increasingly disaffected with CCP authoritarianism and yet deeply invested and steeped in Mao Zedong Thought, they responded eagerly. Directed to cleanse both Party and society of bourgeois-ness and counter-revolutionary conservatism, Chinese youths – the Red Guards, as they called themselves – took the chance to settle old scores with the authoritarian order that had been imposed on China since 1949. Societal order broke down in the face of a radical – often violent – onslaught against the erstwhile institutions of authority, power and tradition.[6] Mao was incapable of controlling the forces he had unleashed, and after the Red Guards turned on each other, in 1968 the People's Liberation Army (PLA) intervened, turning China into 'a garrison state', and sending millions of political undesirables, including students, to be 're-educated' via rural labour.[7] Nevertheless, internal politicking and rivalry between the military and the Party continued to create instability until Mao's death in 1976.[8]

The Cultural Revolution was so-called because Mao and his allies alleged that Chinese culture was a refuge for the bourgeoisie, 'capitalist roaders' and counter-revolutionaries, who concealed their enmity in literary criticism, theatre, opera and other cultural forms. Thus, to return to the 'socialist road', facets of culture that were bourgeois, capitalist or counter-revolutionary – the 'four olds' ('ideas', culture, customs and habits left over by the exploiting classes) – had to be purged.[9] In reality, the 'four olds' became a catch-all term for anything deemed antithetical

FIG. 30
'Dirty goods' (脏物) on display as evidence of bourgeois-ness: note the silk dress, stockings, jacket and leather shoes, Acheng District, Harbin, Heilongjiang Province, China, c.1965

to Mao Zedong Thought, justifying attacks on anyone or anything allegedly bourgeois or counter-revolutionary, including assaults (from verbal abuse to violence) on intellectuals, teachers, writers and artists, and the destruction of cultural objects (see fig. 30).

Fashion and politics

The new climate of radical politics proved to be unfriendly to earlier ideas and expressions of fashion: contemporary accounts describe attacks on so-called bourgeois fashion, incidents of destruction and persecution that histories of the Cultural Revolution have since highlighted in their narratives of the assault on the cultural status quo. Red Guard fashion-shaming attacks on civilians included house raids to find and destroy bourgeois clothes; shaving victims' heads in a yin-yang style (half-clean, half-cropped); hanging wooden boards depicting 'a snake in a flashy dress and high-heeled shoes' on victims; slitting legs of too-tight trousers; and cutting up western shoes. Indeed, as the Red Guards proclaim, in author Ji-li Jiang's memoirs of the Cultural Revolution: 'Tight pants and pointed shoes are what the Western bourgeoisie admire. For us proletarians they are neither good-looking nor comfortable. What's more, they are detrimental to the revolution, so we must oppose them resolutely.'[10] But as historian of design and curator Verity Wilson has noted, contrary to the view that the CCP imposed a sartorial landscape on 'Red China' and 'transformed the people of China into an army of blue-uniformed revolutionaries', 'a sartorial sobriety that verged on the boundaries of a uniform' was not the same as the CCP imposing drab, Maoist uniforms.[11] There was no official uniform; neither Mao nor the CCP tried to impose one. Instead, the uniform appearance – or 'sartorial sobriety' – emerged from the new, radical context, which required appearances to reflect politics. Outfits that recalled military or workers' uniforms were in vogue for their show of solidarity with the revolutionary classes, especially favouring the soldiers (hence, Red Guards).[12] Indeed, quasi-uniforms were politically expedient, allowing their wearers to avoid accusations of decadent bourgeois-ness, and were in line with the frugality (*pusu*) preached by Mao Zedong Thought.[13]

Thus, even if the Cultural Revolution paid 'overt attention to outward appearance' and made 'displays of individuality and eccentricity in dress'[14] politically dangerous, in this context politics intersected with – rather than eradicated – fashion. The fashion historian Juanjuan Wu writes that fashion 'was not killed during the Cultural Revolution – it just donned a different mask'.[15] She points out that fashion was highly paradoxical: people were supposed to shun bourgeois styles and a 'four olds'-like concern for appearance, yet the hyper-ideological climate meant that appearance became paramount, as a 'deviation from the rigid dress code could result in life-threatening consequences'.[16] Fashion in Mao's China was still responsive to trends, albeit politically defined trends. The radical climate made soldiers' uniforms 'the trendiest and most revolutionary look in the Cultural Revolution's sartorial system'.[17] Mao's cult of personality created

demand for 'ideologically correct accessories', such as the Little Red Book, red armbands and – the most popular – Mao badges,[18] 50 million of which were produced each month in 1968 (fig. 31).[19]

Equally, variations in placement and subtle alterations of badges, buttons, collars, pockets and sleeves, and the selection of materials and stitching, suggest that many Chinese people still asserted individual styles and identities. Historian and sociologist Peidong Sun argues that such 'silent and subtle undertaking[s]' were 'a cultural practice of everyday resistance', with 'personalized, gendered and rationalized clothing practices such as altering the sleeves, collars, waists and trouser leg openings' acting as 'major expressions of people's resistance' to the Cultural Revolution's sartorial order.[20] As politics endowed dress with such significance, opposition to the existing order could equally be expressed through clothing: a teen with straight-legged black jeans; a worker with close-fitting clothes; or a 'sent-down' youth who preferred 'more fashionable round-shaped, stand-up, boat and wing collars'.[21]

Such nuanced intersections of politics and fashion during the Cultural Revolution suggest that Chinese fashion history is more complex than is often recognised. In order to offer further evidence of this relationship, this essay draws on both Chinese and American primary sources in order to investigate one of the most famous incidents of the period, the persecution of Wang Guangmei in 1966–7.[22]

Wang Guangmei

Wang Guangmei (1921–2006) was the wife of Liu Shaoqi (1898–1969), the second President of the People's Republic of China (1959–68), or PRC, and the man originally chosen by Mao as his successor. Wang came from a fairly well-to-do, urbane and cultured family; her father was a high-ranking government official and a diplomat, and her mother was a senior educator. She was elegant, stylish, and vivacious – it is said that Wang first caught Liu's attention when she approached the high-ranking Party official for a dance at a party.[23] Wang joined the CCP in the 1940s (becoming a member in 1948) and, as she spoke English, French and Russian (and had a degree in atomic physics from Fu-jen University), she worked as an interpreter in the CCP's wartime-base in Yan'an, where in due course she married Liu. After the establishment of the PRC, Wang served as Liu's secretary, witnessing at first hand the breakdown of relations between Liu and Mao.[24] Beyond that, as China's de facto First Lady, Wang became one of the country's most prominent

FIG. 31
Mao badges on full display, as worn by a soldier of the People's Liberation Army, c.1968

style icons, and images of her in elegant dresses, accompanying her husband on his official duties, were regularly published in the Chinese media (figs 32, 33, 34).

Liu had been Mao's heir-apparent prior to 1966, but by the mid-1960s the two men were increasingly estranged. With the socio-political upheaval of the Hundred Flowers (1956–9) followed by the economic disaster of the Great Leap Forward (1958–61), and as tensions between China and the USSR grew, by the early 1960s Mao's leadership was under question, and the Party's prestige damaged.[25] Liu and other CCP leaders had criticised Mao for the Great Leap, and they also disagreed with Mao about how to fix its legacies. Mao wanted to renew the Revolution and class struggle, to eliminate the obstructive bourgeoisie; Liu wanted to rid the CCP of graft, inefficiency and incompetence. In the ensuing Socialist Education Campaign, Liu's priorities triumphed; over five million CCP members were purged or punished, and 77,000 driven to their deaths.[26] This divergence, and Liu's apparent ascendance, created in Mao a deep sense of insecurity, yet another underlying motivation for the Cultural Revolution.[27]

Given Mao's animosity towards Liu by 1966, Wang was under threat too.[28] Having offended Mao herself, she was a target in her own right. In the Socialist Education Campaign, Wang had led a work team to Taoyuan (Hebei Province), where they compiled information on local cadres who were guilty of either graft or 'incipient capitalism'. After Wang reported her findings in April 1964, 40 out of 46 ranking cadres were purged.[29] Wang's efforts were promoted and lauded by Liu. But Mao did not approve: he resented the 'big fuss' and felt that Wang and Liu were upstaging him.[30] Moreover, Wang's purge of the cadres could be interpreted as an attack on Mao, since he had praised many such rural cadres for their successes during the Great Leap – successes that Wang had undermined.[31]

If Wang's actions during the Socialist Education Campaign were not enough to make her one of Mao's political enemies, her leadership of a work team during the early Cultural Revolution cemented her vulnerable situation. In May 1966, Mao had the CCP Central Committee issue a call to 'hold high the great banner of the proletarian Cultural Revolution' by 'thoroughly expos[ing] the reactionary bourgeois stand of those so-called "academic authorities" who oppose the party and socialism'.[32] Yet, at this point, Mao had left the implementation of the Cultural Revolution to the CCP leadership. Meanwhile, the students responded fervently, and Peking, Qinghua and other universities were soon rife with poster denunciations of rightist, bourgeois, and counter-revolutionary 'backward' teachers and students. Faced with growing chaos, CCP work teams were sent to restore order. Wang Guangmei led a team to Qinghua and, when faced with radicalised students who refused to back down from attacking teachers approved by the CCP, and who criticised the Party for interfering, Wang arrested their leader Kuai Dafu, publicly criticising him and his friends.

OPPOSITE ABOVE
FIG. 32
Liu Shaoqi (left), Vice-Premier Chen Yi (centre) and Wang Guangmei (right) attending the May Day celebrations in Kunming, China, 1963

OPPOSITE BELOW
FIG. 33
Liu Shaoqi (foreground left) and Wang Guangmei (centre) visiting a factory in Kampong Cham, Cambodia, accompanied by Prince Sihanouk of Cambodia, 3 May 1963

ABOVE
FIG. 34
Liu Shaoqi and Wang Guangmei (right) being welcomed at Phnom Penh airport, Cambodia, 1 May 1963

Mao had no interest in suppressing student radicalism; he was counting on it to get his way. Thus, in July 1966, after he announced his return to pre-eminence with a swim in the Yangzi River, Mao sent allies to visit the imprisoned Kuai, and used his wife, Jiang Qing (Madame Mao), to convey his endorsement of the students' actions. Kuai was soon released, and the work teams disbanded. The radical 'rebel' students were exonerated, and the Red Guards were unleashed. Emboldened, Mao seized the momentum to clear the Party leadership of his enemies and promote his allies. By the time a new Central Committee had declared, on 8 August, that the Cultural Revolution was against 'those in power within the party taking the capitalist road', Liu Shaoqi, Deng Xiaoping, and many others had already been purged.[33]

Liu Shaoqi was still President, but this hardly mattered. The next few months saw increasing attacks on Liu and Wang, from public protests by thousands of students to vicious caricatures of Wang depicting her as a 'painted prostitute' and, by 1 April 1967, house arrest and national condemnation in the *People's Daily* (*Renmin Ribao*).[34] The worst, however, was still to come. In the morning of 10 April, Wang was arrested by the Red Guards and taken to Qinghua University campus.

FIG. 35
Transcripts of the 'Three Interrogations of Wang Guangmei' (Sanshen Wang Guangmei), Jinggangshan Regiment, Qinghua University, Beijing, 1967

You must put on that dress!

The Red Guards' plan was to hold a 'struggle session' in Qinghua's square.[35] But before the event, the youths wanted Wang Guangmei to confess her crimes. Ostensibly, the Red Guards of Qinghua University (the so-called 'Jinggangshan Regiment') wanted Wang to confess her political misdeeds, and yet the transcript of her interrogation suggests a distinctly sartorial element to her alleged criminality, and indeed to her counter-revolutionary-ness (fig. 35).[36]

Perhaps the most prominent feature – prop, even – of the interrogation was a dress that Wang had worn during a state visit to Indonesia in 1963. The Red Guards repeatedly demanded that Wang put on the dress, and she refused each time, infuriating the students. When Wang refused to put it on, claiming that 'it [was] not presentable', the students' response was to question why she had worn it in Jakarta. When Wang tried to explain, the students questioned why she had worn it in Lahore, which, in fact, she had not. This might seem like a non sequitur, except when viewed through the tinted lenses through which the Red Guards judged Wang. They were trying to make a broader point. They wanted Wang to wear that dress – whether it was from Indonesia or Lahore – because the dress had come to represent something blameworthy about Wang. When Wang refused yet another demand to put on the dress and suggested to the young comrades, 'Would it not be better for us to discuss things seriously?', the Red Guards erupted in righteous rage:

Who wants to discuss things with you? Let me tell you: you are being strug-
gled against today! ... You are the wife of a Three-Anti Element, a reactionary
bourgeois element, and a class-alien element. You will not be given an iota of
small democracy, let alone extensive democracy! Dictatorship is exercised
over you today, and you are not free.[37]

Wang was certainly not free, but she still refused to put on the dress – 'come what
may', she declared – even if she opened herself to the possibility of 'criticism
and struggle' and even if she had indeed 'committed mistakes'. The Red Guards
insisted: 'You are guilty of crimes! You are being struggled against today, and you
will also be struggled against hereafter. Put it on!'[38]

For the students, there was a clear correlation between the fact (to their
mind) that Wang was 'guilty of crimes' and the dress in question. That link was
made only more concrete by the alleged correlation, at the time, between being
fashionable and being counter-revolutionary. Wang herself seemed to realise that
fashionable dress was both related to 'four olds' behaviour and an example of
a 'four olds' object, obliquely stating, in reference to a fur coat she was already
wearing: 'This is already good enough for receiving guests. It was a gift from
Afghanistan. They had this in mind when they said that I was fashion-minded.'[39]

But the Red Guards again demanded that Wang put on the dress she wore in
Indonesia. When she refused once more, they gave her an ultimatum. Wang tried to
negotiate, first suggesting that she could wear a dress appropriate to the climate
and then, as a sign that she recognised the larger point the Red Guards were trying
to make by showing her publicly in the dress, proposing instead that she put on a
pair of high heels. This, unsurprisingly, was rejected: 'That is not enough! You must
wear everything!' When Wang protested that they had no right to treat her in this
way, the students exploded:

We have this right! You are being struggled against today. We are at
liberty to wage struggle in whatever form we may want to, and you have
no freedom. You might as well forget about your vile theory of 'everybody
being equal before truth'. We are the revolutionary masses, and you are
a notorious counter-revolutionary old hag. Don't try to confuse the class
demarcation line![40]

After which, the transcript notes, the 'Ghostbusters', as they were called, the
name derived from a metaphor for 'capitalist roaders' as ghosts or devils, began
to force Wang to wear the dress.[41] Wang tried to resist, but they pulled it on
over her clothes. Her protests were met with escalating abuse: chanting that 'a
revolution is not a dinner party', the Red Guards made Wang wear silk stockings
and high-heeled shoes, which – along with the dress – had been taken from her
home, and, most bizarrely, a specially made parody of a pearl necklace, a string of
ping-pong balls. The point of this, as Wang knew well, was to use fashion – Wang's
fashion – as evidence of her counter-revolutionary criminality. Wang herself dryly
noted: 'You are making every effort to make me look ugly.' Which, to be sure, the

Red Guards were. But the point of the exercise was to show that the dress and its accoutrements proved her guilt. Indeed, as they responded: 'This is what you have been all the time. Why feel shy about what you have done? All we do is restore your true identity.'[42] Wang was then brought out in front of a mob of 300,000 students, subjected to vitriolic abuse, forced into the 'jet plane' pose for photographs (fig. 36) and filmed for a new documentary.[43]

Despite her humiliation, it is obvious from the transcript that Wang remained remarkably cool-headed throughout. Indeed, once the absurd outfit had been forced on her, she remarked to her young oppressors that 'Chairman Mao says that nobody is allowed to strike, abuse or insult another person' and that by coercing her into that outfit, they had violated his rules. The Red Guards were infuriated:

> Nonsense! It is you who have insulted us. By wearing this dress to flirt with Sukarno in Indonesia, you have put the Chinese people to shame and insulted the Chinese people as a whole. Coercion is called for when dealing with such a reactionary bourgeois element as you – the biggest pickpocket on the Qinghua campus![44]

Fashion-minded

A long-standing interpretation of this incident is that it was carried out on the orders of Jiang Qing. When Wang had accompanied Liu on the state visit to Indonesia in 1963, she had been photographed at diplomatic receptions with Indonesian President Sukarno, wearing an elegant, traditional silk *qipao* (figs 37, 38).[45] This image, and others like it, were well known in China; historian Antonia Finnane suggests that a documentary was filmed in colour, and then shown in cinemas across China after the state visit.[46] Jiang was allegedly 'bitterly jealous' that Wang could 'wear glamorous clothes when she went abroad as the president's wife'; hence, in 1967, she made sure those images were revisited as part of the humiliation of Wang.[47] Prior to the 'struggle session' on 10 April, Jiang told Kuai Dafu that 'When Wang Guangmei was in Indonesia, she lost all face for the Chinese. She even wore a necklace!' And since Wang had worn the *qipao* 'to make herself a whore with Sukarno in Indonesia', Jiang apparently ordered Kuai '[to] find those things and make her wear them'.[48]

To be sure, Jiang harboured deep resentment towards Wang.[49] In fact, Jiang – in the words of the CIA – had 'openly despised' Wang, who had thus ended up 'a special target of the Madame's wrath'.[50] But, according to Kuai, while Jiang had raised with him the allegation that Wang's wearing of the *qipao* had shamed the Chinese people, she did not mention a necklace, or give any instructions on how to humiliate Wang. Kuai admits that making Wang wear the *qipao* had been his idea, while the oversized necklace had been an idea of his comrades, as a real pearl necklace would have been invisible to the public. Moreover, Kuai adds that the Red Guards had deliberately looked for these items of clothing at Wang's home.[51] But if Jiang Qing had not issued the order, why had it been necessary to make Wang wear these items?

FIG. 36
Wang Guangmei's 'struggle session' at Qinghua University, Beijing, 10 April 1967

To the Red Guards, Wang was a 'counter-revolutionary', a 'reactionary bourgeois', and an enemy of Mao and the revolution. They were clearly convinced of it. Wang was indisputably a 'Three-Anti Element' because Mao himself had already prominently identified her as his ideological enemy.[52] And, of course, the reason the Qinghua Red Guards had such hatred for Wang was because of her involvement with the work team that had tried to suppress their revolutionary ardour in 1966.[53] Thus, politics – in terms of Mao's machinations of power, *and* the struggle for the direction (and soul) of the Revolution – was the determinant of the crime(s) of which Wang was accused. But at the same time, Wang's guilty status – indeed her bourgeois criminality – was proven by her choice of fashion.[54]

The CIA had noted that in the run-up to 10 April, posters had appeared in Beijing with caricatures of Wang as a 'painted prostitute'.[55] But this was part of a larger criticism that used Wang's alleged fashionability – both in terms of her dress and her supposed ideas about style – as ammunition for vicious attacks. In March 1966, Wang had travelled to Pakistan with Liu – just as she had to Indonesia and elsewhere – on a state visit. The Red Guards alleged that Wang had taken advantage of this duty, 'feeding on the blood of the people' in a series of fashion indulgences. She is said to have demanded hats with silk streamers

FIG. 37
(From left to right) President Sukarno, Wang Guangmei (wearing a *qipao*), Hartini Sukarno and Liu Shaoqi entering the Presidential Palace in Bogor, Indonesia, during Liu Shaoqi's state visit, April 1963

and lining, out of concern for her 'strange hairstyle', and then ordered replacement hats to be flown over to her when she misplaced the originals. Other expensive clothes were apparently ordered, and workers in the Beijing Friendship Company (the state-run department store) were allegedly told by Wang: 'I am in front of the curtain, you are behind'. The Foreign Ministry's protocol office was instructed by Wang to display all the clothing kept for her to choose from for state occasions, even as she insisted they make custom orders for her of the 'Western and Hong Kong styles', like qipao, coats and capes. Wang was supposed to have ordered a custom cape made of 'fur, with black satin lining, lace borders, and flower-patterned pockets'; to have refused to use local 'Peony Brand' rouge, demanding that her staff find Parisian rouge (as well as the largest pearls to make *that* necklace); and generally, to have 'chased desperately after Hong Kong and Western fashions'.[56]

The Red Guards claimed that such behaviour showed the air of superiority, feudalist thinking and decadent bourgeois-ness in which Wang Guangmei indulged. In fact, the 'old fox spirit' (as the Red Guards called her) had apparently always been that way: when she was a student at Fu-jen University, her vanity and social aspirations had allegedly led her to have cosmetic surgery to give herself double eyelids.[57] Wang's fashion – her 'sartorial past' – was potent proof of virtually all their accusations.[58] Thus the interrogation was peppered with references to the qipao, the necklace, Wang's fashionability, and motifs of appearances, all of which proved exactly how far along the 'capitalist road' she was. And so she would be displayed as such.

It is worth noting that none of the Red Guards' denunciations at Wang's 'struggle session' referred to her alleged sartorial crimes, nor did they allude to what her previous, 'fashion-minded' behaviour proved.[59] Forcing Wang out in public in that outfit – even if it were a parody – would have been viewed as proof enough of her guilt. Indeed, as Elizabeth Perry, scholar of Chinese politics and history, notes of Maoist China, the use of props, and stage-managed public shaming and humiliation, was key in 'a conscious strategy of political and psychological engineering', intended to stir up 'mass passions in service to larger political and economic goals', especially during the Cultural Revolution.[60] Wang's dress and necklace were props intended to prove her criminality against – and provoke mass support for – the prevailing political regime.

FIG. 38
(From centre left to right) Liu Shaoqi, President Sukarno, Wang Guangmei and Hartini Sukarno receiving a traditional Balinese welcome in Bali, Indonesia, during Liu Shaoqi's state visit, April 1963

Style Activism: The Everyday Activist Wardrobe of the Black Panther Party and Rock Against Racism Movement

Carol Tulloch

[T]he significance of the clothes people wore and their body language could not have been estimated at the time; there was no time for distance, things were happening so fast.
Syd Shelton, *A Riot of Our Own*, 2008

This essay is a treatise on style activism, where the styled body is associated with energetic action about a concern. Style activism is the embodied making of a political activist self as statement, whether lifelong or for just one event. I argue here, in reference to the concept of style activism, that the styled body is a sincere identifier of the individual within an activist movement. How someone chooses to style themselves, to construct their sense of self, is agency. It is unquestionably autobiographical.[1] Style activism is another example of this.

Towards a definition of style activism

This definition of style activism emerged for me during a series of projects and critical thinking that I conducted on identities, difference, style-fashion-dress, the styled body, style narratives and activism.[2] It has primarily been inspired by the photographs taken by Syd Shelton of the Rock Against Racism (RAR) Movement, 1976–81 (figs 39, 43),[3] his documentation of contextual events of racist factions, anti-racist demonstrations and 'the lives and landscapes that were defined by others as "different", which often fuelled racist acts of violence by simply being'.[4] Shelton's observation, which introduces this essay, relates the urgency of activism and its documentation at the time. Here, I aim to redress Shelton's concerns that he overlooked the importance of the styled bodies in his photographs, and to consider their possible contribution and meaning to anti-racist action.

I first used the phrase 'style activism' in the preface to *Syd Shelton: Rock Against Racism* (2015):

FIG. 39
Rock Against Racism (RAR) event, Southall, London, 1978
Photographer Syd Shelton

As collective activism, RAR's success was dependent on individual
contributions to fuel the movement's activities across the country.
This unique national, and eventually international, charge incorporated
personalized performativity as another antagonistic tool against
racism. For example, the styled bodies of black and white contributor-
participants at RAR events were acts of style activism – the making of
a political activist self as an embodied graphic statement of anti-racism.
Shelton's images prompt us to remember that the individuals at RAR
carnivals, gigs, and demonstrations were the event – they were RAR.[5]

I employed the term next in the coda of the monograph *The Birth of Cool: Style Narratives of the African Diaspora* (2016), to clarify that there are different aspects to the style narratives of black people, whether quiet activism or more vocal, as in style activism. There, I 'wanted to demonstrate how seemingly innocuous presentations of the styled self can have an equally high octane impact of meaning'.[6]

This thinking, which is effectively also about designing the self, connects with debates on design as activism. Penny Sparke has defined design activism as 'a movement that is rooted in the belief that design has the capacity to change the world, not merely to reflect it'.[7] Guy Julier stresses that 'Design activism is overtly material in that it grapples with the everyday stuff of life: it is also resolutely driven by ideas and understandings. It is a making of politics.'[8] In light of this, the examples considered here articulate the significance of 'self-made action'. The prism of making is central, significantly making the self, making things and, in the context of this essay, individuals as part of a movement making history.[9] I want to emphasise that making and the personal are part of the different ways in which one can protest. The styled body is a significant aspect of this.

Within dress studies there have been developments in the expanded meaning of terms produced to consolidate the significance of individual and group activism. Tanisha Ford, for example, refers to 'soul style' in her quest 'to offer an alternative perspective on the civil rights and Black Power movements' in the African diaspora, with a focus on black women's soul style.[10] Ford speaks specifically of ensembles, garments, accessories and the beauty regimes of African diasporic origins and meaning that came to define specific African diasporic approaches to activism.[11] This essay focuses on two movements: the American Black Panther Party for Self-Defense (BPP), 1966–82 (fig. 40), and the British RAR, the name coined by the photographer Red Saunders.[12] My references to style activism[13] are inclusive of women and men of different cultural groups, black and white. It is important to consider the anti-racist activist connections between black and white people, as it is generally the disconnections between them, due to the effects and affects of racism in its official and everyday guises, dating back to slavery and continuing to the present day, that are emphasised.[14] A further aim of this study is to assess how one can *read* style activism, as captured in the photographs that were vital to the mediation of the concerns and goals of particular activist anti-racist organisations.

FIG. 40
Black Panther Party members
protest outside the New York
City Courthouse, 11 April 1969
Photographer David Fenton

Photography as meaning, photography as activism

This essay concentrates on two activist photographs. The first, taken by Shelton, is of the Anti-Anti Mugging March, which occurred in Lewisham, London, on 13 August 1977 (fig. 45). This was a counter demonstration of some 5,000 local people and anti-racist activists, which included a contingency of RAR members who were protesting against the Far Right Anti-Mugging March of the British National Front Party (NF). The NF made the brazen claim that all muggers were black. Additionally, their march was organised to intimidate the non-white population of Lewisham. Shelton was at the time an RAR (London) committee member. The second image is of the wedding of BPP members Emory Douglas and Judy Graham in 1969, which featured in *The Black Panther* newspaper (see fig. 46). The photographer is not credited. This documentation took place at a significant moment in the history of the BPP, as it was reaching its height in terms of local, national and international impact, with some 10,000 members, chapters in 26 states and international branches.[15] The Party's enduring belief was that 'the most important thing to hold on to in the midst of racist oppression was our revolutionary culture, which was about the need to give the people more economic, political, and social empowerment.'[16]

In the production and mediation of these photographs, one can see their specific relevance to the advancement of activism for their respective organisations. Yet together, despite their different transatlantic locations, the photographs contribute to a mapping of style activism as a vital anti-racist tool for both black and white contributor-participants. I suggest they represent the concept of togetherness – 'a sense of belonging together, fellowship'[17] – from different tangential positions, under the rubric of anti-racism, civil and human rights shrouded in style activism. What marks the two photographs are the subjects' styled bodies and gestures, their styled selves as an embodiment of the activism to which they contributed.

The vast range of photographs associated with RAR and BPP includes images of individuals in clothes worn for a specific event, which convey the sense that the 'photographs were rooted in the fact of the thing' – the activist event that was part of 'a living [lived] experience'.[18] To conduct a reading of the style activism of these two events is to help cement the sense of 'the real' that is the desired hallmark of documentary photography. Style activism, as read in these photographs, is a reminder that the individuals who take part, who contribute to the progression of an activist movement, *are* the movement.[19]

My reading of these two images is conducted within the context of the aims, objectives and aesthetics associated with RAR and BPP, which are discussed later, and the subjective purpose of the photographer. Michelle Bogre has stated that an activist documentary photographer tries to communicate a truth about a situation that is of concern to others.[20] She clarifies this further:

> *The word activism is interchangeable with advocacy ... An activist photograph can be subtle and persuasive, or it can be confrontational ...*

Activist photography is intent and process. It is an act and a filter through which a photographer perceives the world ... An activist photographer ... is driven both by history and the desire to change an inequity, underscored by the belief that it can be changed.[21]

The photographs of the BPP and RAR's associated participation include this range of desired activist intent and hopeful impact on potential viewers. Simultaneously, they are dominated by the styled bodies of anti-racist activists and the range of 'ordinary' clothing is clear to see, suggesting that these looks are created from a personal wardrobe, which by extension could be called an activist wardrobe. What is especially enticing is the contexts in which these styles were formed and the meanings associated with their use. Therefore this essay also explores what conceptual artist Victor Burgin designates as the *meaning* of the image in the photographs, specifically the styled bodies.[22] To engage in such a practice, 'in order to develop critical perceptions which can be brought to bear upon photographic practices, historically and now',[23] is to be aware that due to photography's 'heterogeneity, it is clear that photography theory must be "inter-disciplinary"'.[24]

This latter advice is useful with regard to the images at the centre of this study. In the case of Shelton's activist documentary photographs, they are of black and white contributor-participants in Britain taken by a white photographer of working-class origins. While the other, by an unknown photographer, is of black members of the BPP. Art historian Erina Duganne's advice as to how to work with photographs of black people applies equally to the images of black and white anti-racist activists. Duganne proposes that a study of photographs that are solely of, or include, black people can be done from the vantage point of 'the specific ways in which the racial meanings of their representations shifted according to the social and historical turns of their production and reception'.[25] My approach to the reading of photographs associated with the BPP and RAR is comparable to Duganne's guidance, which emphasises:

The careful attention to the complexities of the historical moments and social relationships in which these images were produced and received ... but also those more private and elusive attitudes, desires and interpersonal relationships that influenced the manner in which these representations came to acquire meaning about race and self during this period ... [for] race, subjectivity and documentary photography ... especially as an index of the 'real' ... not only produced one another but were inescapably intertwined in postwar America.[26]

Rock Against Racism and Syd Shelton: style activist dynamics in black and white
RAR was a collective creative engagement between black and white designers, writers, actors, musicians, performers and activists that resisted the violent, and sometimes fatal, racism of the 1970s. The main trigger for the formation of the movement was a racist rant by Eric Clapton during his concert at the Birmingham Odeon, on 5 August

1976, that 'Britain [was] becoming "a black colony"', further aggravated by his support of Enoch Powell, the British right-wing Conservative politician who in 1968 had made the 'rivers of blood' speech, which pre-supposed that this would be the outcome for Britain if immigration of black people continued.[27]

In response Red Saunders instigated the writing of a letter,[28] signed by friends and sent primarily to the music press, which declared in the pages of *Sounds* magazine: 'We want to organise a rank and file movement against the racist poison in rock music – we urge support – All those interested please write to: Rock Against Racism, Box M, 8 Cottons Gardens, London E2 8DN. P.S. "Who Shot the Sheriff" Eric? It sure as hell wasn't you! – Signed Peter Bruno, Angela Follett, Red Saunders, Jo Wreford, Dave Courts, Roger Huddle, Mike Stadler, etc.'[29] The letter was also published in *Melody Maker, New Musical Express* and *Socialist Worker*. According to David Widgery, socialist RAR (London) committee member and GP, for whom the central provocation that energised his activism was the racist murder of Altab Ali, a 25-year-old Bengali clothing machinist on his way home from work,[30] there were some 140 letters 'the first week, all enthusiastic', in support of the call for the movement.[31]

RAR recognised that the chronic rise of racism in the 1970s was a legacy of British slavery, colonialism and imperialism, the effects of which were still felt by African, Asian and Caribbean migrants and immigrants to Britain, and their descendants born in Britain after the Second World War. RAR's activism took the form of demonstrations, carnivals, music, gigs and design. Their activities took place on the street and in parks, town halls and pavilions across Britain. RAR's form of activism was illustrative of what a collective creative engagement between designers, writers, actors, musicians, performers and supporters can achieve. RAR emphatically represented collective activism, dependent on the individual contributions of those who were taking part, who expressed their concerns about Britain and so cemented the meaning of RAR.[32] The movement's activities were what author and political activist Barbara Ehrenreich calls an 'ongoing community',[33] which spread across the country, as documented by Shelton, and eventually reached Europe and the United States. RAR, uniquely, combined the chronic issues of combating racism with the 'collective joy' of music; various forms of individualised and group performance, and performativity, where the styled bodies of contributor-participants were one of the 'essential elements' of such an endeavour.[34]

FIG. 41
Anti-racist skinheads, cover of RAR newspaper *Temporary Hoarding*, no. 6, 1978
Photographer Syd Shelton

Interestingly, RAR did not have an official photographer, but Shelton took hundreds of photographs of anti-racist and racist subjects and activities between 1976 and 1981, resulting in the largest collection of photographs of the movement and its social-cultural contexts.

He used photography, he says, 'as a graphic argument, enabling me to be a subjective witness of the period that could, hopefully, contribute to social change'.[35] Shelton's photographs are visual quotes from this period of intense racism and anti-racist activism. Many of his photographs were used in the RAR newspaper *Temporary Hoarding* (fig. 41). Shelton's photographs communicate the embodied actions of RAR contributor-participants: from the designer-makers of the wide range of RAR material to the people who wore RAR badges or styled their bodies for RAR events, from the people who bought *Temporary Hoarding* to those who carried and read RAR banners. These were enmeshed forms of self-expression in opposition to the National Front. RAR's numerous forms of activism – including Shelton's photographs – were indicative of French philosopher Paul Ricoeur's observation that each contributor-participant to such activism is '"entangled in stories"; the action of each person (and of that person's history) is entangled not only with the physical course of things, but also with the social course of human activity' (fig. 43).[36]

Indeed, a rich materiality, particularly a sense of 'intellectual and physical touch',[37] emanates from Shelton's images. For me, the evocative marks of presence and the enduring trace of energetic participation made by individuals who contributed to RAR events are personal quotes derived from actually being there, from being part of something worthwhile. His evocative photographs of crowds at outdoor RAR carnivals resemble a textile design – an imprint of cohesive collectivity and activism (fig. 42). By 'imprint' I mean 'a character impressed upon something, an attribute communicated by, and constituting evidence of some agency',[38] which can be said to be the agency of RAR. Individuals made unique imprints that left marks on the space where they performed, as when the clothed body of John 'Segs' Jennings of The Ruts created an imprint in the dry foam that covered a Bradford stage during a performance on the RAR Militant Entertainment Tour in 1979 (fig. 44).[39]

This is my interest here. A moment in a life when the styled self is captured in activist activity. I am encouraged further in this proposition of style activism as a legitimate genre of style practice by social and cultural historian Paul Gilroy's response to Shelton's collection of photographs and graphic design associated with RAR, which he believes can help in the following way:

FIG. 42
RAR Carnival, Brockwell Park,
London, September 1978
Photographer Syd Shelton

OVERLEAF
FIG. 43
Contributor-participants in the
RAR Movement and contextual
demonstrations, London,
Cromer and Leeds, 1976–81
Photography and montage
by Syd Shelton; images
selected by Carol Tulloch

[To] discover a new appreciation of the extent to which British politics was actively and deliberately racialised during those difficult years ... Shelton's archive is also a means by which to grasp the strategic significance of anti-racism and to understand its value as both a substantive political disposition and a grounded philosophical framework. That emphasis is now unfashionable. It yields expanded conceptions of what comprises authentic politics and of where cultural factors have decisively shaped important outcomes. In other words, new ways of thinking about the incorrigible power of noisy, electronic culture and inchoate, youthful resistance are still pending in this marginal history.[40]

This essay is a proposition of ways in which one can expand on these 'marginal histories' through style activism.

The photograph of the Anti-Anti-Mugging March protestors, both black and white, on New Cross Road, Lewisham[41] begs analysis (fig. 45). At first glance there is nothing seemingly radical or subversive in the individualised styles of these Anti-Anti-Mugging demonstrators: jeans worn in popular designs, either flared or with a straighter leg and rolled hem; demure skirts; footwear from pumps to flip-flops to jellybean sandals; headscarves worn by black women as a recognised sign of black consciousness. The gamut of style genres range from workwear-based

FIG. 44
John 'Segs' Jennings of
The Ruts, RAR Militant
Entertainment Tour,
Leicester, 1979
Photographer Syd Shelton

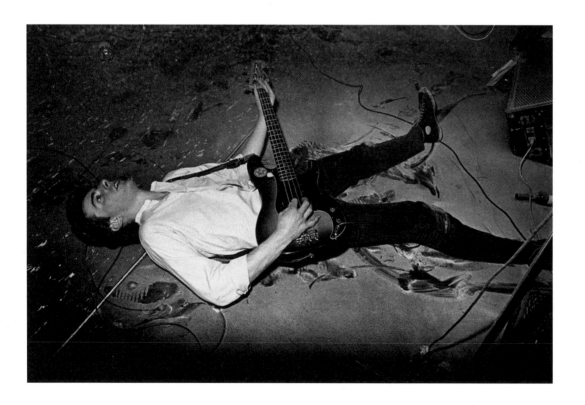

FIG. 45
Anti-Anti Mugging March,
Lewisham, London,
13 August 1977
Photographer Syd Shelton

dungarees to an army surplus-style shirt. Perhaps the most visibly creative personal styling is the man on the right, with his long hair, beard, and sleeveless V-neck jumper worn over a shirt and jeans, who is wearing a drop earring. Fundamentally, it is the combination of very familiar garments, items that were once directional and had now become the basic elements in the daily practice of *being,* and the unanimous gestures of protest culminating in a concert of embodied graphic argument against racism, which makes this photograph so compelling.

The young black woman on the left of the photograph, who has tied her denim jacket around her waist in such a way that it becomes an impromptu apron, summarises this for me. She is not the only Anti-Anti-Mugging protestor to tie clothing around that part of the body in this group, but it is the resultant mini apron that grabs my attention. It triggers connections with previous observations I have made on the apron associated with black lives.[42] A seemingly mundane object,[43] the apron has historical and political significance that on the one hand absorbs, protects and projects demands for rights as worn by British suffragettes, while on the other hand becomes a symbol of segregation as the badge of demarcation of black American female domestic servants or black South African maids during apartheid – thereby becoming an 'activist tool'.[44] It was these expanded meanings underlying the cultural relevance of the apron that led me to view the young black woman's version of an apron as an activist shield. Her repurposing of a denim jacket, worn like an apron while she makes political gestures in harmony with her fellow anti-racist demonstrators, provides a rich photographic composition of activist action that Shelton captured as it happened – 'a living experience'[45] that provides a sense of 'the real'.

Additionally, these gestured movements, and the anti-racist context in which individuals chose to express themselves, were documented and supported by the activist photograph, which cemented their actions as part of the geographical and political landscape of Britain at the time, and subsequently its history. The raised fists, punching into the air as the protestors sing and chant,[46] animate the graphic fist illustration at the centre of the 'Socialist Workers Party Bristol' banner to the right of the photograph. This is a significant example of co-agency. The act and process of gesture 'arises from a mingling of inside and out, the result of physical and psychological emotion', 'the resonance of *feeling* bodies – alone and in community'.[47] Further, it can be a connection with and between others, as gesture 'points to a moment in time and a movement in space';[48] 'gestures *migrate*' and 'undergo appropriations and enjoy afterlives that change their initial function',[49] as illustrated in Shelton's photograph. Such unconscious, yet profound, styling details as a denim jacket, tied around a woman's waist whilst she demonstrates with others, encourage the aptitude to *see* into activist photography anew, and, as John Berger says, '[to] again and again, register surprise'[50] at how styled activism embodies the intent of anti-racist action.

What I find motivational is the sense of excess in Shelton's body of work around RAR, which connects with the contextual frame of graffiti that is present in his work. Sometimes boldly independent, at other times graffiti can be background noise to a portrait (see fig. 43, bottom left) that echoes how such graphic exaltation imprints itself on society. Graffiti, Norman Mailer has explained, is a graphic expression by those 'in the know', who experience and understand what they are commenting on, where 'the courage to display yourself is your only capital'.[51] Shelton's image of the Anti-Anti-Mugging demonstration, like graffiti, was a dialogue with society, a reaction to an issue that required swift, militant style response, and encouraged others to join in.

Shelton's photographs are about lives that matter, not only those that were being marked by racism, but also those that contributed to and supported RAR's activities and other anti-racist movements. The contemporary cultural understanding of, and democratised reliance on, photography has enhanced the historical value of such images. This, in turn, places RAR contributor-participants and other anti-racist activists as necessary visual reminders of action against racist ideologies, so evidently 'us' against 'them'.[52] In the languid space of historical reflection, Shelton's photographer-participant act can be seen as a cypher for the enmeshed urgency and agency of lived contributions and experiences that fanned the momentum of RAR. The role of style activism here is to emphasise the fact that the activist *was* the argument.

FIG. 46
'A Wedding of Revolutionaries',
The Black Panther newspaper,
Saturday 23 August 1969

A Panther wedding: an iteration of Black Panther activism

The 23 August 1969 issue of *The Black Panther* newspaper carried a full-page feature titled 'A Wedding of Revolutionaries', which recounted the marriage of Emory Douglas, the BPP Minister of Culture, and Judy Graham, an editor on *The Black Panther*, held at St Augustine's Episcopal Church, Oakland – a primary meeting place for the BPP (fig. 46). This was the third of four such weddings in 1969, which featured in the newspaper.[53] The main photograph of the couple at the altar could be defined as 'subtle activist photography', as referred to by Bogre previously. It is a respectful head-and-shoulders shot of a significant moment in a couple's life – the decision to make a public declaration of their wish to share their lives with each other. Nonetheless, there is activist, or, more precisely in line with the aims of the BPP, revolutionary intent.

Every aspect of this news feature emphasises that life can be lived differently through the lens of Black Nationalism according to the BPP. In the main, the couple wear similar garments and hairstyles, recognisable items of the BPP uniform: black leather jackets, black shirts and Afro hairstyles. They both wear badges, of what appears to be an image of Huey P. Newton, co-founder of the BPP, the kind of badge that was produced for the 'Free Huey' campaign following his imprisonment in 1967. Yet their styles are individualised. Graham wears, apparently, prescription glasses of a generous size that follow the line of her expertly shaped eyebrows, which are in turn accentuated by earrings. Graham's meticulous presentation of her face for the wedding trumps former Black Panther member Erika Huggins statement that 'Panther women were not concerned with their appearance, and "the best thing we could say about our clothing was that it was clean."'[54] To mark himself, Douglas wears a chain resting diagonally across the chest of his black shirt, while strident sunglasses draw attention to his face, to him, a look made complete by a well-groomed goatee beard. Douglas's choice of accessories brings an expression of contemporary, grass roots, black male glamour to the proceedings.

Here was an inventive, modern ceremony building on the foundation of a traditional ritual. At first glance this wedding appears unusual due to its negation of traditional bridal wear, yet it was in keeping with the cultural zeitgeist of the 1960s. Wedding outfits of the late 1960s reflected the trend for the rejection of 'conservative' dress.[55] Fashion curator Edwina Ehrman and dress historian Avril Lansdell refer to the late 1960s vogue of 'dressing up' by brides and grooms, which included references to historical dress designs and details resulting in '[P]op interpretations of nineteenth-century styles and fabrics.'[56] In relation to this, Bellville Sassoon stated: 'It was the art of clothes to get you noticed.'[57] Ehrman describes 1960s fashion in general as 'flamboyant' and adds that fashion magazines such as *Queen* marked a shift in thinking. The 1970s bride was perceived as 'a person not just a fashion cipher, part of a tradition but very much herself',[58] thinking that could equally be applied to this BPP wedding ensemble.

Douglas and Graham were not 'dressing up'. They wore what I see as a 'wedding uniform' that signified the embodied evidence of their allegiance to, and participation in, the BPP. The easy, streetwise air of the Panther uniform was redolent of its origins, an outfit that Huey Newton wore for a meeting with Bobby Seale, his BPP co-founder. Seale recalls:

> Huey happened to be dressed in a sports-style leather jacket, black slacks, and a blue shirt. I stepped back, looked at him in the nice California sunshine, and said, 'Hey, Huey, wait a minute. That should be our uniform, just the way you're dressed right now, with the black shoes nice and shiny.' The next evening we were watching an old movie about the French underground resistance to Hitler's occupation. The characters in the film were wearing berets. I said, 'Huey, let's wear berets, man.' The uniform was an important part of our image. Huey and I understood that good visuals – the graphics in our posters and newspapers and the use of photographs like Stephen Shames's – were part of how we could successfully communicate and capture the imagination of the people.[59]

Seale's recollection of how the Panther uniform was constructed from personal items, the resultant look so well crafted by Newton as to create wonderment in someone who knew him, demonstrates how a style could affect others due to its 'blinding visibility', to draw on Krista Thompson's term.[60] Equally, therefore, Graham and Douglas in Panther wedding uniform radiated a blinding revolutionary visibility to the wide readership of *The Black Panther* newspaper.[61] Additionally, Douglas was the paper's 'revolutionary artist, "a critical part of the liberation struggle", artistic director, graphic designer and illustrator'.[62] Writer and artist Colette Gaiter states that Douglas was responsible for the 'branding' of the Panthers as '[t]he Panthers were adept at creating recognizable signifiers and icons that identified their members and eventually represented their ideology',[63] which includes the leather jacket as worn by Graham and Douglas at their wedding.

The couple may have maintained allegiance to wearing 'recognizable icons' of the BPP, but of the differentiating personal items the couple chose to style their wedding outfits, Douglas's sunglasses stand out. Fashion historian Vanessa Brown argues that sunglasses support a look and the spirit of the wearer,[64] but when Panther members wore sunglasses for their public activist talks, she states:

> [I]t seems the Black Panthers sacrifice the ability to communicate 'openly' with the live audience in front of them, for a statement which is in fact aimed at the American audience at large, in a use of sunglasses which suggests ... [an] 'unhidden hidden gaze'... The masking of the eyes states clearly that the Black Panthers disallow their audience to fully read what that might be. For a group to do this en masse, in a uniform, indicates that this unknown intent is shared by the group.[65]

But could there be alternative meanings behind the use of dark sunglasses that shield the eyes of these militant black men other than concealment? On a practical level, was the wearing of sunglasses by the Black Panthers, particularly in Oakland, done to combat the bright light of the Californian sun? In the case of Douglas, wearing sunglasses as part of his Black Panther wedding uniform, I offer another possibility of use. In the main photograph of the couple, and in additional images of them holding hands or standing with the best man at the wedding, Bobby Seale, one can see Douglas's eyes through the dark lenses. This visibility, from behind and within, I read as a style choice that Douglas wants to make while at the same time staying openly communicative about the revolutionary goals of the BPP.

Togetherness

In addition to the standard marriage verses, the officiant of the Graham and Douglas wedding, Father Neil (the BPP's spiritual advisor), read passages from the final chapter of *Soul on Ice* by Eldridge Cleaver (1968):

> *To all black women, from all black men*
> *Queen – Mother – Daughter of Africa*
> *Sister of My Soul*
> *Black Bride of My Passion*
> *My Eternal Love*
>
> *I greet you, my Queen, not in the obsequious whine of a cringing Slave to which you have become accustomed, neither do I greet you in the new voice, the unctuous supplications of the sleek Black Bourgeoisie, nor the bullying bellow of the rude Free Slave – but in my own voice do I greet you, the voice of the Black Man. And although I greet you anew, my greeting is not new, but as old as the Sun, Moon, and Stars. And rather than mark*

a new beginning, my greeting signifies only my return. But put on
your crown, my Queen, and we will build a New City on these ruins.[66]

This excerpt is taken from the chapter in which Cleaver concludes his complex feelings about his attraction to white women and his own sense of self. The book is a journey of self-discovery for Cleaver: his advocacy for love of, and commitment to, black women and the coming together of black men and women at this time, in the 1960s, were paramount as a form of survival. Ideally, such a union was a bid for a different black future.

Paul Alkebulan, once a member of the BPP, references these weddings in *Survival Pending Revolution: The History of the Black Panther Party* (2007). He discussed them in the chapter 'Women and the Black Panther Party', under the section heading 'Sexual Relationships'. By placing an overview of the weddings here, Alkebulan draws attention to the complexity of such relationships within the party – the desire for the development of loving relationships between black men and women, and the reality that 'multi-partner relationships were common in the BPP'. He adds that '[A]lthough the weddings united two people, sexual fidelity was an individual decision.'[67] A reading of the feature 'A Wedding of Revolutionaries' necessitates recognition of such contextual observations.

As mentioned previously, the Douglases worked together on *The Black Panther* newspaper. They were what Marie Corbin calls 'a unit', whose identity can be regarded as 'interchangeable'.[68] Corbin's definition of a couple includes the way the pair act in public: '[T]heir relation is marked off from others, acquiring some degree of exclusivity. Because they define themselves as a "couple" they may feel that they ought to behave in certain ways – to meet, to do things together – and that their relationship should have some precedence over others.'[69] Additionally, Corbin explains that 'Sometimes the deliberate demonstration to others in a community that the proprieties are being observed, the specifically public nature of social interaction, may also be extremely important.'[70] Similarly, dress historian Katrina Rolley argues that to dress alike is to raise comment and cause viewers to look again, to emphasise a couple's 'special closeness and their difference from the rest of society'.[71] In light of this, and in the wearing of the BPP uniform for their wedding, this 'revolutionary couple' accentuate their united presence, one that is symbolic of BPP aims. They challenge perceptions of what black aesthetic power can look like. This pensive moment is also the embodiment of togetherness as activism. Fundamentally, my intimation of togetherness underwrites the materiality of co-agency through the couple's style activism and the sanctity of the wedding event. As feminist scholar Maria Tamboukou has remarked, an 'event ... a continuum wherein past, present and future co-exist, an unfolding time, wherein events as forces that effectuate changes, emerge',[72] is something that cannot be underestimated in terms of personal and collective meaning to the bride, groom and Black Panthers in general.[73]

Conclusion

The two case study photographs represent fragments of activist time that make up the pivotal periods in anti-racist, anti-fascist, human and civil rights history. They achieve the primary objective of this essay – to illustrate that style activism is a contributory methodology of activist co-agency, as it is the material and aesthetic practice of individualised action under the banner of a specific activist group concern. Equally, it is another arsenal in the graphic argument of the fundamental importance of difference. The choice of garments, of supposedly ordinary components from an individual's wardrobe in order to style themselves for taking part in an activist event, as in the anti-racist demonstration and BPP wedding outlined previously, is also a matter of taste and habitus, the practices of everyday life that help negotiate individual agency and being, a concept originated by Pierre Bourdieu.[74]

I have argued that taste is a distinctive trope with which to assert difference as part of everyday life. That when practiced by black people, it is fundamental to making a life, to a sense of survival and freedom that has resulted in expanded meanings of taste: taste as necessity, taste as a statement of autonomy, a tactic of activism, taste and belonging ... taste as 'us-ness', intimacy as an aesthetic of taste, taste in the definition of a life.[75] Habitus is far from being invisible:[76] 'One can actually see habitus in the effect it has on others who are *affected* by the social and cultural relations between individuals and groups, particularly through objects.'[77] The photographs explored here demonstrate the visibility of habitus on the body as style activism in public spaces and intimate activist ceremonies. In turn, such visibility is a contributory factor to the 'consciousness attention'[78] that is generated in its making, its choice and use by individuals and cultural groups to graphically express, through style activism, the everyday concerns of anti-racism, human and civil rights.

III

Bodies and

Borders

Bombshell: Fashion in the Age of Terrorism

Rhonda Garelick

Fashion, and the related realms of women's material culture, including magazines and cults of celebrity – can appear to some as unserious, cordoned off from global politics. Yet, these realms do the unsuspected work of inducting women into politics, of enabling their communicative participation in the political unconscious. For this reason, examining fashion as it appears at key political and cultural moments – in political debates, on the runway, on the red carpet, and as represented by artists of several media – casts new light on how terrorism, and the responses it evokes, plays into, heightens, and finds expression in codes of feminine sexuality and gender politics.

Terrorism has existed for millennia. Here, though, I shall be referring mainly to the period beginning with the 9/11 attacks of 2001, and to the cultural sphere of Europe and the United States (with the exception of work by Palestinian filmmaker, Sharif Waked).[1] And beyond specific or delineated acts of terrorism, I am especially interested in the broader phenomenon of 'the culture of terror', a term coined by Henry Giroux to describe the overarching atmosphere of suspicion and violence that permeates all sides and includes the mentality and the techniques adopted in principle to combat terrorism, but which often mirror or replicate terrorist tactics. These include invasive surveillance practices, attacks on civil liberties, and an internalised culture of fear, militarism and heightened racism.[2] This essay argues that women's material culture cannot be cordoned off from these effects but offers, instead, another portal to surveying a cultural dimension of terror.

Jean Baudrillard has written that terrorism is causing the West to terrorise itself.[3] It might be more incisive, though, to say that terrorism often provides an excuse for the West to perpetuate terror upon both itself and others. Jacques Derrida offers an especially apt metaphor for the self-inflicted violence inherent in terrorism: he understands it as a kind of autoimmune disease – as the body politic attacking itself from within.[4] In figuring terrorism as a medical problem, Derrida foregrounds the essential connection between the global, political disruption of terrorism and its effect upon literal bodies of flesh and blood. This connection between terrorism and the body is precisely the site on which we can position a discussion of terrorism and that most embodied form of art, fashion.

FIG. 47
Marilyn Monroe (with Steve Smith, brother-in-law of John F. Kennedy) wearing a transparent Jean Louis gown with rhinestones, the first 'naked dress', 19 May 1962

Terrorism – violence visited upon civilian populations by non-state actors – can be an intimate phenomenon, far more physical and more deeply bodily than traditional warfare. Terrorism alters conceptions of the body; and it consequently implicates fashion, which absorbs and re-interprets these shifting conceptions. Fashion, in fact, often serves as a site for the displaced, deflected anxieties that attend terrorism, becoming a kind of dark fun house mirror, reflecting, perpetuating and exaggerating terrorism's effects on and relationship with bodies, especially women's bodies, as well as the metaphoric, collective body we all occupy: the body politic.

Political precursors, displayed and hidden:
two iconic garments from the 1960s

The past will illuminate the present here; hence, I shall begin by considering two iconic garments, markers of two cultural-historical events from 1960s America. Together the garments lay the terrain for a discussion of the contemporary relationship between fashion and terrorism. Both items find their provenance in the presidency of John F. Kennedy, the glamorous 'Camelot' era violently ended by assassination, an act officially labelled 'domestic terrorism' by the FBI. The garments are Marilyn Monroe's transparent, rhinestone-embellished Jean Louis evening gown (fig. 47; designed by Bob Mackie, a 19-year-old assistant at the time), in which she famously sang 'Happy Birthday' to JFK at a fundraiser held at New York's Madison Square Garden; and First Lady Jacqueline Kennedy's fuchsia pink bouclé Chez Ninon suit (a line-by-line Chanel copy), which she wore in Dallas, Texas, on 22 November 1963, the day of the assassination.

Monroe's gown was worn without undergarments, and has been called the first 'naked dress'.[5] Under the bright stage lights of Madison Square Garden, the paper-thin silk gauze became a transparent screen through which shone Marilyn's nude body, glittering with 8,080 strategically placed, hand-sewn rhinestones.[6] Although held until recently in a private collection, out of public view, the dress remained vividly in our cultural imagination for over 50 years, thanks to the countless circulating photographs and the much replayed, grainy film footage of Monroe, singing breathily to the president, her breasts, abdomen and derrière often clearly visible.

In 2016, the dress itself re-entered the public eye when Ripley's Believe it or Not Museum bought it for over five million dollars, making it the most expensive dress ever purchased at auction. Ripley's promptly capitalised on its investment by featuring the dress as the star attraction of a highly publicised, touring exhibition in 2017, commemorating Kennedy's 100th birthday. Fifty years later, Monroe's 'naked dress' still served as a provocative lure for audiences: 'Monroe just shimmered and sparkled on stage,' says Martin Nolan, who organised the sale to Ripley's. 'The audience … thought "She's wearing nothing." And that's what she wanted.' The dress was 'made to shock audiences,' explained a Ripley's official in a press interview, clearly hoping to entice modern audiences with the same shock value.[7]

If Monroe's dress represents extreme visibility – both literally (in its transparency) and figuratively (as a high-profile Ripley's attraction) – Jacqueline Kennedy's pink suit represents the opposite: extreme invisibility. Physically, the suit was modest, providing no glimpse or even outline of the First Lady's body. Boxy, square, and made of opaque wool – in the classic Chanel style – it loosely skimmed and covered Mrs Kennedy from shoulders to knees. And while photographs of it do exist, the suit itself remains un-seeable to this day: although Mrs Kennedy refused to take it off on the day of her husband's assassination, for the 55 years since, the blood-stained suit (fig. 48), minus the matching pillbox hat, which has disappeared, has been kept entirely out of sight. It remains hidden underground, stored in a vault at the National Archives, unavailable for public viewing.

The National Archives holds a wide collection of artefacts related to the Kennedy assassination, which scholars may view and examine. These include garments worn by killer Lee Harvey Oswald; Oswald's rifle; the bullet-shattered windshield of the President's limousine; and the famous 8mm film, shot by private citizen Abraham Zapruder (who had only intended to film a home movie of Kennedy's Dallas visit), depicting the entire ghastly scene. Only Jacqueline Kennedy's suit may never be viewed – at least not for nearly another century: it will not be released from its vault until 2103.

The official reason given for keeping the suit locked away was to avoid bringing 'dishonor to the memory of Mrs. Kennedy or President Kennedy', an explanation that feels inadequate.[8] Why would the suit dishonour the Kennedy family when none of those other assassination-related artefacts does? Why bury it away? In an interview, fashion curator Phyllis Magidson offered a curious answer: 'It would produce hysteria if placed on view.'[9] But what exactly is this hysteria? Placing the suit in dialogue with Monroe's dress offers some answers that will prove highly relevant to an analysis of contemporary fashion's relationship to terrorism.

To start, the pink Chez Ninon suit presents a complicated gendered semiotics: while it revealed little of Jacqueline Kennedy's body, it did reveal bodily truths of a different kind. After the assassination, while the jacket remained largely intact, the skirt was badly stained with blood. In itself, that might not be shocking; skirts often wind up stained with a woman's own menstrual blood. Every woman has dealt with this annoyance. Blood on trousers or a skirt 'codes' as a sign that a woman's sexual, reproductive interior has somehow overflowed, overrun the usual constraints (feminine hygiene products, undergarments) meant to contain and conceal it. But Jacqueline Kennedy's suit was stained not by *her* blood, not with traces of her bodily interiority, but with her husband's. The skirt bore indelible evidence of the President's shattered body, specifically of the interior of his exploded head – his brain – which had sustained the fatal bullet wound. When he was shot, President Kennedy slumped over into his wife's lap, soiling her skirt. Nothing less than the literal Head of State, a symbol of power and strength, had exploded onto a woman's skirt. In this way, the stained suit testifies to the vulnerability – the 'explode-ability'

– of the national body politic, demonstrating its unsettling proximity to the realm of the corporeal, and to the feminine. Here, then, may lie the reason why the pink suit stays locked away: it announces a perilous loss of national honour and the defilement of power. President Kennedy's head, the seat of his reason, was reduced to a menstrual-like stain on a lady's skirt. We see now what may have prompted Phyllis Magidson's choice of the highly gendered term 'hysteria' to describe the uproar the suit risked causing if exhibited. Magidson's word, 'hysteria', suggests that displaying the stained suit would reveal the fragility, the feminisation of the body politic, and thereby incite a particularly female chaos, provoking a kind of 'uterinisation' of the body politic by contagion. The suit must remain buried in the vault in order to conceal the terrible damage done to the nation, to the body politic, by domestic terrorism. We bury that garment away, just as we tend to bury consciousness of our own organic, bodily frailty, and the revulsion, or abjection, it can provoke. Abjection, as Julia Kristeva explains, 'is what does not respect borders'. And in the matter of Jacqueline Kennedy's blood-stained suit, multiple borders have in fact been transgressed: the border between the exterior and interior of the presidential body; the border between male and female bodies (as his organic matter splattered onto her); and ultimately, the borders of the body politic, which suffer transgression as well, having been symbolically disrupted by the terrorist act of assassination.[10]

Compare these circumstances to those of Monroe's dress: freely exhibited in public and celebrated because, despite its transparency, it has never revealed anything dangerous, tragic or politically destabilising, only female body parts, without mishap, rupture or overflow. In fact, rather than suggest the slightest bodily irregularity or excess, the gown outlined, highlighted, contained (but only barely – Monroe had to be sewn into it) and presented the intact body of the woman widely suspected at the time to be the President's mistress, thus reminding the public of his libidinal appetites, his virility.[11] Monroe's gown, then, confirms not only her own intact feminine desirability, but also the intact masculine functioning of the presidential body and, by implication, the intact potency of the State – precisely the opposite of what Jacqueline Kennedy's suit conveyed.

Account must also be taken here of Monroe's particular persona. More than just an actress, Monroe embodied a kind of potential erotic explosion, conveying an extravagant female sexuality often described with metaphors of violence or death: she was a 'bombshell', a femme fatale. But that skintight Jean Louis gown, worn to honour the President (and commissioned especially by her for this occasion), reassuringly harnessed Monroe's erotic explosiveness in symbolic service to national, masculine (patriarchal) power. It packaged her symbolic explosivity as a gift offered up for the pleasure of the President, and all those watching the event in Madison Square Garden and on television.

Monroe had established her erotic explosivity, of course, on film, and it seems clear that Bob Mackie and Jean Louis designed the dress with Monroe's

FIG. 48
Jacqueline Kennedy (with Attorney General Robert F. Kennedy) at Andrews Air Force Base, Maryland, in her blood-stained Chez Ninon suit, 22 November 1963

cinematic quality in mind. In fact, she had specifically requested a gown that 'only Marilyn Monroe could wear'.[12] With its finely woven mesh material and thousands of flickering crystal beads, the dress resembled nothing so much as a movie screen – projecting Monroe's body in all its glory. In this way, the gown underscored her role as the pre-eminent example of Hollywood's special brand of idealised, commodified female sexuality, which was (and perhaps still is) the American film industry's prime global export. The dress, then, highlighted not only Monroe's sex appeal, but also her role as a screen spectacle and symbol of America's international cultural influence. That this universally known movie idol might also have 'belonged', in a sense, to President Kennedy only intensified the peculiar blend of Eros, popular culture and patriotism assembled to mark and celebrate JFK's 45th birthday – and all so perfectly encapsulated, gift-wrapped even, by that single, flickering tube of silk.[13]

The presumptive freedom of shopping: fashion and nationalism

In the ensuing half-century, national anxieties about power, female sexual explosivity, and political violence – especially terrorism – have continued to find symptomatic expression in the domain of women's fashion. In 2001, in the wake of the 9/11 attacks, President George W. Bush famously exhorted citizens to 'go shopping' as a form of resistance, reframing terrorism as an aggression against American capitalist 'freedom', which could be countered somehow by spending more money at the mall. The fashion world promptly seized upon this idea as a way of shoring up its own industry: in 2001, Editor-in-Chief Anna Wintour launched an anti-terrorism campaign called 'Fashion for America: Shop to Show Support', writing in American *Vogue* about the need for 'fashion in these difficult times'.[14] Fashion and media scholar Minh-ha T. Pham, who labels such rhetoric 'fashion-as-a-right discourse', makes the case that 'Wintour's formulation of consumerism interarticulates biopolitics and national politics so that the care of the self is made coextensive with the care of the nation.'[15] In other words, the self-adorned shopping woman stands in for a fortified nation. Hence, in a symbolic sense, women's fashion, used correctly, combats terrorism. Conversely, one might infer, fashion misused or abused (as in the case of Mrs Kennedy's suit) signals a nation's weakness, its susceptibility to terrorist attack.

The discourse of 'fashion-as-a-right' (and by extension, 'fashion-as-bulwark-against terrorism') has continued to resurface in the aftermath of terrorist attacks. Often, sexually provocative clothing specifically – understood as proof of western freedoms – comes to represent resistance to Islamic terrorism, which is interpreted (self-servingly) as an expression of Muslim condemnation or envy of these ostensible freedoms. In an interview after the November 2015 Paris terrorist attacks (which killed 130 people), model and fashion designer Inès de la Fressange embraced this theory: '[T]here's solidarity against bloodthirsty cowards ... We'll need even more luxury, short skirts, and extravagance – everything totalitarians reject.'[16]

In other words, the best resistance consists in doubling down on European women's provocative allure, consumerism and self-indulgence.

Such views are not limited to western-born women. In a widely read 'Open Letter to Daech [ISIS]', written also in the wake of the November 2015 attacks, a young Tunisian-born French Muslim woman, a law student, echoed de la Fressange's remarks. The text, published anonymously, posited the author's own westernised fashion and (unveiled) coiffure as forms of resistance against Islamic terrorism: 'I like dressing as I please, in flowing, short dresses in summer ... I like to style my hair and to feel the wind caress it ... I love my life, and do you know what I owe it to? My country, France ... I am a woman and I do not fear you.'[17] Here, again, the presumed pleasure in exposing the female body (pleasure accessible to the woman herself as well as to those observing her) – the mini-skirted legs, the blowing hair – signifies pride in nationhood and opposition to terrorism. Note that both de la Fressange and the French-Tunisian author mention short skirts specifically: feminine sexual allure consistent with European norms of bodily exposure has morphed here into a patriotic refusal of terror.

This curious proximity of sexy fashion to anti-terror campaigns makes sense when we recall the deeply bodily nature of terrorism, and specifically its relationship to bodily explosion. At its most basic level, terrorism operates via the haunting, pervasive fear that any or all bodies can explode or shatter without warning, through contact with another body – a suicide bomber, for example. Such explosion occurs randomly and often, contiguously, via body-to-body contact, in a kind of contagion of explosion. Such violence is triggered not by warplane or battleship, but by the intimacy of a body potentially next to yours at the airport, in a nightclub or at a soccer match – a body that will likely explode along with yours. The greatest potency of these acts, furthermore, extends far beyond the actual victims: it consists of the fear they instill in *everyone* – fear of our bodies' fragility and susceptibility to explosion or destruction, fear of just how closely we adjoin not only death, but also physical disintegration. Terrorism thrives by producing a kind of 'border anxiety': a state of hyper-awareness of our bodies' vulnerable borders, of the potential dissolving of the border lines between our interior and exterior selves, the possibility that our skin won't hold our interiors in – a possibility disturbingly confirmed by Jacqueline Kennedy's blood-splattered suit.

Terrorism creates a parallel brand of 'border anxiety' as well: the anxiety of disrupted *national* borders. By threatening to harm the body politic from within (in the manner of autoimmune disease, as Derrida pointed out), and by upending traditional notions of what constitutes identifiable foreign enemies (perpetrated as it is by non-state actors), terrorism undermines our understanding of the frontiers that separate and define nations, blurring the distinctions – the border lines – between enemy states and allies, between friend and foe. Baudrillard puts it succinctly: 'We cannot draw a demarcation around "[terrorism]".'[18] The 'war on terror', then, is an a-territorial, borderless (not to mention apparently unending) pursuit. Understandably, responses to this menacing amorphousness, to this dissolution of borders, often involve a compensatory insistence on redefining and re-affirming national borders, on redrawing the bodily silhouettes of countries in an attempt to keep out dangerous outsiders. Two recent examples of this kind of nationalist ardour for border maintenance and control include the United Kingdom's June 2016 Brexit vote to exit the European Union and President Donald Trump's ongoing attempts to build a wall along the United States border with Mexico.

In his analysis of terrorism, W.J.T. Mitchell also raises the issue of border anxiety, and the shapeless, un-delineated nature of terror: 'Terror[ism] produce[s] a different kind of battlefield, [which] has no front or back,' he writes.[19] He thus invites the question: What does, reassuringly, have very clear fronts and backs within the given discourse of terrorism? An answer: Bodies. Especially women's bodies. And here we find increasing clarity. In response to terrorism's border anxiety, its threat of formlessness, the 'culture of terror' finds reassurance in a compulsive policing and redrawing of the human (often female) bodily silhouette. This leads to a shift in focus from national borders to bodily contours, to the intense scrutiny and policing of individual persons, in an effort to make visible the invisible, to make sense of the unknowable bodies around us. It leads to airport X-ray scanners and bags being rifled through, to strip searches and pat downs, to garments being opened and manipulated, and bodies palpated and scrutinised through those garments.

Here again, fashion enters: terrorism's greatest power lies in its undetectability, in its capacity to resist visual recognition. Terrorists look like anyone else. Their clothes manipulate semiotics. *Terrorism, that is, scrambles fashion codes*.[20] Consequently, we find an increasing compulsion for visibility and clarity, for looking, a hunt for the sartorial data that terrorism either refuses, redirects, or renders illegible. The culture of terror yearns to render the body visible; it is obsessed with physical transparency, with laying bare.

In the wake of twenty-first-century terrorist attacks, such obsession with physical transparency and bodily exposure has dramatically infiltrated the entire cultural sphere surrounding fashion. This leads often to what amounts to a *mise en scène* of compulsive looking – both through and with clothes – in a symptomatic attempt to conjure a controllable body politic. We find evidence of this in a variety of arenas including fashion photography, the arts, political debates around dress codes and, of course, couture design. In what follows, using examples taken from each of these arenas, I shall offer analyses of 'compulsive looking' and its multifarious political, psychological and aesthetic implications within the 'culture of terror'.

Terrorism as a fashion shoot motif

Sometimes compulsive looking takes a very literal form, as in Steven Meisel's controversial 2006 photo shoot for Italian *Vogue*, which commemorated the fifth anniversary of 9/11. Entitled 'State of Emergency', the Meisel shoot absorbed and re-purposed scenes of terrorism culture (including Abu Ghraib), staging scenarios of bodily surveillance, torture, disrobing, bodily violation and female sexual display – with a dose of BDSM.[21]

Meisel's 'State of Emergency' literalises the phrase 'fashion terrorism', featuring scantily clad models in the role of potential terrorists, being wanded by airport security, cowering before menacing attack dogs, intimately probed by policemen, and violently smashed to the ground or onto cars.

The models also get to play soldier, pointing machine guns while lying prone in body suits and high heels. The same models, that is, appear as both suspected terrorists and as warriors against terror, a confusion that highlights the slippage of fashion codes, their double agency within a culture of terrorism. Meisel's magazine spread invites us to wonder which side of the terrorist divide the models are on. Are they victims or perpetrators? The answer is, in clear scramble mode, both.

'State of Emergency' plays also with the notion of fashion itself as a kind of terrorism, suggesting that a beautiful, chicly dressed woman – a model – could be a form of terror. The spread extends the fashion-as-terror metaphor in its fetishistic quality, the mildly pornographic violence it conveys through its multiple images of women captured in liminal states between covered and uncovered, dressed and undressed. This was not just mindless provocation or titillation by Meisel. Rather, 'State of Emergency' aptly gestures toward fashion's participation in a process of compensatory unveiling, a show of compulsively rendering visible the packaging of fetishised, fragmented, commodified female sexuality. Unveiling and offering up women's bodies for scrutiny in this way replays the security surveillance procedures of terrorism culture. However, it does so in manageable, recognisable, commodified and commercial doses, channelling the terror of violent bodily harm through a kind of chic sado-masochism, facilitating the analogous relationship between the explosion of female sexuality and the explosion of terroristic violence.

Israeli-Palestinian politics on the catwalk: Sharif Waked's *Chic Point*

In 2003, Palestinian artist Sharif Waked explored the surveillance procedures of terrorism culture in a film entitled *Chic Point: Fashion for Israeli Checkpoints*, which created a fictional runway fashion show – for men, meant as an ironic commentary on the rituals of bodily surveillance undergone by Palestinian workers who cross into Israel daily. Such surveillance is intended, ostensibly, to ensure that the Palestinian men are not terrorists.

Waked channels some of the same kind of commodified, fetishistic sexual display we see in the Meisel photographs, only here the bodies on display are men, the male models who walk what Waked called 'the Occupied Runway'. Since the Palestinians at the Israeli checkpoints are subjected to strip searches or forced to disrobe, fully or partially, Waked designed fashions that provide literal 'windows' into the wearer's naked body. A business suit, for example, features a peekaboo midriff opening (see pages 148–9); a shirt has a bias-cut zipper that spirals all the way around the torso for easy removal of the bottom half. In another example, Waked sewed two men's shirts together vertically to create a makeshift dishdasha (the traditional, long white robe worn by men throughout the Arabian Peninsula), turning the open collar of one shirt into a kind of ship's portal for the body beneath (fig. 49). Another shirt operates like louvred venetian blinds and when the model pulls an attached cord, the shirt front rises in pleats to expose the wearer's chest.

It is genuinely startling to see these clothes on a runway – not least because heteronormative men's clothing does not generally fetishise or expose bare flesh in this way. To eroticise a man's lower abdomen or back is immediately to code the event as gay or somehow gender ambiguous. At least one outfit veers into BDSM – a latex or Spandex hooded crop top with a lattice-work mesh that exposes the midsection, worn with skintight bicycle shorts. The film ends with a series of still photographs of actual checkpoints where Israeli soldiers force Palestinian men to unbutton or raise their shirts, kneel naked, or otherwise undress (page 149).

Waked's video points not only to the general indignity and humiliation of these checkpoint practices, but also expressly to the emasculation involved. Viewing this 'fashion' show, we cannot help noticing that the models occupy stereotypical feminine roles: they are offered up for our visual delectation, presented not as unitary signifiers of maleness (as men usually are), but as a series of the kind

FIG. 49
Sharif Waked,
Chic Point, 2003
Video still, depicting traditional robe with added 'window opening'
Colour video, with sound, 5:27 mins

of fragmented body parts into which women are typically compartmentalised by fashion. The eroticised exposure of men in *Chic Point* is feminising, ergo undignified, and represents, Waked suggests, the Israelis' attempt to *de-fuse* and *contain* the presumed weaponisation of Palestinian bodies. For Waked, such an attempt amounts to a fetishised framing and display of the men's bodies, treatment usually reserved for women. And so Waked pushes that idea to its limit, filters it through the discourse of fashion, and ends up with sexy male catwalk models in *déshabille* – an ironic commentary on the sexism of the fashion industry as well as on terrorism.

Waked demonstrates here how effectively fashion functions as a symbolic mirror of the culture of terrorism, using fashion to contemplate the treatment of the Palestinians at the hands of Israeli border guards. His film makes a powerful statement about the way the culture of terror responds to its fear of violent explosion by, instead, foregrounding erotic explosion, fetishising and fragmenting bodies in a symptomatic attempt to transform a perceived threat of violent explosion into the manageable, familiar and containable spectacle of commodified sexuality. Walking Waked's runway, the male models – stand-ins for Palestinian workers – are exposed in pieces. Their bodily borders are transgressed. With their suggestive glances and sexy catwalk swagger, the men are 'explosive' in the metaphoric sense; they 'smoulder'. But this brand of 'firepower' is familiar, banal and controllable – the kind we see daily in advertisements.

At the real checkpoints, the Israelis' racialised suspicion and fear of violence leads them to subject Palestinians to humiliating rituals of bodily exposure, containment and transgression. As the Palestinians cross the frontier, their own bodily borders are disrupted, along with their sexual integrity – that is, their masculine privilege to remain whole subjects rather than morselised, denuded body parts. These disruptions find apt and concise dramatisation on Waked's 'Occupied Runway'.

Language of containment: sex, bombshell fashion and the conceptual art of Ivana Spinelli

Everyday metaphoric language betrays how deeply entrenched is the idea of clothing as a control mechanism, as bodily containment, of fashion as a buffer against bodily explosion. We speak, for instance, of people 'bursting their buttons' with pride. Someone arrogant is 'too big for his britches'. Journalist Ida Tarbell, writing of President Theodore Roosevelt (who assumed the presidency in the wake of an act of domestic terrorism, the assassination of McKinley), described the energetic Roosevelt as someone 'whose clothes might not contain him. He was … so ready … to attack.'[22]

Tarbell's remark calls to mind a recognisable metaphor of male, ejaculatory power bordering on violence. But the concept of erotic excess that wields violent power applies as well to women. The term 'bombshell' refers uniquely to women, of course: to the kind of voluptuous women, such as screen icons Jean Harlow, Marilyn Monroe, or Jayne Mansfield, whose garments seem figuratively, or even literally ready to burst. 'Bombshell' is a concept occupying the realms of both

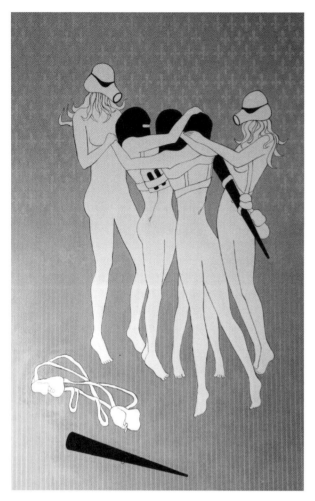

Eros and Thanatos; so, too, is fashion. Walter Benjamin knew well the closeness of fashion and death, writing 'fashion ... affirms the right of the corpse over the living', so reminding us that fashion, whose inorganic adornments tend to outlive their wearers, functions as a memento mori.[23] In this, fashion resembles terrorism, haunting us with the fatal weakness of our mortal fragility, our vulnerability beneath the surface. Stark and vivid reminders of fashion's haunting quality (as a marker of lost humanity), and its relationship to terrorism, appear often in the media after terrorist attacks – in the countless photographs published of clothing devoid of its wearers: coats and jackets on the ground, empty shoes, abandoned handbags, overturned hats.

Like Steven Meisel, but far more ironically, Italian artist Ivana Spinelli has literalised this connection of fashion, sex, consumerism and terrorism in her cartoon series 'Global Sisters' (fig. 50). Critic Franco Speroni describes Spinelli's posse of glamorous, terrorist Barbie-doll-like action heroines as 'global pin ups ... blending the televised icon of a Miss Italy with the Graces of the Renaissance and bodies traversed by the chronicles of terror and the images of seduction of the globalised ... mediascape'.[24] The Global Sisters boast bombshell figures and wear *literal* bombshell fashion accessories – suicide vests, hand grenades, balaclavas and other paramilitary gear. Since they are meant to be creatures of screen culture, sometimes Spinelli portrays them performing in mediatic situations, such as beauty pageants. At other times, she depicts the Sisters in quasi-erotic situations, as when two embrace while one fingers the grenade pin on the other's suicide vest, clearly on the verge of 'exploding' her. Spinelli has also begun expanding her concept into merchandising. Global Sisters handbags, dolls and other fashion items are now available for purchase, in an ironic commentary on the neo-liberal capitalist linking of women's shopping, fashion and terrorism, and in a subtle critique of the way we police and control women's bodies and fashion in a deflected attempt ostensibly to forestall terrorism.

Examples of such attempts are myriad and include the ongoing headscarf wars in France, the 2017 banning of the veil in Germany, the bloody attack in the American state of Oregon in the summer of 2017 (which began with a white nationalist harassing a young girl for wearing a hijab) and the so-called 'burkini bans' in France in 2016, which will offer an excellent case study.[25]

FIG. 50
'Global Sisters', illustration by Ivana Spinelli, 2005

The Burkini Ban: policing fashion, controlling bodies

In the wake of a major Islamic terrorist attack in Nice on Bastille Day, 2016 (when a cargo truck rammed deliberately into pedestrians on the Promenade des Anglais, killing 86 people and injuring hundreds more), some 30 French Riviera towns banned the burkini – the modest swimming costume consisting of tunic, pants and headscarf, worn by some Muslim women.[26] When a number of burkini-clad women on French beaches were fined, harassed and even made to disrobe by police officers, official explanations could ill-disguise the racist, anti-Muslim sentiments that seemed to underlie the ban. Some officials argued that by publicly displaying a religious affiliation, the burkini flouted France's famous secularism laws, or 'laïcité', and were 'not compatible with French values', as then-Prime Minister Manuel Valls put it. Valls even attempted to put a feminist spin on the ban, claiming that the burkini 'represent[ed] an archaic vision of a woman's position in society … the enslavement of women'.[27] Echoing these sentiments, Representative Valérie Boyer, of France's Bouches-Du-Rhône region, condemned the burkini (and all other Islamic women's garments) for negating the three famous cornerstones of the French Republic: '[It constitutes] … a prohibition of liberty, a prohibition of equality, a prohibition of fraternity.'[28] (Critics quickly undid this argument, noting that Catholic nuns, for example, fully covered by their habits, and swimmers in full-body wetsuits, could freely walk French beaches, and were never accused of harming either laïcité or feminist principles.)[29] A summons issued to one woman cited her for not wearing 'an outfit respecting good morals'.[30]

More specific and overtly political justifications crept into the debate as well. Some officials suggested that the burkini itself could lead to chaos or violence. While no one exactly accused the women of being terrorists, the implication that the modest swimsuits might provoke hostilities, perhaps even crime, hovered over the proceedings. The Nice tribunal declared the burkini 'a defiance or a provocation, exacerbating tensions felt by the community'. The Mayor of Cannes, David Lisnar, feared the burkini 'could risk disrupting public order';[31] and another Cannes official explained the ban was necessary 'to prohibit ostentatious garments that announce an allegiance to terrorist movements that are waging war against us'.[32] A socialist mayor in French Corsica saw the burkini ban as a means 'to protect the people's security', since they were 'sitting on a powder-keg'.[33] And former President Nicolas Sarkozy (who was planning another presidential run in 2017) announced that 'Wearing a burkini is a radical, political gesture, a provocation … testing the resistance of the Republic.'[34]

As these explanations make plain, the burkini bans (which were repealed later in 2016, after an outcry from groups such as the Collective against Islamophobia in France, or CCIF, and Human Rights Watch) had redirected the fears surrounding terrorism onto women's clothes, as if the burkinis themselves held the power to 'disrupt', 'provoke' or otherwise aggress the nation.[35] (This fear of the destructive impulses a women's garment might unleash in others recalls Phyllis Magidson's concern about Jacqueline Kennedy's suit inciting public hysteria.) More curiously, in their justifications, officials seemed also to invert criminals and victims, penalising innocent beach-going women for the destructive reactions their garments might provoke in others. The public's potential for violence (a latency defining terrorism) was being attributed to the garment and those wearing it. In the summer of 2016, the burkini became the screen onto which were projected fears of terrorist violence. Modesty, covering the feminine body, had become, ironically, a crime – a perfect 'cover' for the underlying racist agenda here.

Regulation or containment of women's fashion – of the sort exemplified by the burkini ban – turns up repeatedly as a method for gesturally controlling or warding off terrorism. That this measure is possible speaks directly to how women's fashion functions metaphorically in a manner analogous to that of anti-terror campaigns, in that it regulates, contains and releases, in acceptable doses, a form of explosiveness

– the erotic firepower or 'bombshell potential' of the female body, its provocation (to borrow President Sarkozy's term for the burkini).[36] The burkini affair perfectly illustrates how attempts to control women's sexual power and display often stand in metaphorically for attempts to control or forestall political violence against a nation.

If the ban deemed the modest burkini offensive, even un-French, would the opposite proposition also be true? Would a revealing swimsuit, say, a bikini, be the best choice? The most 'French'? Marine Le Pen, President of the extreme right-wing, anti-immigrant group, the National Front, suggested as much in an interview: 'The burkini,' she said, did not 'represent the "soul" of France ... France does not lock away a woman's body. The French beaches are those of Bardot and Roger Vadim.'[37] In other words, the most appropriately patriotic and law-abiding beachgoer would be a white woman in a bikini: a knowable, containable blonde bombshell of the 1960s, Brigitte Bardot – an icon to France, in much the same way as Marilyn Monroe was to America (fig. 51). Bardot's iconicity was so deeply rooted, we should recall, that she was the first celebrity chosen as the 'face' of Marianne, the allegorical figure of the nation.[38]

Note that Le Pen finds re-affirmation of Frenchness, the national soul, not exactly in Bardot the woman, but in Bardot the screened, cinematic image, as seen through the camera lens of Roger Vadim. The burkini ban was in effect an attempt to process racism and fear of terrorism via the regulation of female bodies and fashions – a figurative attempt to fortify national borders (the national 'silhouette') by legislating how women could define their silhouettes in public. And as we saw with Monroe's gown, a mediatic, bared and highly commercialised female sexuality can be far more reassuring than a modest garment. A bikini renders a woman controllably provocative (Eros); a burkini is a political provocation, conjuring literal bombshells (Thanatos) instead of cinematic ones.

FIG. 51
Brigitte Bardot sunbathing,
French Riviera, 1960s

Screened bodies: security surveillance and fashion

Exposed bodies and screened silhouettes appear routinely in the surveillance culture of terrorism, for what do airport security scanners produce but a near-infinite stream of pixellated screen images of nude bodies? Beginning in 2009 (in response to the so-called 'underwear bomber' incident, when an alleged member of al-Qaeda was convicted of attempting to bring down an airplane with explosives hidden in his undergarments), thousands of X-ray scanners appeared in every American airport and across the world, granting security staff full front and back views of passengers' naked bodies – breasts, genitals, buttocks, external medical devices, etc.[39] (fig. 52). Here we see again a symbolic, visual restitution of terrorism's battlefield, recovering the missing 'front' and 'back' of which W.J.T. Mitchell wrote.[40]

Unsurprisingly, far from remaining neutral security devices, the scanners led to an increase in the sexual harassment of passengers, as agents would single out those (usually female) passengers whose bodies they most appreciated, leading to incidents of airport disruption, lawsuits, anger and embarrassment. In the name of protecting the population from foreign enemies, the female half endured aggression from domestic sources.[41] In the United States, those passengers opting out of the scanners are subjected to physical pat downs, which have led to accusations of sexual misconduct as well.[42] These examples offer instances in which terrorism culture shores up retrograde sexual politics.[43] Just as the nostalgic image of the nearly nude Brigitte Bardot on a screen was posited as a symbolic remedy for the terror anxieties swirling around burkinis, so at the airport, bodies are being denuded and projected onto screens, where men (mostly) can ogle them – in the name of combatting terrorism.

Recently, on the runway (fashion not airport), we have seen a style phenomenon curiously comparable to the spectacles of airport scanners and related bodily surveillance. I am referring to the strong fashion trend of at least the last three years which we might call the 'super-naked dress' – not just sheer or revealing dresses, but dresses that are little more than tubes of tulle or netting with *de minimis* beading or embroidery. These are by far among the most revealing dresses in memory. Tamer versions, sheer or peek-a-boo dresses, have long existed, of course, and recur in cycles: there were sheer, bosom-revealing dresses in the late eighteenth century; there were some in the 1960s and 1970s. And there was a brief vogue for see-through beach dresses in the early 1900s, when they were called 'X-ray dresses' and banned in several American states.[44] 'X-ray dresses' may be a fitting name to resurrect today. Or maybe we could call those ultra-revealing numbers 'airport scanner dresses', since their effect reads as a symptomatic or compulsive repetition of surveillance culture.

These dresses flooded the runways in the wake of bursts of terror panic – the Charlie Hebdo murders in early 2015, the multiple later attacks in Paris, in Brussels and in Nice. And they have come to be associated also with highly photographed, big name celebrities, such as the Kardashian sisters, top models such as Gigi and

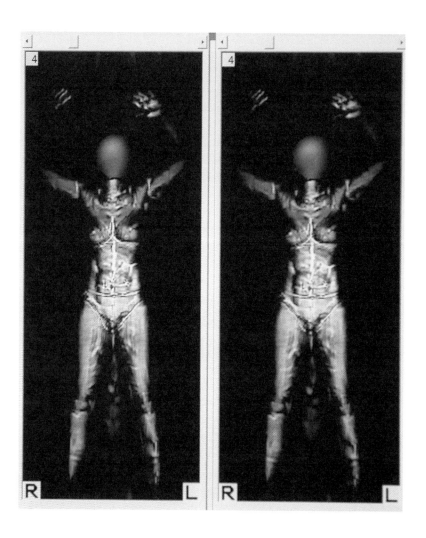

FIG. 52
TSA (Transportation Security
Administration) whole body
imaging system, Los Angeles
International Airport, 2008
Photographer David McNew

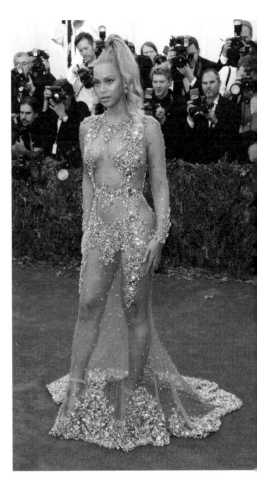

FIG. 53
Bella Hadid in sheer, crocheted catsuit by Alexander Wang, 'Rei Kawakubo/Comme des Garçons: Art of the In-Between' Costume Institute Gala, Metropolitan Museum of Art, New York, 4 May 2015 Photographer John Shearer

FIG. 54
Kendall Jenner in 'fishnet' La Perla gown, 'Rei Kawakubo/ Comme des Garçons: Art of the In-Between', Costume Institute Gala, Metropolitan Museum of Art, New York, 1 May 2017 Photographer Theo Wargo

FIG. 55
Beyoncé in sheer dress by Riccardo Tisci for Givenchy, 'China: Through the Looking Glass', Costume Institute Gala, Metropolitan Museum of Art, New York, 4 May 2015 Photographer Larry Busacca

Bella Hadid (fig. 53), and pop stars such as Rihanna and Beyoncé. Nearly all of these dresses are made of mesh, or glittering net. In other words, they allow viewers to peer through a physical screen, a material grid, and find a naked body. They turn women into techno-spectacles of unveiled body parts. These dresses are, in fact, barely clothes at all; they are not worn for the occasion at hand, but rather for the technological replaying of the occasion in photographs, on video, and especially, on social media. That is, they turn the wearer into a kind of screen image in preparation for her subsequent technological after-image, her appearance on other technology screens. About Beyoncé's Givenchy gown (fig. 55), for example, a New York Times journalist wrote, 'You couldn't really call it a dress ... This wasn't fashion, it was an Instagram moment.'[45] The subtitle of the Metropolitan Museum exhibition and gala event for which Beyoncé wore this gown, 'Through the Looking Glass', takes on special resonance here: she is visible as if through a video screen, the grid-like pattern of the tulle anticipating her screened appearance later on Instagram.

Still more provocative was the La Perla 'naked' gown worn by Kendall Jenner for the 2017 Met Gala (fig. 54). La Perla's creative director, Julia Haart, specified that the dress was not made of fabric at all, but cut from 'one piece of string. A very strong, very flexible, incredibly thin piece of nylon, and we've strung 85,000 crystals onto it.'[46] In other words, Jenner was not exactly wearing a dress so much as she was caught and held like prey, like a glamorous fish in a sparkling, video-screen-like net.

In this rising trend of highly revealing, pixellated-screen-style dresses, we see the discourse of fashion absorbing and reinterpreting the surveillance culture that saturates our 'war on terrorism'. All the containing, packaging and screening of celebrated nude female bodies registers as a compulsion to detect the obscured, see the veiled, master the interiority of the body, now so keenly aware of its vulnerability. We have seen the rationing of acceptable doses of 'bombshell' culture. And we may note that among the most famous wearers of these dresses – including the Kardashians, Jennifer Lopez, Rihanna and Beyoncé – are also the most bombshell-like of public personalities. As manageable bombshells, they grant the sensation of espying the hidden, the unknowable, and thereby allaying the terror of that other kind of undetectable bodily explosiveness. Consider, too, how often we use other terms of violence in describing fashion and beauty: a 'killer' dress or body, 'slaying' on the runway, 'stunning', a 'knock out'.[47]

In considering these 'emperor's new clothes', we need also to consider the perspective of those who wear them and those who aspire to do so. To don one of these 'airport scanner' outfits is to freely cast aside any bodily modesty. For some, this can be a feminist gesture. I am not so sure though. On the most obvious level, only vanishingly few people can wear these. They require a punishing degree of bodily perfection, self-policing, fanatical exercise and devotion to a fitness regime – another form of what we might call fashion terrorism, which again replicates its self-policing body culture of terrorism: call it 'Pilates terrorism'.

Beyond the physical oppression brought by the super-naked dresses, there is also the loss of a more abstract concept of the personal, of keeping anything private, which goes along with the technological panopticon we now inhabit. As journalist Leslie Camhi writes in American *Vogue*, about the fad for highly revealing clothes, 'while some fourth-wave feminists are putting women's breasts on the front lines of the battle for sexual equality, another battle is being waged, almost without our knowing it, a daily hammering away in this culture of oversharing, at the expense of privacy so vital to intimacy.'[48] The naked-dress trend glamorises the abandonment of bodily and personal privacy and, by extension, dares us all to do likewise. The trend is the sartorial equivalent of the way Google, Facebook, Instagram, Snapchat and the like, all make it seem so natural for us to sign away our most intimate lives in exchange for the pleasures of self-display.

And here we see a final irony. As terrorism breeds, even encourages, a tenuous grip on our bodily integrity, threatening us with dissolving borders of myriad kinds, fashion steps up, seemingly to allay or control these anxieties, while actually reproducing symbolically the very things we fear, normalising and encouraging an internalised (unconscious) culture of surveillance. Via the trappings of luxury, celebrity, feminine beauty and indulgence, this internalised culture constitutes a stratum of the political unconscious. We might, in this context, also call this register of unspoken but symptomatic cultural eruptions the 'sartorial unconscious', and ask: What other registers of cultural practice – of gender politics – get shunted aside in examinations of terrorism? And at what cost do we dismiss or trivialise them, turning a blind eye to their potentially constitutive role in the culture of terror?

Insurgent Trend: The Popularity of the Keffiyeh

Jane Tynan

In 2017, the Museum of Modern Art in New York staged an exhibition titled *Items: Is Fashion Modern?*, a display of 111 items of clothing and accessories chosen for their impact on twentieth- and twenty-first-century culture. It was no surprise to find that the keffiyeh had been included. However much it has been appropriated and transformed by popular culture, the keffiyeh[1] – originally a simple headscarf worn by peasants in various regions in the Middle East – continues to have extraordinary power. In this essay, I explore whether the popularity of the keffiyeh, particularly as a fashion object, has enhanced or obscured its political potency. If the militarising of the keffiyeh has given it special meaning within and beyond the Middle East, does this history of protest explain its popularity amongst western fashion consumers?

Here, I adopt anthropologist Daniel Miller's approach to material culture, in order to understand how 'form itself is employed to become the fabric of cultural worlds'[2] in relation to the dramatic life of the keffiyeh. The temporary and ephemeral nature of fashion allows us to explore the multiple lives and various transformations of material objects. Indeed, fashion is itself a process of materialisation, which, as sociologist Sophie Woodward argues, comes into being through 'the longer-term relationships people have to fashionable garments, and also the possibilities of change and fluidity'.[3] This discussion explores what people 'do' with the keffiyeh, in order to understand why it has undergone various processes of materialisation, which perhaps can only be understood through the historical events that made it meaningful.

The keffiyeh in the Arab revolt, 1936–9

While initially a traditional Middle Eastern peasant headdress, the keffiyeh was arguably re-created as an artefact of modernity through the part it played in a key conflict in British Mandate Palestine in the 1930s. Palestine had been placed under British control by a mandate, obtained from the League of Nations in 1922 and incorporating the Balfour Declaration of 1917, the document that declared British support for the creation of a Jewish homeland there. The mandate state grew increasingly restless, leading to the 1936–9 Arab revolt (known as 'The Great Revolt') against British colonial rule, an uprising that holds a special place in the history of Palestinian resistance to colonialism and occupation. In April 1936, the Arab Higher Committee, a new union of Palestinian political parties, was formed. It called for a general strike and the non-payment of taxes in support of the

FIG. 56
A Bedouin sheikh, photographed by John D. Whiting (member of the American Colony in Jerusalem) on a trip to Trans-Jordan, 14–16 August 1937

demand for national government. Jewish immigration, officially enabled by a British government susceptible to Zionist pressure, was frustrating and provoking Palestinian nationalists. During the strike, which formed the first stage of the revolt, attacks were made on British troops, police posts and Jewish settlements, with the result that the British administration imposed curfews and called in troop reinforcements and other emergency measures to quell the rebellion. The British government appointed a Royal Commission to investigate the causes of the disturbances, and it recommended the partition of Palestine into Arab and Jewish states, which led to the second stage of the revolt from July 1937 to March 1939. Viewed as a whole, the uprising represented the first sustained rebellion by Palestinian Arabs as a unified nationalist movement.

The history of headwear in the region is critical to understanding why the keffiyeh became part of the conflict and thereafter a symbol of Palestinian self-determination. Prior to this event, only the peasants – *fellahin* – and the Bedouin wore the keffiyeh, not only for reasons of modesty but also to keep out the cold and shield their heads from the scorching sun (fig. 56). Urban Palestinians, who began to adopt European-style clothing from the end of the nineteenth century,[4] wore a variety of headwear. It was headwear that marked men as city dwellers, villagers or Bedouin, and indicated their religious affiliation and socio-economic position. Palestinian Bedouin headwear was distinctive and 'comprised a square cloth (*hattah* or *kaffiyyeh*) folded diagonally over the head and held in place with black ropes (*agal*) made of goat or camel hair. The *hattah* or *kaffiyyeh* were made of cotton or fine wool and were either white or white with black or red designs.'[5] The keffiyeh was a marker of low status, distinguishing the *fellah* – peasant – from the *effendi* – the educated middle-class men of the town, who wore the maroon-coloured *tarbush* or *fez*, introduced in the 1830s by a reforming Ottoman government to erase variance in ethno-religious identities. Dominating and displacing the *fellahin* appeared to be a cornerstone of Zionist policy; they lacked access to government, which meant that their customary rights to the land were often blocked.[6]

In the 1930s Arab revolt, the keffiyeh was an important part of the 'uniform' of guerrilla fighters; wrapped close to their heads it provided anonymity when they wandered the countryside,[7] but it made them conspicuous in the towns and targets for arrest by the British army. To resolve this problem, in 1938 the rebel leadership commanded all Arabs in urban areas to also wear the keffiyeh. While this made it impossible to know whom to arrest, the widespread adoption of the cotton headdress intimated that everyone in the country was a rebel.[8] In 1938, *The Times* newspaper reported that hundreds of armed rebels had infiltrated Jerusalem, their presence disguised by the adoption of the keffiyeh as a result of this long-standing campaign for all men, regardless of affiliation or social position, to adopt it as their uniform:

> *For some time they had been coming in from outside unarmed, and passing inconspicuously among ordinary Arab civilians, as all alike now wear the keffiyeh or headscarf and camel's hair agghal or rope-like bands to hold*

it in position. These intruders, once inside, were provided with arms
which had previously been smuggled in and were ready for service.[9]
In his memoir Robin Martin, a new recruit to the colonial police in 1930s Palestine, describes how the keffiyeh was becoming a critical part of the rebels' military strategy: 'It was felt that if everyone wore the *hatta* and *agal* it would make identification much more difficult and easier for any of the rebels coming in from the country to pass among the crowds unobserved.'[10] Enlisted as a weapon of war in this way, the keffiyeh had to be supplied in high numbers; it is thought that large consignments arrived from Iraq.

Guerrilla fighters were thus enlisting the whole of Arab society in their sartorial disguise. As historian Raymond Betts argues, nationalism in the colonial world imbued localised protest with a strong ideology to gain the support of both the urban and rural dweller: 'No successful protest movement was made without ideology and without peasant support.'[11] In British Mandate Palestine peasantry and the bourgeoisie came together to resist occupation; a sense of nation was fostered when both groups adopted the keffiyeh, collapsing markers of identity. According to anthropologist Ted Swedenburg, the central role of rural men in the 1936–9 revolt meant that the *fellahin* and their dress came to epitomise anti-colonial struggle.[12] Thus, a certain strand of popular memory, of which the keffiyeh is emblematic, is commonly rooted in these events of the 1930s, when a symbolic change took place through the dress practices of Palestinian villagers and urban dwellers alike.

In fact, all social markers were shifting as a result of the conflict. Women linked to Palestinian nationalism also reflected their allegiance in their appearance. For instance, a photograph of 1937/8 of young women in Nablus, Palestine, collecting donations for nationalists, shows them wearing their headdresses keffiyeh-style, rather than the traditional form of a veil held in place with a headband.[13] Transmuted from peasant dress to a symbol of Palestinian nationalism, the keffiyeh became a modern aesthetic form.

While this play with the rooted meanings associated with the headdress might have represented a disruption of the traditional order, in fact the keffiyeh's new status relied on both old and modern meanings. Events demanded that clothing and adornment be mobilised in the waging of war and thus the keffiyeh became a material object embodying the revolt. Insurgency relies more on political vision than military organisation; it embodies the energy of peasant rebellion combined with the ideology of modern revolution.[14] Rebels not only improvised a 'uniform' from peasant dress; they also employed the modern military practices of camouflage through their use and misuse of the keffiyeh.

The keffiyeh and insurgency, 1940s–90s

The story of the keffiyeh reflects how material objects can mediate political flux. Already a highly mobile object, as discussed, the keffiyeh was mobilised again for insurgent action at mid-century within an Arab nationalist movement built on the popular memory of the earlier revolt. By 1948, Zionists were ahead with their nation-building efforts, leaving Palestinians behind, largely because their experience of political mobilisation was not built on ideation but rather was confined to acts of resistance to Zionists or the British.[15] With British withdrawal from Palestine in 1948, the United Nations was tasked with dividing Palestine into an Arab state and a Jewish state.[16] Meanwhile, a newly formed state of Israel was seizing a significant amount of territory not assigned to them and intervention by Arab states, to prevent partition and protect the rights of Palestinians, led to the first Arab-Israeli War of 1948 (also known as 'The Catastrophe' or *Al-Nakba*). From this point onwards, Palestinians clearly saw the value in nurturing symbols of national self-determination, of which the keffiyeh became one. There was some regional variation in keffiyeh colour, but by this time the distinctive net or dog-tooth pattern in black and white was firmly linked with the cause of Palestine.

However, the keffiyeh only starts to feature prominently in visual images – in posters, in particular – in the 1960s. Yasser Arafat, chairman of the Palestine Liberation Organisation (PLO), which sought to establish a Palestinian state, from 1969 until his death in 2004 made a political statement with the keffiyeh, by carefully arranging the scarf in the shape of a triangle over his right shoulder to resemble the shape of Palestine (fig. 57). For the PLO, as it had been for rebels earlier in the century, the symbolic use of the keffiyeh was an ideal mechanism for collapsing differences between rich and poor, urban and rural and, importantly, to erase social class in the pursuit of national unity. These memories of equality were rooted in the 1930s Arab revolt, but were of course selective: rebels were not above imposing sartorial restrictions on women, in particular those that forbade the adoption of European fashion.[17] Once Fatah, the Palestinian national liberation movement, was established in the late 1950s – a coalition of Palestinian nationalist networks already active in refugee camps, a global diaspora of Palestinian students, and Palestinian communities in the emerging Gulf states – there was a clear sense that it sought to embrace an image of pluralism. Thus, the keffiyeh, which had been militarised as a form of disguise for male rebels during the Arab revolt of 1936–9, eventually began to be worn around the world by various social groups, including women, as a mark of solidarity with the Palestinian cause.

Population transfers and dislocations, the result of massive land expropriation and with it the decline of agricultural activity, led Palestinians to search for symbols that opposed the very material reality of settler colonialism. If Zionist actions jeopardised the relationship between peasant and land, political groups for Palestinian liberation sought to utilise the peasant as a sacred figure, as seen in the elevation of olive trees in national symbolism – in poetry and song – and in the fostering of traditional crafts.[18] Later the keffiyeh was also incorporated into political posters, whose visual messages intensified the sense of the sacredness

FIG. 57
Yasser Arafat, Chairman of the Palestine Liberation Organisation, at the Arab League Summit in Rabat, Morocco, 1974

of Palestinian soil, as is evident from the 1981 poster *For the Land – Palestine*, designed by Ismail Shammout for Fatah, which depicts a stylised image of a man wearing a keffiyeh firmly planting an olive tree in the earth.[19] Here, the keffiyeh is *the* form chosen to become, as Daniel Miller puts it, 'part of the fabric of cultural worlds'. Having gained meaning and significance locally as a material object involved in insurgent action, here it undergoes a further transformation to become a key symbol internationally of the plight of Palestinians.

In the Middle East and elsewhere, the wearing of the keffiyeh was consolidating a recognisable image for the Palestinian cause. Arafat came to global prominence when in December 1968 *Time* magazine featured a youthful image of him on its cover wearing the distinctive black-and-white keffiyeh, sunglasses and combat jacket, with the cover line 'The Arab Commandos – Defiant New Force in the Middle East'.[20] Behind him a menacing figure with a gun has his face completely covered, perhaps signifying the requirement that insurgents wear disguise when in combat. If the 1930s Arab revolt was being evoked by Arafat, the contemporary Palestinian leader, through the wearing of the keffiyeh, he was transforming it from a local reference point to 'an international symbol of Palestinian identity and nationalism'.[21] Disguise and subversion took on positive associations in the form of the keffiyeh but as an object it also held a range of other connotations. Arafat and other activists were mindful of the meanings it had accrued over difficult times for Palestinians: tradition, modesty, agriculture, homeland, improvised identity, strength, and solidarity forged in adversity.

By the 1960s and 1970s, many of those who formed the Palestinian diaspora – both women and men – could be seen wearing the keffiyeh.[22] Political posters, created by various activist groups after the 1960s, often incorporated the keffiyeh, either depicting members of both sexes wearing it, or using the graphic potential of the pattern to signify resistance and the assertion of rights over the land of Palestine. The keffiyeh was a symbol employed within Palestinian visual culture that also embodied the very material reality of conflict. A photograph that circulated internationally, from 1969, shows Leila Khaled, a member of the Popular Front for the Liberation of Palestine (PFLP), wearing a keffiyeh and holding an AK-47 after an attempt to hijack an American passenger jet en route from Rome to Tel Aviv (fig. 58). This mediated image offers a sense of what the keffiyeh would later become: an edgy and somewhat glamorous depiction of youthful defiance. The appeal of such images reflects the growing fascination, particularly in Europe and North America at this time, with militarism, and in particular with insurgent action. This was not the sole preserve of Palestinian freedom fighters but they did offer a particularly compelling image of insurgency.

By the 1970s, western popular culture was regularly looking to military conflict for compelling images of defiance and rebellion aimed at a youth audience. Army clothing had become part of the vocabulary of protest, and various military garments and accessories were adopted and repurposed by emerging youth

subcultures, a form of working-class resistance to dominant capitalist culture.[23] Media theorist Dick Hebdige in particular interpreted British subcultural style as an interruption of the normal social order through the subversive styles adopted by young people.[24] Through deviant style 'spectacular subcultures' were creating alternative ways of being, which enabled young people to be in a constant state of voyage through a complex array of identities and stylistic possibilities.[25] This offers insights into how and why the keffiyeh was adopted and worn by young people outside the Middle East, certainly from the late 1970s on (they were found on market stalls, or in second-hand shops, or wherever young people shopped for subversive style), as a symbol of solidarity with the Palestinian cause, and by extension with any groups who saw themselves as oppressed by colonial and capitalist power. Military clothing, often surplus, was cheap and an ideal adornment for young people who sought to desecrate symbols of power. Rather than being a military symbol of colonial powers, the keffiyeh represented those who, against all odds, rose up against them. This authentic military object, in real material terms, held memories of a successful revolt against a powerful force.

Indeed, the difficulties of Palestinians spoke directly to young people throughout the second half of the twentieth century. The First Intifada of 1987–91 – a Palestinian uprising against the Israeli occupation of the West Bank and Gaza – saw the meaning of the keffiyeh shift, from a symbol of solidarity with the Palestinian cause to a style choice for hip young people in Europe and North America. It is worth considering fashion as a process of materialisation in order to understand the reasons for such change and fluidity, and in this case how wearing a scarf with such material memories might, for many western young people, reflect a consciousness of specific historical events pertaining to the Palestinian struggle. After an Israeli Defense Forces (IDF) truck collided with a civilian car in 1987, killing four Palestinians, civil disobedience erupted in the form of boycotts, graffiti and stone throwing at the IDF within the West Bank

FIG. 58
Leila Khaled, member of the Popular Front for the Liberation of Palestine, at her guerrilla base in Amman, Jordan, after the hijacking of an American TWA passenger jet in Damascus, 29 August 1969
Photographer Eddie Adams

and Gaza Strip. Israel retaliated by deploying military might, which killed a large number of Palestinians. Images of soldiers attacking and beating young people, many of them wearing the distinctive keffiyeh, were shown on global media. Throughout its life the headdress was transposed from civilian to military and from military to civilian use; it mobilised interest in the 'idea' of a Palestinian state as part of a visual guerrilla strategy to create a counter-discourse to colonialism and occupation. Young people in various parts of the world wearing the keffiyeh could not embody the same plight as their counterparts facing the realities of occupation, but the popularity of the object at this time suggests that it could highlight their own struggles beyond the original locale of conflict.

If the Zionist movement claimed Palestine was uninhabited land, and there for the taking, for many western young people the wearing of this headdress as a

simple scarf was a gesture of solidarity with people under siege, and one that contained the claim of that people's connection to the land. Thus, anti-colonial struggle characterised by local and improvised conflict to oppose military might, reminiscent of 'peasant rebellion', was powerfully re-enacted through the wearing of keffiyehs. This integration of history with popular cultural forms is in fact a powerful insurgent strategy. The re-appropriation of historical Zionist posters by Palestinian activists, such as Jaafar Alloul, highlights subaltern methods of resistance, drawing attention to how 'Palestinian voices continue to defy the "disciplined" cage that is enforced on them through intelligent visual guerrilla techniques that challenge Israel's dominant settler-colonial technology.'[26] Discourses of counterterrorism de-legitimised Palestinian violence, but by embodying various iterations of anti-colonial struggle, the material presence of the keffiyeh challenged that narrative, offering an alternative – one of revolt and resistance – that circulated and resonated within global visual culture. By the 1980s and 1990s, the keffiyeh materialised a left-wing position on global politics. The meanings of the keffiyeh are extended each time a new group adopts it. Social movements from Civil Rights to Occupy have since perpetuated the sense that the keffiyeh is *the* symbol of political solidarity for all oppressed groups (fig. 59).

Fashioning the keffiyeh, 1970s to today

The move from political statement to fashionable accessory is not easy to explain, but there is a sense that the malleability of the keffiyeh arises directly from its complex 'life' as a material object. The 'biography of a thing,' as the anthropologist Igor Kopytoff puts it, becomes the story of the various 'classifications and reclassifications in an uncertain world of categories whose importance shifts

FIG. 59
A demonstrator is arrested by police, following a protest march outside the International Monetary Fund and World Bank conference on Hauptstrasse, West Berlin, 29 September 1988

with every minor change in context'.[27] Such is the biography of the keffiyeh, which, with every change in context, shifts in terms of meaning. In 2007, a story in the *New York Times* began by acknowledging that the keffiyeh, once associated with Arafat and Palestinian countrymen, 'has lately shown up on the shelves of adventurous boutiques in the United States and even mainstream retailers like Urban Outfitters'. This shift in context and meaning was greeted with surprise, but the journalist was also keen to reassure readers that 'Its newest wearers, who wrap it around the neck like a scarf, say they are less Fatah sympathizers than fashion party

FIG. 60
Raf Simons, 'Riot, Riot, Riot'
Collection, Autumn/Winter
2001–2

FIG. 61
Givenchy, Collection for
Spring/Summer 2010
Designer Riccardo Tisci;
photographer
Dominique Charriau

crashers.'[28] This article contains the sense of inevitability that the keffiyeh is continually renewed by transformation, this time by mainstream fashion. Military style, which articulated youth rebellion in the 1970s and 1980s, by the end of the century had become a routine identity marker for young fashion consumers drawn by a popular culture that 'has demonstrated a fascination with the aesthetics of militarization'.[29]

The soft power of popular culture might have normalised militarism by aestheticising its objects and symbols, but it does not necessarily mean that the fashionable appropriation of the keffiyeh is implicated in such techniques, particularly since it has been carrying a message of opposition and resistance to colonial power for so long. Mixing subcultural references with high-street staples has in the past allowed young people to negotiate a complex array of identities and style options through, for instance, combining army jackets with jeans or slogan T-shirts with fashionable footwear.

Nevertheless, the keffiyeh is no longer confined to street style and there is a range of recent examples of its appropriation by high fashion labels, such as Balenciaga, Givenchy and Chanel. Belgian fashion designer Raf Simons's Autumn/Winter 2001–2 collection, presented in January 2001, used versions of the keffiyeh to give menswear a masculine styling that echoed the edginess of streetwear (fig. 60). In *The Guardian*, Charlie Porter declared in response that 'terrorist chic' was one of the strongest messages of the season, and also pointed to Simons's mix of cultural references, which intensified the message of rebellion that keffiyeh scarves could convey: 'When styled aggressively with the clothes of May Day rioters, translated on to the catwalk in Simons's skinny black drainpipes and bulky army surplus coats, the scarves become a fiery symbol.'[30] Here, in the context of high fashion, the keffiyeh signifies rebellion, but the move from politics to fashion is somewhat expected, given Simons's history as a designer who fuses subcultural style with masculine tailoring. At this stage, his designs not only embodied the 'outsider' but also powerfully recreated the wearer as a positive figure capable of instigating transformation and renewal. Simons's work is interdisciplinary and is about the convergence of opposing worlds; this particular use of the

FIG. 62
Artist Scott Tyler, sporting
Mao T-shirt and keffiyeh,
among activists protesting
against a ban on the
desecration of the
American flag, Washington
D.C., October 1989
Photographer
Cynthia Johnson

keffiyeh was interpreted as a bold statement that 'led to the collection being read
politically'.[31] The keffiyeh, in particular, offers Simons an opportunity to grapple with
contradictions that inevitably come with any item of clothing that has played a part
in conflict.

Some fashionable appropriations of the keffiyeh work with the history
of insurrection, while others completely transform its meaning. For instance,
Balenciaga in 2007 re-constituted the keffiyeh as dresses with the familiar tassels
swinging from the hemline, a mix of craft and luxury that sidelines its radical history.
In 2010, Riccardo Tisci created a collection using the keffiyeh pattern for a range of
garments for Givenchy, without any connotations of Palestine, militarism or protest.
The collection used a distorted version of the keffiyeh print on trousers, dresses,
bags and shoes, creating a kind of optical illusion (fig. 61). The designs, no longer

presented as a scarf, are nonetheless recognisable as keffiyeh-inspired, evidence of the global visibility of this intriguing material object. Similarly, in 2015, a black-and-white, keffiyeh-patterned tweed and sequined Chanel cruise jacket, clearly a luxury item, bore none of the supposed rebellious history of the original keffiyeh.

While guerrilla fighters in the 1930s creatively enlisted the whole of society in their sartorial disguise in order to defy a colonial power, that narrative, inspirational though it may be for many, has been transformed and co-opted by the fashion system. As sociologist Nashwa Salem argues, the high-street chain Urban Outfitters re-coded the keffiyeh in order to appropriate it 'as a nameless object of cultural exotica', which she claims the chain further achieved by calling it an 'Anti-War Woven Scarf' and moving away from the black-and-white design.[32]

One of the biggest casualties in its transmutation from political statement to fashion accessory might be the keffiyeh's association with methods of subaltern resistance. An article in *The Guardian* in 2008 sensationally asks whether the keffiyeh is still considered to be 'Jihadi Chic', since it has become a surprise fashion staple in Tel Aviv, evidence that its revolutionary symbolism has been finally forgotten.[33] In 2015, during Tel Aviv fashion week, Israeli fashion designer Ori Minkowski presented keffiyeh-derived dresses to symbolise the peaceful co-existence of Israelis and Palestinians. *The Times of Israel* declared that this must be the moment 'when the keffiyeh turned couture'.[34] Jordanian designer Ghada Zada also used them and Danish fashion label Cecile Copenhagen regularly transforms the keffiyeh pattern into dresses for western fashion consumers.

Re-constituting the keffiyeh might reflect an attempt to neutralise the history and radical meanings of the scarf, but the ubiquity of fashionable references to it might equally be the result of its materiality and its cultural currency in contemporary society. Material culture looks to the ways in which everyday objects can evoke larger ideas and, importantly for this discussion, how the past can reside in the present. If, for some, the keffiyeh has very situated meanings, in a place and time, for others part of the spirit of rebellion is retained in vague references to resistance and protest. It is difficult to focus on questions of authenticity while also exploring the larger meanings that flow from significant historical moments. The keffiyeh is caught up in such a dilemma, as is the Che Guevara T-shirt, worn by many young people who might have only a vague notion of what the Cuban revolution meant and Guevara's part in it, but are nonetheless interested in laying claim to his ideas of equality and social justice. There is no reason to believe that either a keffiyeh or a Che Guevara T-shirt cannot act as carriers of popular memory of revolutionary struggles.

In 1989, the artist Scott Tyler protested against a United States constitutional amendment banning the desecration of the national flag, following the controversy aroused by his 1988 art installation *What is the Proper Way to Display a U.S. Flag?*. By wearing a Mao T-shirt and a keffiyeh, this mix of revolutionary signifiers reflected his position on freedom of speech and his opposition to American state

FIG. 63
Yasser Herbawi in his
keffiyeh factory in the
West Bank city of Hebron,
Palestine, May 2008
Photographer Joe Klamar

FIG. 64
Fashion blogger Sidya Sarr
demonstrates contemporary
street style including a
keffiyeh and a Zara top, Paris,
December 2016
Photographer Edward Berthelot

power (fig. 62). Kurdish teenagers wear the black-and-white checkered *pusi* scarf, an object bearing a strong similarity to the Palestinian keffiyeh, not only to express opposition to policies repressive to the Kurdish minorities in Europe, but also to make a fashion statement.[35] Its political significance, in this context, does not diminish its status as a fashionable object. What the material life of the keffiyeh reveals is the mutual constitution of objects and bodies; when bodies take it on, its meaning is altered, and the wearer too is similarly transformed by its power. The wearing of the keffiyeh may now be part of fashion discourse, but as a material-embodied practice it has the capacity to continually re-enact rebellion at various times and in many locations.

The question of appropriation in fashion, though, deserves attention, and Salem has a point in arguing that Urban Outfitters negated the Palestinian cause by calling the keffiyeh an 'Anti-War Woven Scarf' – a perverse name given its history – and selling it in colours that deny the specificity of its material history. Questions of appropriation are particularly relevant in relation to a place such as the Occupied Palestinian Territories, where geography and culture are contested, where land is appropriated but so too are cultural narratives, words, food, folk traditions and crafts. As explored, the story of the keffiyeh itself is one of subversion and re-appropriation. If the keffiyeh emerged as a weapon of war, its continuous re-appropriation first by guerrilla fighters, then by Arab leaders, and later by the Palestinian diaspora became a subaltern strategy of resistance.

It is unlikely that this rich history can be neutralised by fashion, but the keffiyeh's re-styling is perhaps symptomatic of attempts to incorporate it into western modernity. The keffiyeh is a disruptive symbol for settler-colonial technology, particularly considering how the 'dichotomy modernity/tradition has been another master narrative of Zionist state ideology', whereby 'military technology, democracy, attitudes, architecture, dress styles' are pitted against 'feudalism, sheikdom, patriarchy, architecture, folk costume'.[36] The keffiyeh not only evokes memories of an insurgency against Zionist modernity; it also celebrates improvised forms of power and knowledge. The craft tradition that the keffiyeh represents could not be further from the modernity that created a fashion society. And yet, the paradox of the keffiyeh's popularity must be its failure to bolster craft production in Palestine. The Herbawi textile factory in Hebron, which has been weaving keffiyehs since 1961 and still produces a small quantity, has lost business despite the global surge in sales of the scarf (see fig. 63).[37]

The edgy, glamorous image of youthful defiance that the keffiyeh represented in the 1970s may no longer be in evidence (see fig. 64), but when clothing brand Zara included in their Summer 2014 collection a pair of mini-shorts clearly derived from the black-and-white keffiyeh design associated with Palestine, they received a barrage of negative criticism on social media and removed the item from sale. Similarly, in 2017, Topshop's keffiyeh-inspired 'scarf playsuit' was removed from sale due to much social media outrage in Britain about cultural appropriation and accusations of theft.[38] The point must be that while fashion design and media processes may wilfully ignore the meanings that material objects, such as the keffiyeh, have accrued over time, they are not capable of completely devouring and defusing their radical histories and disruptive potential.

Despite its new status as 'military chic', then, might the popularity of the keffiyeh be a sign of the dissolution of social structures, whereby young people see fit to choose not the uniform but a deregulated, desecrated version of military masculinity? Media interest in the keffiyeh highlights the extent to which it has become an anti-establishment statement, borne of a desire for change and renewal; a statement that celebrates a particularly disorderly form of militarism that terrifies the establishment. What fashion does especially well in the case of the keffiyeh is dramatise the temporality and instability of meaning that attaches to material objects. As we have seen, this is also precisely what made the keffiyeh politically potent throughout the twentieth century. When media reports on the popularity of the keffiyeh ask whether it is a fashion trend or a political statement, it is tempting to suggest it is both.

Acknowledgements
I would like to thank Pasold Research Fund for supporting the archival research that contributed to the development of this essay.

Photo Essay

The Uniform, the Subject, the Power

Gabi Scardi

Art is an active way of thinking about the world. It has always gained energy and urgency from its porous relationship with reality. Many artists, sensitive to new contexts and values, to the social tensions and transformations of their day, structure their work in relation to other disciplines. Fashion, for one, allows them to embrace the complexity of the present.

Within the vast theme of fashion and dress, there is one category – the uniform – that is inherently and explicitly political. The uniform brings into focus the question of the forces that shape us – the forces to which we are subject. The uniform is a regulatory item of dress. To adopt it, either compulsorily or spontaneously, is to conform to a code of belonging or behaviour, norms that play a decisive role in the psychological and socio-political dynamics of individual and collective identity.

Be it prescribed as a direct and formal expression of the official, or adopted on the basis of individual and seemingly independent choices, a collective garment that strives to abolish social differences in the name of democracy, equality and inclusivity, or a direct expression of hierarchical structures – the uniform demonstrates just how relative our autonomy is.

Reflecting on uniforms and their related rituals through the works of artists, as this visual essay does, helps us to look at the construction, representation and exercise of power, and its relationship to dress. But through uniforms artists also refer to the irreducibility of the individual, to moments when the energy of difference clashes with the allure of the group or with an authority – from the mass media to the more directly ideological political party – that intends to shape the individual and bring her or him in line. The individual always retains a subjectivity that resists simplification and tends to elude all rules, a sense of self that cannot be totally obligated, bridled, contained or shared.

ABOVE
Leon Golub
Mercenaries II (section III), 1975
Acrylic on linen,
194.3 x 236.2 cm

RIGHT
Mercenaries II (section I), 1975
Acrylic on linen,
259.1 x 152.4 cm

Köken Ergun, *I, Soldier*
(Ben Askerim), 2005
(video stills)
Three video stills from a
two-channel video projection,
colour, sound, 7:14 mins

Artur Żmijewski,
KR WP, 2000
Five video stills from
single-channel video, colour,
sound, 7:10 mins

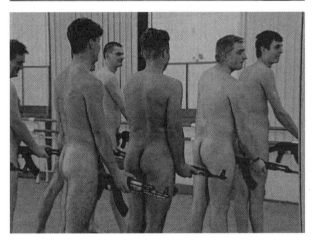

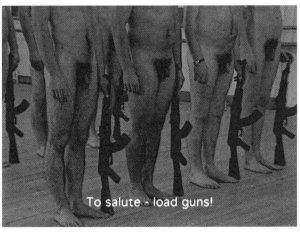

To salute - load guns!

Sharif Waked,
Chic Point, 2003
Four video stills from colour
video, with sound, 5:27 mins

Al-Khalil, 2001

Sharif Waked,
To Be Continued..., 2009
Video still from colour video,
with sound, 41:33 mins

after which he returned, gave orders for departure, and journeyed to his brother's capital.

Rineke Dijkstra,
Shany, Tel Hashomer,
Israel, May 18, 2003, 2003
Chromogenic print,
126 x 107 cm

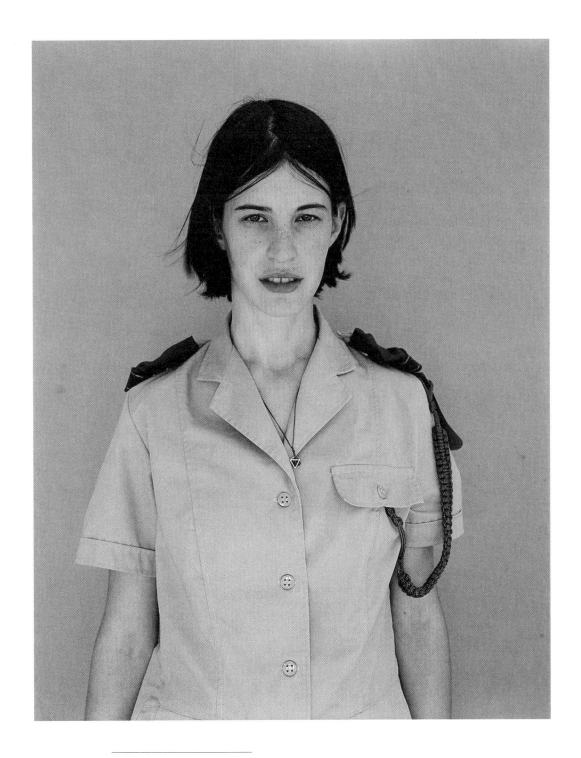

Rineke Dijkstra,
Shany, Herzliya, Israel,
August 1, 2003, 2003
Chromogenic print,
126 x 107 cm

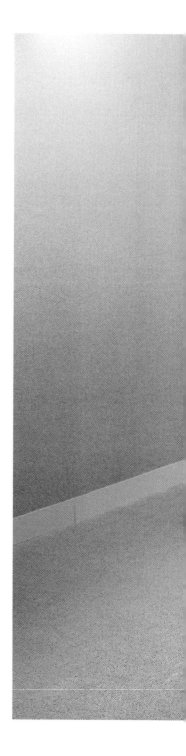

Do Ho Suh, *Uni-Form/s:*
Self-Portrait/s:
My 39 Years, 2006
Fabric, fibreglass resin,
stainless steel, casters,
169 x 254 x 56 cm

Yoshua Okón,
Parking Lotus, 2001
Lightjet c-prints,
each 101.5 x 76.2 cm

Mella Jaarsma,
The Warrior, 2003 (detail)
Sixteen shredded military
outfits, seaweed, miso soup,
monitor and DVD

OPPOSITE
Mella Jaarsma,
The Follower, 2002
Embroidered emblems
Photographer Mie Cornoedus

Kader Attia,
The Dead Sea
(La Mer Morte), 2015
Installation comprising
second-hand blue clothing
and three lightboxes, each
130 x 160 x 18 cm
Photographer Henning Rogge

Leon Golub
*Mercenaries II
(section III)*, 1975
*Mercenaries II
(section I)*, 1975

The American artist Leon Golub sees an inalienable correlation between ethics and aesthetics, and between power and violence. In his view, power corrupts. Tirelessly his work bears witness to a world in which violence reigns supreme, and reacts against the abuses generated by power games and the tragedy of war. His paintings – realistic yet monumental, adhering to facts but universal in meaning – are images of defeat, scenes of extraordinary eloquence in which victim and executioner are unmistakable thanks to the uniforms worn by standing armies, corrupted police or mercenaries.

Köken Ergun, *I, Soldier (Ben Askerim)*, 2005

Here we see uniformed soldiers and officers in a dramatised parade. A battle is clearly evoked through a complex choreography that combines an agonistic spirit and the idea of sacrifice, and condenses practice and representation, aesthetics and a sense of masculine and heroic togetherness. Uniform is essential to the effectiveness of this spectacle. By referencing Turkey's National Youth and Sports Day, a state-controlled event that marks the anniversary of the Turkish War of Independence in 1919, artistic expression is here aligned with national politics. Through a seemingly neutral documentary-like language, Köken Ergun highlights how this dramatisation emphasises rhetoric and therefore how identities are politically controlled and defined by the display of a nationalistic, militarised, highly codified visual repertoire.

Artur Żmijewski, *KR WP*, 2000

For KR WP Artur Żmijewski asked soldiers from the Polish Army's Honour Guard (Kompania Reprezentacyina Wojska Polskiego) to execute their drill ceremony on the parade grounds in full uniform, and then repeat it naked, in a ballet studio. With a demystifying gesture, Żmijewski strips his soldiers, undressing them: of the uniform they share, of their sense of power and safety, and thus of the assertiveness the uniform usually confers on them. The body, deprived of the uniform that is also an instrument of subjective affirmation, reveals itself in its unalienable singularity and vulnerability, forced always to march. Human pride is tenacious, though, and renouncing all its signs may be too much: the soldiers keep on their boots and retain their weapons. The result is a caustic work: an anti-rhetorical and grotesque counterpart to the official image that authorities such as the army wish to display.

Sharif Waked, *Chic Point*, 2003

The vulnerability of bodies that are sites of confrontation – not only cultural and political but also armed – inspires the work of the Palestinian artist Sharif Waked. For Waked, creating a fashion collection is an opportunity for redemption and reclaiming personhood in dehumanising situations such as the current reality in the Middle East. In the video *Chic Point*, male models emerge from a dark background onto the catwalk. The clothes they wear have openings, zippers, buttons. We catch sight of parts of their bodies. The video dims to a close and the viewer is transported from fashion show to the West Bank and Gaza. A series of stills invoke the immediacy of photography – images in which we see Palestinian men approaching an Israeli checkpoint, forced to raise their shirts, jackets and tunics in front of armed Israeli soldiers in uniform to prove they are not concealing weapons. This is a form of surveillance that causes humiliation on a daily basis. In response, the artist wishes to restore respect and dignity, as well as beauty and desirability, to these people.

Sharif Waked, *To Be Continued...*, 2009

Waked courageously refers to the apparatus of terror in the video *To Be Continued ....* Borrowing the ritual format that radical Muslim terrorists use to record their last will and testament in preparation for a suicide bombing, he stages the declaration of intent of a jihadi, dressed and armed for the occasion. The moment of preparation is dragged out endlessly, and the attack is delayed, as the jihadi, instead of the usual ideological protestations, starts to recite stories from *One Thousand and One Nights*. There is an evident schism between the necessity of carrying out the act for which, as evidenced by the clothes, the jihadi has been so carefully prepared, and the attraction of life, and the desire to survive, expressed by the central character of Scheherazade. War is underway, but life continues to be clung to. Referring to geopolitics, while simultaneously seeing the jihadi not as the representative of a category – a criminal or a hero – but rather as an individual, Waked allows a dense series of considerations to emerge. Among these is the sense that expressiveness, by means of which Scheherazade saved her life, is still a possible antidote to brutality.

Rineke Dijkstra,
Shany, Tel Hashomer,
Israel, May 18, 2003, 2003.
Shany, Herzliya, Israel,
August 1, 2003, 2003

In her *Soldiers* series, Dutch artist Rineke Dijkstra portrays a young Israeli recruit, Shany, over a period of time from her first day in the army until she quits. In these simple, larger-than-life-size portraits, we see her first wearing her ordinary clothing and then trying on her uniform, which is still stiff and new. We sense a moment of deep psychological transformation: the tension between a feeling of unflagging certainty and loyalty, which the uniform aims to convey, and the posture, still unsure, which denotes a moment of emotional vulnerability. This discrepancy will vanish when these young recruits find themselves fully in their role as soldiers, with everything this entails in terms of power, responsibility and public position.

Do Ho Suh, *Uni-Form/s:*
Self-Portrait/s:
My 39 Years, 2006

Korean artist Do Ho Suh highlights the life-shaping forces that a person experiences as he or she ages. *Uni-form/s: Self-Portrait/s: My 39 Years*, a rack displaying all the uniforms worn by the artist

throughout his life, shows how social conventions and political structures – from education to the military, from family to career – contribute to the process of regimenting age and generating 'conforming' citizens. The uniform acts as a vehicle for this process: related to the idea of order, made in series and imposed even in its less martial aspects, it is deployed with the goal of disciplining individuality, reducing it to a mere role.

Yoshua Okón,
Parking Lotus, 2001

For *Parking Lotus* security guards around Los Angeles were asked to meditate in a yoga position in the parking lots where they work. The Security Guard Meditation Movement had recently been initiated by the local branch of the Union of Security Guards of America. Yoshua Okón blends staged situations with documentation, video installations with photographs. Here he captures a sense of paradox, the discrepancy between the guards' bodies dressed in uniform and the feelings of introversion and exploration of the self expressed by meditation. His work not only highlights how the standardising effect of the uniform reaches its limit in the uncontrollable singularity of the body. It also suggests the huge effort needed to maintain – or rediscover – that self-identity within a mandated, and often frustrating, uniformity.

Mella Jaarsma,
The Follower, 2002
The Warrior, 2003

Dutch artist Mella Jaarsma creates body-covering artworks that recall the burqa: as restrictive as shrouds, they are as protective as cocoons. These coat-tents cling to the shape of the body like a second skin; they also envelop and conceal it. Made of a patchwork of logos, as in *The Follower*, or scraps of military uniforms, like *The Warrior*, they evoke disequilibrium, conflict, the contradictions of the global economy and the power play linked to the circulation of goods and capital. But while these clothes conceal the face and most of the body, they leave the eyes uncovered: a sign of vital energy, singularity and resistance.

Kader Attia,
The Dead Sea (La Mer Morte),
2015

The uniform is not just military; we all live in uniforms of one kind or another. French artist Kader Attia's installation, *The Dead Sea*, recalls the flotsam and jetsam left on a beach when the tide has retreated, the jeans, sweaters and T-shirts resembling those commonly worn by migrants and fugitives during their journeys. Strewn on the ground, these garments in shades of blue both evoke the sea and bear witness to an all-too-frequent tragedy. The installation is a site of bereavement. Jeans, created as an egalitarian and universal type of clothing, thus become a symbol of a society based on inequality, in which the individual is no longer valued.

IV

Resistance or

Recuperation

Dressing the Opposition: Sartorial Resistance on Europe's Political Left

Anthony Sullivan

This essay argues that dress and the fashioned body matters to oppositional politics. On the contemporary European left, anti-austerity radicalism combined with vestimentary disruptiveness has emerged as a cultural dominant. Unconventional attitudes to dress, manifested as style choices, have become emblematic of a rejection of the status quo and the political challenges mounted by insurgent, anti-establishment figures, from Pablo Iglesias, the leader of the populist left Podemos party in Spain, to Alexis Tsipras and Yanis Varoufakis of the Greek radical left reformist party, Syriza. In Britain, too, political outsider Jeremy Corbyn rose from obscure backbench dissident Member of Parliament to become head of the Labour Party, and – in defiance of those who predicted that the grey-haired, bearded and 'dishevelled' 'scruff'[1] would preside over an electoral meltdown – showed that Labour was a contender to defeat the Conservatives.

Sartorial insouciance as oppositional trope

Beginning with an outline of the role of the suit as a key site for the sartorially embodied contestation of political power, this essay moves on to a more detailed analysis of the way in which the self-presentation of each leader has worked to anchor their oppositional politics. In that discussion, I distinguish between the often-conflated terms 'dress', 'fashion' and 'style',[2] arguing that it is the agency embodied by these individual leaders that produces their 'style', understood as their personal interpretation of dress codes within or against fashion. More specifically, it is against the clean-cut corporate suited look, which still dominates the cycle of fashion in contemporary political dress, that the nuances of their oppositional style must be understood. Joanne Entwistle argues that since dress and fashion are situated bodily practices, style evolves through the way individuals creatively negotiate the 'tension between structure and agency as structures such as the fashion system impose parameters around dress'.[3] For Carol Tulloch '"style" is a matter of personal agency and the construction of self through the assemblage of garments, accessories, and beauty regimes that may, or may not, be "in fashion".'[4] Importantly, then, in relation to my argument – and paradoxically, given the left's impoverished sartorial reputation as 'sandal wearing quacks', as George Orwell famously put it [5] – the style

FIG. 65
Pablo Iglesias, leader of Podemos, at a campaign meeting in Madrid, 2015

of Europe's new left leaders, created within and against the corporate suit, has emerged as a persuasive factor in the credibility of their oppositional political stance.

Whilst by no means limited to European left political leaders, as US President Donald Trump's larger-than-life dress aesthetic shows – his outsize suits, oversize golf jackets and slacks combined with his infamous comb-over hair together signify a rejection of the vestimentary precision of his predecessor Barack Obama – it is the former figures' cultivation of sartorial insouciance as oppositional trope that is my focus.

The suit as a site of power and resistance

The suit's role as the embodiment of elite political power and the acceptable mode of dress for bourgeois male politicians emerged in the late eighteenth and early nineteenth centuries. Europe-wide struggles for democracy led by the bourgeoisie, whose productive ownership of capital made them the revolutionary class of their day, set them firmly against the inherited wealth and wastefulness of the aristocracy and nobility.[6] As Entwistle suggestively argues, 'except in France, for the most part this [class] challenge was fought out obliquely less with swords than through symbols, of which dress was one of the most significant.'[7]

Psychologist John Carl Flügel's 'Great Male Renunciation' thesis proposed that in the shadow of the French Revolution, bourgeois men, having actively participated in fashion in the eighteenth century, gave up on it in the nineteenth and twentieth centuries: 'in as far as clothes remained of importance to them men aimed at being "correctly" attired, not at being elegantly or elaborately attired'.[8] Valerie Steele explains how in this context the suit came to represent 'Parliament and Constitution (versus royal prerogative and corruption), virtue (versus libertinism), enterprise (versus gambling, frivolity and dissipation)'.[9] She emphasises the class dynamics of the suit as the means to display ascetic restraint, and embody bourgeois man's political power. Christopher Breward, too, argues that 'the growing cultural clout of the mercantile classes'[10] was reflected in their mastery of what Anne Hollander calls 'the pants-jacket-shirt and tie costume'.[11] So Victorian conduct books[12] enabled the bourgeois public man to 'signify adherence to the rules and values of the mainstream'.[13]

But this only gives us a partial picture of the changing relationship between bourgeois men, politics and fashion. We must allow for the criticism made of Flügel by Breward[14] and Hollander, namely that men did not renounce fashion completely but rather participated less ostentatiously in 'a different scheme'.[15] The view of the suit as, in Foucauldian terms, purely a means of disciplining and controlling the embodied self fails to capture the complexity of its history. Indeed, Michel Foucault's argument that 'power is [diffused] exercised from innumerable points', and that resistance to power is 'never in a position of exteriority to it',[16] suggests that power works through human bodies and practices including fashion and dress,[17] in this case the suit.

Crucially, as Breward shows, 'some suit wearers far from dressing to conform to hegemonic demands … instead chose to use the suit as a weapon of style …

incorporat[ing] and adapt[ing] the uniform of power as a vehicle for dissidence and disruption.'[18] The 'subversive possibilities'[19] of the suit were used in the eighteenth century by the Macaroni (the term given to fashionable young aristocrats recently returned from the Grand Tour), in an exaggerated and excessive mode, to queer the pitch of bourgeois decency and disrupt its emerging codes of masculine respectability. Peter McNeil's recent account of these 'Pretty Gentlemen' shows that in Europe's cities, Macaroni dress subverted the suit with tight breeches, colourful brocaded silk waistcoats and elaborate accessories such as high wigs, buckles, buttons and canes. Such dress marked out '"homosexual" or same sex subcultures',[20] and in wearing it the Macaroni announced a form of resistance to rigidly prescriptive ideas of gender and sexuality.

Moreover, as the complex fashion repertoire of 'the original macaroni' Charles James Fox[21] demonstrates, these subversive possibilities also contained much more explicitly political and party political dimensions. McNeil argues that Fox, a Whig opponent of royalist absolutism who served as both British Foreign Secretary and Leader of the House of Commons, donned elements of 'French aristocratic dress without the autocratic agenda'.[22] So to signal his support for the French and American revolutions and his opposition to both his Tory arch-rivals and King George III, Fox, whose style evolved from foppish 'coxcombry to slovenliness',[23] appeared in London's The Mall 'in a suit of Paris-cut velvet, most fancifully embroidered, and bedecked with a large bouquet; a head dress cemented into every variety of shape, a little silk hat, curiously ornamented; and a pair of French shoes, with red heels'.[24]

Breward demonstrates how the suit was further worked and reworked, deconstructed and reconstructed by nineteenth-century dandies, bohemians and Wildean aesthetes and twentieth-century nationalist political leaders. With regard to the latter, in 1915 the Indian anti-colonial leader Mohandas Gandhi swapped his English-style suits for simple loincloths and shawls made from homespun 'khadi' cotton, an ensemble that became iconic of the struggle against British imperialism and its devastating economic effects.[25] Pandit Nehru, India's first Prime Minister, adopted and adapted his mentor Ghandi's oppositional style. The khadi fabric was, as Breward explains, cut and sewn into 'a tailored version of the Kasmiri sherwani',[26] or closed-neck coat worn over trousers. Despite its complex vestimentary genesis, which drew on both the traditional *qipao* or *cheongsam* and the uniform adopted by China's nationalist leader Sun Yat-sen, the Mao suit, with its signature 'blue grey or olive green khaki cotton or wool, five buttons, four symmetrically placed patch pockets and square cut trousers', represented a further iteration of the basic scheme of the suit. Set against the 'softer surfaces', 'sleeker form and lighter weight' of the lounge suit, which had become de rigeur 'business wear by about 1910',[27] Breward argues that the Mao suit provided 'perhaps the most compelling and effective sartorial challenge to the hegemony of the English suit … and symbolised resistance to Western imperialism and materialism'.[28] Since then, the creative and resistant rendering of the suit has continued, whether in the voluminous wide cut of the wartime American 'Zoot Suit', the colourful fabrics of the Congolese Sapeurs or the fetishistic precision that marked out its 'subcultural twisting'[29] in British Ted, Mod and post-subcultural styles.

Today, the suit as contemporary political dress, which originated in and evolved from the intersection of gender, sexual, class, national and political dynamics outlined earlier, has, despite youth-driven shifts in fashion towards pluralism and casualisation,[30] seen a strengthening of its normative disciplinary codes. The dominance of neo-liberal ideology has brought with it the incursion of its 'values', discourses, practices and, more pertinently here, its sartorial style: the business suit, now globally hegemonic. In the 1980s, Conservative British Prime Minister Margaret Thatcher restyled herself as a power-dresser in line with 'the dress for success' principles of John T. Molloy.[31] In the following decade, the British Labour Party under three-times premier Tony Blair followed suit, rebranding the party as 'New Labour' and embodying its upfront infatuation with the City in its modernised image. Signalling their ease with 'profit' and acceptance of Thatcher's neo-liberal imperative TINA ('there is no alternative to the market'), and fixing the template for today's political fashion, New Labour politicians adopted the sartorial style of the 1980s: the designer suit – and more particularly Giorgio Armani's famously 'eviscerated' version of it.[32] Paradoxically, then, the very hegemony of the corporate business suit as political fashion provided the backdrop for the disruptive style of insurgent leftist politicians today.

Political and sartorial resistance to neo-liberal corporate hegemony: Spain and Greece

Deep global, political and social turbulence forms the context for the rise of Europe's new left oppositional leaders like Iglesias, Varoufakis and Corbyn. Recent historical events have confounded Francis Fukuyama's Hegelian end-of-history thesis, which argued that capitalism, liberal democracy and free markets had triumphed.[33] The Great Recession of 2008 to 2009 (which followed the global financial crash of 2007), the worst slump in the world economy since the Great Depression of the 1930s, has formed the backdrop to a series of social and political crises.[34] These have centred on a combination of resistance to neo-liberal austerity policies (severe cuts in public spending to reduce the social wage and government debt) and a widening and deepening opposition to the rule of what are widely perceived to be corrupt mainstream parties and politicians. Here David Harvey's characterisation of neo-liberalism is acutely apposite: a post-war anti-social-democratic and counter-hegemonic political and economic project that aims to transfer wealth from the poor to the rich 'to restore and reconstruct the power of economic elites'.[35]

In Spain the crash of 2007 created a sovereign debt crisis, to which the government responded with severe cuts in state spending. With one in four people unemployed and more than 150,000 families evicted from their homes between 2009 and 2014,[36] a wave of protest developed against the socially damaging effects

FIG. 66
Albert Rivera, leader of liberal reform party Ciudadanos (left), Socialist Workers Party general secretary Pedro Sánchez (centre) and Podemos's general secretary Pablo Iglesias (right) before the electoral debate held at the headquarters of the newspaper *El País* in Madrid, November 2015

of austerity pursued under Spain's de facto two-party parliamentary system. These mobilisations included most notably the city-centre occupations by 'the Indignados' movement of 15 May 2011, or M-15. In this tumult the Spanish left was reborn, soon to realign itself with the formation of the anti-austerity party Podemos in March 2014.[37] In contrast to the two dominant mainstream parties – the right-wing Popular Party (PP) and the left-wing Spanish Socialist Workers Party (PSOE) – Podemos had at its helm two youthful and sartorially strikingly, unbuttoned academics from Madrid's Complutense University – Pablo Iglesias and Iñigo Errejón.

Alongside Errejón's casual dress, Iglesias's dress style in particular (fig. 65), together with his bodily comportment, fitted both the form and content of the anti-austerity movement. Beard, long pony-tail, no tie, linen or checked shirts, their sleeves rolled to reveal leather wrist bands, and belted blue jeans – an off-the-peg amalgam of chain-store 'normcore' and subtle signs of hippy oppositional dress as anti-fashion[38] – Iglesias's signature look came to vividly embody rejection of the two-party establishment. It also made him stand out and apart from the homogeneous style and corporeal stiffness of his besuited political rivals (fig. 66). The leadership of the old guard of Spanish politics typically adopted the global uniform of the business elites, the main beneficiaries of the neo-liberal political consensus: the corporate suit complemented by short, well-cut hair, fastidious grooming and attention to epilation. Importantly, then, Iglesias's stylistic disruption announced itself against the bland homogeneity of mainstream political fashion, which, as will be explored, is based on a very narrow rendering of the many and often subtle possibilities for expression offered by the suit – which, as Breward demonstrates, can be an unparalleled 'vessel for creativity'.[39]

Iglesias and Errejón dressed in keeping with a conscious political trajectory. Together they had formulated a Gramscian strategy[40] based on the tactics and experiences of the early Hugo Chávez in Venezuela,[41] before a fall in oil prices led to economic collapse and a tide of repression under Chávez's successor, Nicolás Maduro.[42] Podemos combined the initial hope inspired by Chávez with theory drawn from the Argentinian post-Marxist Ernesto Laclau and the Belgian political philosopher Chantal Mouffe, for whom 'populism [meant] the creation of a people ... and the establishment of a boundary between an "us" and a "them", the people and the establishment'.[43] Such a perspective required a leader to articulate this 'us' feeling, so as to embody a new collective will.[44] In pursuit of this goal, Iglesias's distinctive casual, vernacular style, along with Podemos's popular profile, was carefully and successfully built using the platform *La Tuerka*, an online news show that became the voice of M-15, achieving over 60 million views on its YouTube channel in eight years.

From his new media base, Iglesias projected his sartorially disruptive, oppositional stance as celebrity insurgent leader further, by winning slots on popular television chat shows as the voice of anti-austerity and anti-corruption politics. In a series of moves which culminated in the decision to put a photo of himself on Podemos's ballot papers – a first in Spanish electoral history – Iglesias's image as the figurehead of a Spanish left populism was carefully cultivated and embodied sartorially.[45] Andy Brown concludes that 'the party used his image as the political signifier of the anti-establishment feeling he expressed',[46] cutting through and fighting against an image-based celebrity politics too often dismissed by the left as necessarily disempowering.[47]

Meanwhile, in Greece in 2015, Syriza, a new left political alliance that had emerged a decade before, won two key election victories to defeat the established left party, the Panhellenic Socialist Movement (PASOK). Along similar lines to those pursued by Iglesias and Errejón – a neo-Gramscian strategy inflected with the revisionist Marxist state theory of Nicos Poulantzas[48] – Syriza proposed that the existing state, far from being a barrier to social transformation, could be used to benefit all the people. Between 2008 and 2014 Greeks became on average 40 per cent poorer, as a result of Greece's sovereign debt crisis and the massive cuts to public spending demanded by the Troika (the EU, IMF and ECB) to secure further bail-outs or loans.[49] Against a backdrop of popular resistance to deepening austerity, including 32 widely observed General Strikes between 2010 and 2014,[50] on 6 July 2015 Varoufakis resigned as Finance Minister rather than do the Troika's bidding. Shortly afterwards, as the Greek Prime Minister Alexis Tsipras pressed ahead with further austerity measures, Varoufakis parted company with Syriza too.[51]

FIG. 67
Greek Prime Minister
Alexis Tsipras and German
Chancellor Angela Merkel
at a news conference in the
Federal Chancellery, Berlin,
March 2015

In the case of Syriza questions of style also came to the fore. Just before the first election in 2015, Tsipras told the *New York Times*: 'We [Syriza] haven't assumed this mentality of establishment parties, with specific ways to dress, to act.'[52] For Tsipras, it was the tie that became the key signifier of the redundant two-party system and its supplication to capital (fig. 67). As Farid Chenoune and other historians of male dress have argued,[53] the tie evolved from the cravat as part of the dress code of the respectable bourgeois gentleman in the nineteenth century, as outlined earlier. Avoiding ties for years because of a neck rash, 'Tsipras realized the symbolic power associated with his decision, and wielded it unabashedly', turning his missing tie into the absent vestimentary presence that defined his personal style.[54]

Varoufakis, Tsipras's political second-in-command, developed his style by making use of what Jean Baudrillard tellingly identified as the possibilities for fashionable resistance through 'plus petit difference marginale',[55] the deft adoption of small differences in the detail of his dress – and more specifically his creative interpretation of the suit. A self-styled 'erratic Marxist',[56] Varoufakis became known for his characteristic mix of verbal bluntness and poetic allusion – he described the austerity imposed on Greece as 'fiscal waterboarding' and the political choice for humanity as lying vividly between a socialist utopian *Star Trek* or the dystopian capitalism of *The Matrix*.[57] This he complemented with expressive details and excessive accessories, marking out his oppositional political stance by dressing in a rebellious repertoire of sartorial insouciance. The contrast between the old

politics of austerity and the new left insurgency was vividly, sartorially personified, whether by way of the infamous Burberry check scarf that wrapped up his tie-less look when meeting IMF President Christine Lagarde; his signature mode of wearing jackets and coats with just enough upturned collar to expose a flash of red lining when entering or leaving the austere corridors of power (fig. 68); the spectacularly colourful shirts he wore against the sombre beige background of the Greek Parliament; his donning of biker leathers or, his pièce de résistance, the long 'madchester drug dealer's coat'[58] that he wore to meet British Chancellor George Osborne in Downing Street in February 2015 (fig. 69).

What is fascinating about Varoufakis's dress moves in particular, as these examples show, is that 'the emerging rock-star of Europe's anti-austerity uprising'[59] embodied resistance by riffing on and against the staidness of the business suit, and in doing so reprised something of the stylish ebullience of the Macaroni politician Charles Fox. Thus Varoufakis's style recalls Michel Foucault's argument that 'where there is power, there is resistance',[60] and prompts us to more deeply understand the suit as 'a complex vessel of meaning' whose 'adaptability', as Breward contends, makes it 'an icon of both mainstream fashion and of oppositional style'.[61]

Jeremy Corbyn: post-auratic style as embodied political defiance

The political trajectory of Jeremy Corbyn, a Labour MP since 1983, has been, like that of his European comrades, avowedly leftist and anti-neo-liberal. Like his mentor, former Labour minister Tony Benn, Corbyn aimed to win socialist change through Parliament, but he also believed that extra-parliamentary struggle was necessary to fight austerity, war[62] and racism. An image of Corbyn being arrested at an Anti-Apartheid demonstration in London in 1984 (fig. 70) captures the essence of his politics and the enduring elements of his style. Tie-less and bearded, he wears a loosely fitting jacket with non-matching trousers and clumpy shoes. In a sign of things to come, not long after, Corbyn was criticised for his 'scruffy' style in an interview on the BBC's current affairs television show *Newsnight*. Framed next to Tory MP Terry Dicks, arch-critic of parliamentary sartorial impropriety, who appeared fully suited and conventionally groomed, Corbyn wore a brown casual jacket, Co-op shirt and a jumper knitted by his mother.[63]

When, in April 2017, Conservative Prime Minister Theresa May announced there was to be a general election in Britain in June, Labour lagged 20 per cent behind the Conservatives in the opinion polls. Standing out and apart from his parliamentary peers, both sartorially and politically, Corbyn was labelled a 'mutton-headed old mugwump'[64] by the ex-Mayor of London Boris Johnson. Typically, the

FIG. 68
Greece's Finance Minister Yanis Varoufakis leaves the Institute for New Economic Thinking as Greece makes an International Monetary Fund payment, April 2015

FIG. 69
George Osborne and Yanis Varoufakis outside 11 Downing Street, London, the residence of the Chancellor of the Exchequer, February 2015

Daily Telegraph newspaper commented: 'the clothes may maketh the man, but his dishevelled outfit at the Battle of Britain memorial service just shows his poor judgement.'[65] Corbyn, the newspapers proclaimed, was about to lead Labour to catastrophic election defeat. *The Times* headline was typical: 'May Heads For Election Landslide.'[66] Yet Labour polled 40 per cent, its biggest increase in vote share between two elections in the post-war era.[67]

As well as misjudging the popular potential of Corbyn's anti-war, anti-austerity and anti-cuts programme – the half-trillion-pound bail-out of Britain's banks in the wake of the 2007 crash and 2008 recession drained resources from both welfare provision and vital public services – pundits, experts and pollsters have consistently misread Corbyn's 'image', or rather his unwillingness to present one acceptable to the establishment. They failed to consider how his distinctive embodiment of an anti-political-fashion style might also differentiate him as a party leader with a left alternative agenda, one that might connect with the third of people who did not vote, often on the grounds that politicians are 'all the same'. Although beset by serious problems and criticisms of his leadership,[68] which contributed to the fact that Corbyn was not popular enough to unseat May, and Labour lost seats such as Mansfield, a mining town devastated by Conservative de-industrialisation policies,[69] the election result was significant. And, as with Iglesias and Errejón, Tsipras and Varoufakis, the defiance embodied in Corbyn's personal sartorial style reinforced his standing as an insurgent, anti-establishment socialist leader.

When Corbyn first faced Prime Minister David Cameron at parliamentary Question Time in September 2015, the difference in the two men's appearance could not have been greater. Cameron wore a well-cut, made-to-measure blue suit, combined with a starched white collar and a tie, set off by his signature haircut by leading British hairstylist 'Lino' Carbosiero (fig. 71).[70] Grey-haired, bearded and bespectacled, Corbyn donned a beige, off-the-peg, over-sized suit jacket accompanied by a loose gold and bronze tie and a coffee-and-cream-coloured striped shirt (fig. 72). Five months later, when the two men clashed in the House of Commons over the National Health Service, the incumbent literally dressed down the challenger, demanding 'put on a proper suit, do up your tie and sing the national anthem'.[71] But in so doing, he also inadvertently helped to copper-fasten Corbyn's

FIG. 70
Jeremy Corbyn, being arrested at an Anti-Apartheid demonstration in London, 1984

insurgent appeal by turning the Leader of the Opposition's suits into symbols of his political defiance rather than compliance.

Two days into his general election campaign, in a speech that set out his left-populist insurgent agenda, Corbyn drew on the class-infused tropes of British dress culture to proclaim of the establishment: 'they think there are rules in politics, which if you don't follow by doffing your cap to powerful people, accepting that things can't really change, then you can't win.'[72] In a powerful sense, then, Corbyn's personal dress style, largely unchanged since his 1984 *Newsnight* interview, anchored his political difference and his authenticity against the sartorially homogeneous political fashion of his opponents, in what Dick Pels usefully suggests is the era of the 'post-auratic politician'.[73] Drawing on Walter Benjamin's diagnosis of the loss of aura attached to works of art in the industrial age,[74] Pels argues that the 'halo' of the 'professional politician faded'[75] with the spread of new technologies relating to image reproduction and circulation. As Joshua Meyrowitz suggests,[76] this meant, contradictorily, that the era of the constantly mediated 'celebrity politician' is one in which the 'loss of their aura of greatness precisely is a result of the familiarizing, even banalising effects of continuous media exposure.'[77] Pels expands the point, adding that in such a world, 'the barriers between politicians' traditional front and back regions are eroded'.[78] The result is that the mediated or parasocial closeness that we now feel to such figures, especially through social media, closes the gap between their public and ordinary selves, subsuming the latter in the former rather than demanding their elision in the figure of the 'superhuman persona'.[79]

Corbyn's election was fought as much through the everyday world of social media as through set pieces like Prime Minister's Question Time. He was, then, well placed to ride out the hostile old-media storm that surrounded his every move – both rhetorically and sartorially. Using his 'extraordinary ordinariness', a quality which Pels argues 'characterizes modern [political] celebrity',[80] he won over audiences and managed to deflate the presentational puffery and highly conventionalised self-presentation of Cameron and his successor as prime minister, Theresa May – tellingly nicknamed 'Maybot' by journalist John Crace.[81] The Corbyn campaign's adept use of social media helps explain why, for example, the derision and invective directed against his quotidian, quirky, uncoordinated style rebounded on its sources. Drawing on the networked collective social intelligence of the Internet as a knowledge machine, the 'general intellect',[82] which Marx presciently identified as a possibility some 150 years earlier, Labour's online activists effectively targeted the young.[83] Social media likes and reposts of key events, such as Corbyn's old-fashioned town centre mass rallies, amplified his reach to millions,[84] co-creating from the bottom up an alternative meaning for him as an insurgent Labour leader.

FIG. 71
Prime Minister David Cameron leaves 10 Downing Street for Prime Minister's Question Time, September 2015

Archetypal news images showed a cycling, shell-suited Corbyn, or an 'off duty' (back stage) Corbyn in baggy shorts and trainers or slider sandals, accompanied by text that continually inferred scruffiness equals incompetence. In a prima facie case of the relevance of Roland Barthes's approach to fashion in *The Fashion System*,[85] and also of critiques of his overestimation of the importance of rhetorical codes in the making of fashion's symbolic meaning – these features and commentaries failed to anchor the meaning of Corbyn's style. They also failed to recognise its alternative significance,[86] which was that dress, albeit a language, is a much more open and contested system of meaning, which emerges in an embodied contextual relation to both normative dress codes and wider cultural and ideological shifts. In short, in the case of Corbyn, his opponents' mastery of the old-media frame did not equate to control of the communicative meaning of his longstanding 'ordinary' personal style, which in new contexts, including those now shaped by social media, was read as a mark of his political credibility and authenticity.

Conclusion – oppositional politics and style

This essay has shown how oppositional politics are enacted in part through oppositional style. It is perhaps not such a surprise, then, that in the aftermath of the global crash, the Great Recession and on-going austerity, the European left's assault on the political orthodoxies of neo-liberalism has been mirrored by an iconoclastic sartorial irreverence. In the case of Iglesias and Errejón, although maintaining momentum has not proved easy,[87] their rise in Spain developed from popular mobilisations boosted by the use of an online news platform, which maximised the political visual impact of their casual, unbuttoned dress aesthetic. For the tie-less Tsipras and the sartorially insouciant Varoufakis, their ascendency and subsequent split were ultimately shaped by both the depth of the crisis and the level of resistance to austerity. With regard to Corbyn, forming the next UK government is a real possibility but far from certain.[88] Social media, I have argued, has helped to bind the link between his anti-political fashion style and his anti-austerity politics. As a post-auratic left leader, his progress has demonstrated how the relationship between Barthes's 'vestimentary' and 'rhetorical' codes produced conflicting views as to the meaning of his clothes, and a contest that establishment politicians and mainstream media have clearly struggled to win. Finally, though, while an understanding of sartorial power as subtle and diffuse in the Foucauldian sense has been shown to be useful, the ability of these leaders to defy concentrations of political and economic state and interstate power – especially when its defenders are in office – is a very different matter.

FIG. 72
Leader of the Labour Party
Jeremy Corbyn at Prime
Minister's Question Time,
September 2015

Three Pairs of Khaki Trousers, or How to Decolonise a Museum

Erica de Greef

Three pairs of trousers in the collections of the Iziko Museums in Cape Town, South Africa, shape this essay – the first pair are plain, khaki workwear trousers repurposed as a display prop, the second are conservative everyday office wear, and the third are cheap, mass-produced trousers beaded and embellished to be worn in a rite of passage.[1] Sartorial objects in museums – removed from the bodies of their original owners, wearers or makers, and the social frameworks of their original lives – rely on the architecture of meanings created in museums by classificatory systems and museal practices, and in exhibitions.[2]

In this photo essay, I show how, through intended and unintended slippages of both sartorial and museal boundaries, each pair troubles the museum practices that aim to classify, stereotype and sometimes limit their sartorial complexities. Drawing on historian Carolyn Hamilton's term 'biography', which describes the life of archival material from when it is 'first engaged with a view to it entering some form of preservatory housing', I propose that all three khaki trousers present unique and disruptive biographies.[3]

South Africa's first 'free and fair' elections in 1994 led to the end of apartheid, to a new democracy, and to transformation imperatives spanning public institutions such as museums.[4] Previously segregated clothing collections held in the Cultural History Museum, the South African Museum and the National Gallery were amalgamated in the merger of these three museums, together with eight other, smaller museums to form Iziko Museums in 1999. This merger was an effort to redress the apartheid and colonial legacies of these museums, particularly evident in the division of black sartorial histories from white material culture and identity narratives, as the three pairs of trousers attest. I show how these trousers, if considered critically, can interrupt the reproduction of limited historical narratives and cultural identities, and offer ways of re-thinking fashion collections in South African museums in the twenty-first century.

Photographs by Andrew Juries

Plain khaki men's workwear trousers, front view
Cotton, with classic pockets, button-fly front and belt loops
First displayed in South African Museum, 1978

Purchased as a display prop and exhibited in the South African Museum for almost 40 years, this pair of cotton men's workwear trousers with classic pockets, a button-fly front and belt loops was displayed on a body-cast of Archie Khusu in the 'Sotho' display cabinet of the Ethnography Gallery from the Gallery's inception in 1978.[5] Khusu was one of several volunteers in the museum's body-casting project in the 1970s, which aimed to create realistic casts that would showcase specific ethnic identities in line with the apartheid ideologies of the time.[6]

Public controversy around the use of body-casts in ethnographic museums in post-apartheid South Africa, and in particular those displayed in the well-known Bushman Diorama, also at the South African Museum, led to a 're-dressing' of the Ethnography Gallery display in 2012 when all eight body-casts were replaced with life-size black wire figures.[7] The khaki trousers remained on display on the wire figure until 2017. The final closure of the Ethnography Gallery in 2017 was in response to #Rhodes Must Fall, the student protest movement, which, amongst other demands, called for the decolonisation of South African sites of knowledge reproduction such as memorials, museums and universities.

The plain khaki trousers were never accessioned by the South African Museum, yet they featured in the representation of the museum's 'traditional' cultural identity narrative shown together with the conical, woven straw hat with distinctive top-knot, and the boldly patterned wool blanket with iconic contrast stripe, both considered to be symbols of national 'Basutho' heritage and identity. Altogether, these objects corroborated the gallery's traditional dress narrative of a black South African, tribal identity, largely frozen in an imaginary 'other' time.

The exhibition of so-called traditional sartorial objects – such as the 'Basutho' hat and blanket, and elsewhere in the gallery 'Zulu' beadwork and 'Ndebele' beaded aprons – sustained ideas of rigidly segregated ethnicities. In this way, the South African Museum's Ethnography Gallery exhibited the same racial and political ideals that underpinned key segregationist apartheid policies of the time, separating identities, education and governance of land, and alleged 'group' areas, as well as on more intimate levels, the use of beaches, beds and benches. Tradition was separated from modernity, black sartorial identities from white, and local cultures from global histories.

Surrounded by the other objects and wall texts – collectively an exhibition constructed to show tribal identities, within a museum itself considered as a site for the material culture of ethnographic 'others' – these trousers came to signify tradition. The khaki trousers' identification as contemporary and western, and not authentic or traditional, was completely overwritten by the dominant claims of their context.

Photograph of body-cast of Archie Khusu with plain khaki workwear trousers, 'Basutho' hat and blanket
First displayed in South African Museum, 1978

Plain khaki men's workwear trousers (detail of rope with buckle and waistband)

My request to photograph selected pairs of trousers for this essay gave me the opportunity to access these display trousers, in storage since the dismantling of the gallery in 2017. It became evident that the museum staff in the 1970s had applied coloured shoe polishes to the obviously unworn trousers in an effort to present the store-bought trousers as an appropriate, and 'authentic', prop for the ethnographic display.

Techniques of ageing and, in this case, 'authenticating' the trousers to look soiled and used, contradict the conservation ethics that otherwise govern museum collecting policies and practices. The museal interference with the object, in this case a display prop, troubles this pair of trousers' supposed authenticity, and thereby its legitimacy as a collectable object. The bogus 'scuffs' at the knees, 'dirt' at the pocket mouth and manufactured 'stains' on the inner waistband contrast strangely with the otherwise crisp seams, stainless-steel buckles and unscuffed hems.

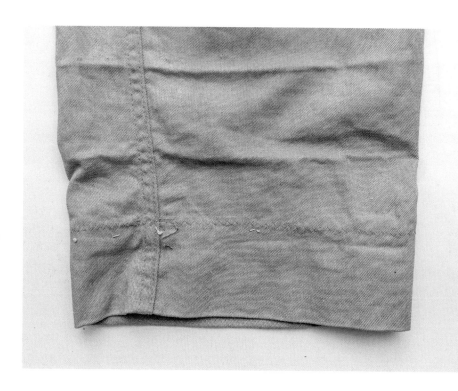

Plain khaki men's
workwear trousers
(detail of cuff folds at hem)

Plain khaki men's workwear
trousers, back view
Cotton; stitching of turn-ups
removed for extra length

A second curatorial intervention became obvious while
closely observing the artefact
when it was photographed. In
the initial display of the trousers, as worn by Khusu's body-
cast, the trousers were given
neatly folded turn-ups, hand-
stitched in place with white
cotton thread. In the swift
'redress' of the entire gallery
in 2012, nothing was changed
in the exhibition, except for
the removal of the body-casts,
which were replaced by new,
custom-made wire figures.
These wire figures were simply
re-clothed with the same
exhibition items, within the
same exhibitionary frame-
work. However, these trousers
were found to be noticeably
too short for their new wire
support. The wire figure had
outgrown the display trousers.
The small white stitches se-
curing the turn-ups had been
hurriedly snipped. However, the
threads and folds remained as
witnesses to the almost four
decades of being on display
on the body-cast. The silenced
trousers with their folds and
white threads went unnoticed,
and unattended, for a further
five years. Although recently
international museums and
galleries have shown interest
in sartorial object 'biographies',
and traces of imperfection and
signs of wearing, shortening or
mending are valued by curators
and collectors, such close,
careful or critical attention
has not as yet materialised
at Iziko Museums.

**Plain khaki men's office
wear trousers, back view
Wool-polyester blend, with
classic pockets and belt loops
Acquired by the South African
Cultural History Museum,
1982**

In a 2016 interview, South
African Museum anthropology
curator Gerald Klinghardt
suggested that these khaki
display trousers 'are now
probably worth accession-
ing as an example, if there is
nothing similar from the 1970s
in the clothing collection' of the
South African Cultural History
Museum. The Cultural History
Museum, established in 1965
as a collection dedicated to
western clothing solely of
white South Africans, was
amalgamated with the South
African Museum and other
cultural institutions to form
Iziko Museums in 1999.

There is in fact a pair of
plain khaki trousers in the
Cultural History Museum
collection. This pair, however,
differs considerably from
the artificially 'aged' khaki
trousers from the Ethnography
Gallery display. The Cultural
History Museum pair of well-
worn khaki, wool-polyester
blend trousers had belonged
to Rene Immelman, who had
worn them during his tenure as
chief librarian at the University
of Cape Town from 1930 to
1970.[8] The accessioning of
these trousers – together with
12 other, rather commonplace
items from Immelman's
personal wardrobe – affirmed
the sartorial identity narrative
of a white academic at the
height of South African
apartheid.[9]

The acquisition, four years
after the purchase of the
display trousers, underlines
the double silencing of the
South African Museum's
unaccessioned trousers.
Firstly, plain khaki workwear
trousers worn by black South
Africans were never considered
collectable. Secondly, the
trousers that were purchased
for the display were instead
treated with polishes to
'authenticate' them so as to
fit with the invented identity
narratives of the Ethnography
Gallery. In this regard the
librarian's trousers present
a significantly different
biography – in relation to its
museal acquisition, as well
as its radically distinct life
and labour narrative – to that
of the everyday, heavy-duty
Lybro-branded trousers worn
by black South African workers
throughout the twentieth
century.[10] Although both
trousers share similar
features, the comfortable
office life of Immelman's
trousers differs markedly
from that of those worn by
often-migrant labourers
enduring physical hardships
and hard labour.

Had anthropologists,
collectors or dealers in
the late 1970s considered
western trousers worn by
black South Africans in both
rural or urban settings to be

**Plain khaki men's office wear
trousers (belt detail)**

appropriate for collection
in either ethnographic or
costume museums, they would
have purchased such plain
workwear trousers and these
would have entered museum
collections as authentic
African sartorial objects.
However, the artificial division
of objects according to the
classifications of 'traditional'
(the sartorial artefacts of

black South Africans) and
'western' (the artefacts of
white South Africans) denied
them entry into any museum
collection. The current
troubles, almost 50 years
later, present yet another
slippage of museal boundaries
as these trousers await
their possible future in the
museum. They do not meet the
criteria for 'authentic' African

artefacts in the South African
Museum collection, and yet
their display as 'traditional'
artefact aggravates their
possible inclusion in the
Cultural History collection.
These are the challenges that
face the trousers despite Iziko
Museums' current efforts to
integrate the collections.

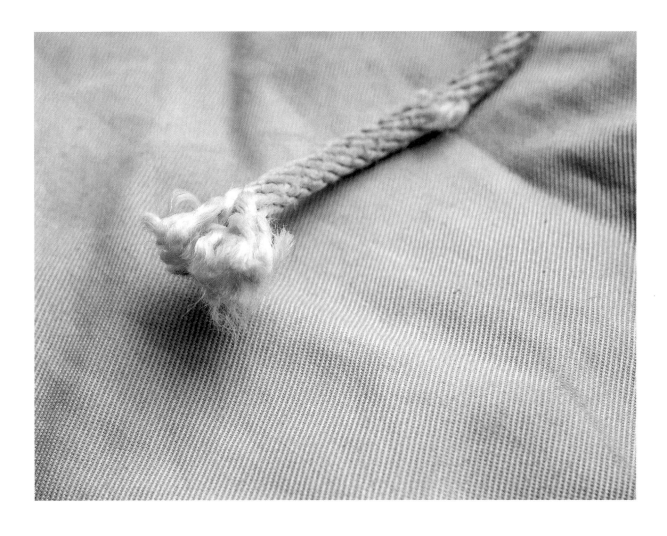

Plain khaki men's workwear
trousers (belt detail)

Beaded 'Xhosa' khaki men's knee-length trousers, front and back views
Polyester-cotton, with embellishments
Acquired by South African Museum, 1991–4

Beaded 'Xhosa' khaki men's knee-length trousers (repair detail)

The South African Museum did, however, collect some khaki trousers originally worn by black South Africans. These were neither plain nor workwear. Instead, responding to a distinctive, albeit stereotypical characteristic of African adornment, the Museum purchased four pairs of beaded 'Xhosa' trousers between 1991 and 1994.[11] As beaded artefacts, these modern western trousers were deemed authentic and traditional enough for the Museum's collection. One pair of khaki polyester-cotton trousers is cut off below the knee with a rough, serrated, zigzag hem and extensive all-over beadwork in red, white, blue and black, some of which is haphazard, some trained along the garment's edges, seams and hems, while other beadwork spells out different 'Xhosa' first names and initials.[12] According to the Museum's catalogue card, the 'tattered and wild style reflects the attitude of youths at [an] irresponsible stage before initiation'. More 'Xhosa' first names are handwritten in thick, uneven black, red and blue *khoki* (fibre-tipped) pen on the back of the trouser legs.

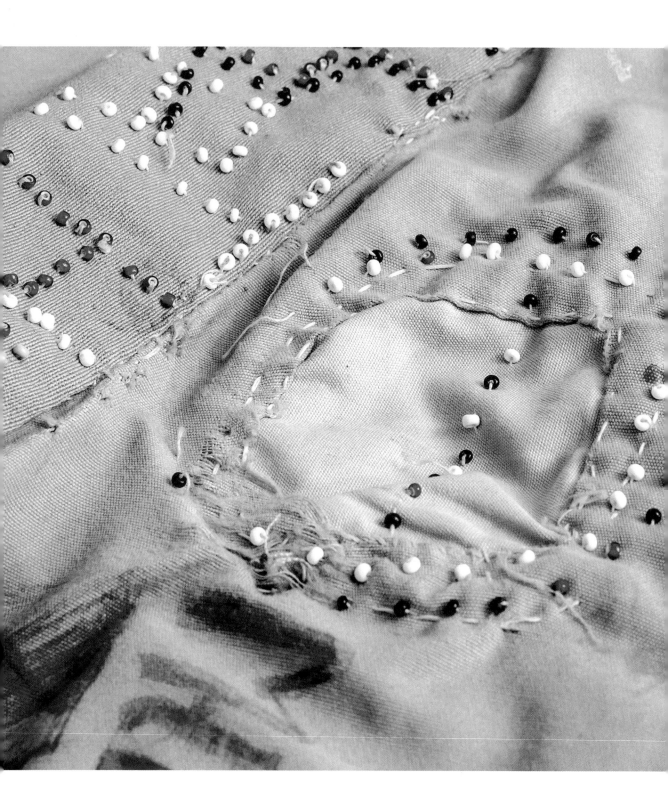

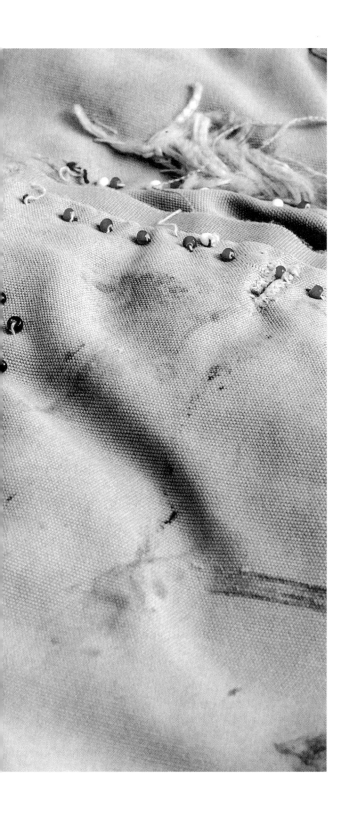

This overwriting and re-purposing of the cheap, mass-produced trousers marks a negotiation with new hybrid forms of identity and makes bold claims by the wearers to notions of ownership. The graffiti-like trope of tagging identities is performed on this garment's surface. The different individual names assert a shared, collective experience and perhaps even a mutual ownership of a single sartorial item. Together, the literal use of penned text and the symbolic use of beaded patterns blur the boundaries in this object between past and present, between tradition and modernity, and between western and African.

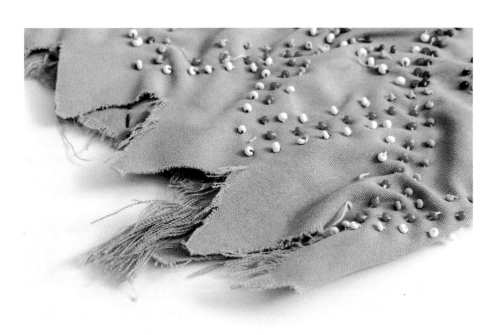

ABOVE
Beaded 'Xhosa' khaki men's knee-length trousers (jagged hem detail)

RIGHT
Beaded 'Xhosa' khaki knee-length trousers (zip detail)

With large numbers of men seeking work in South African cities, whether as migrant miners, labourers or industrial workers, an increasingly complex sense of identity developed in the twentieth century that was often played out through 'collaging European and indigenous forms of dress'.[13] Due to these labour movements and increased political oppression, rural women were often left to negotiate new social, economic and familial structures as a result of these social shifts.

Art historian Anitra Nettleton suggests that, instead of being deemed traditional and un-modern, beadwork largely performed by women is, in fact, 'a representation of modernity'.[14] Through bridging the handcrafted and machine-stitched, the urban and rural, tradition and modernity, these beaded trousers offered, at the time, ways of speaking back to, and beyond, the oppressive colonial and apartheid regimes. The cutting, re-stitching and beading of the manufactured trousers simultaneously re-purposed the object and fashioned new, contemporary hybrid identities. Although their makers and wearers are 'unknown', their presence is made tangible in the materiality and tangibility of these expressive forms of re-crafting and remaking.[15]

'Thrown Away Like a Piece of Cloth': Fashion Production and the European Refugee Crisis

Serkan Delice

During an appearance on the US TV talk show *Late Night with Seth Meyers* on 13 April 2016, Anna Wintour, the editor-in-chief of American *Vogue*, used the phrase 'migrant chic' to describe, and praise, Kanye West's new fashion collection. She was recounting her attendance at the event in New York's Madison Square Garden where West had debuted his new album, *The Life of Pablo*, and his *Yeezy Season 3* fashion line. After receiving 'a firestorm of criticism' for her 'insensitive' comments, Wintour recanted, saying: 'I apologise if my remark was offensive in any way. The migrant crisis is real, and I didn't intend to trivialise that issue.'[1]

Indeed, there are now more people displaced than at any time since the Second World War. The media have been proclaiming a 'global refugee crisis', especially after 19 April 2015 when at least 800 refugees[2] drowned while attempting to cross to the Italian island of Lampedusa. But, as Alexander Betts and Paul Collier argue, this, in reality, was 'a European crisis. And it was a crisis of politics rather than a crisis of numbers'.[3] In this harsh, hostile and downright destructive environment, human catastrophes are at best registered, and increasingly normalised, through a largely quantitative, and at times fleetingly compassionate, language of humanitarian crisis. But the lives, health and well-being of migrants and refugees are in serious jeopardy, not only due to the absence of a worldwide humanitarian support system that should protect both the 10 per cent who try to reach – often under perilous conditions – the 'developed' world and the 90 per cent who remain – and mostly suffer from destitution and discrimination – in the 'developing' world.[4] They are also threatened by the violence of what Nicholas De Genova calls the 'Border Spectacle', that is, a spectacle of border enforcement and immigration policing at increasingly militarised and securitised European borders, whereby a whole regime of migrant 'legality' and 'illegality' is produced in order to protect and sustain the capitalist-nationalist world order.[5] Through 'national' borders, De Genova reminds us, 'national' states 'legally and politically *produce* and *mediate* the social and spatial differences that capital may then capitalise upon and exploit'.[6] In other words, capitalist globalisation, as Slavoj Žižek usefully captures, relies on 'the idea of a self-enclosed globe separating its privileged Inside from its

FIG. 73
Boy in small clothing
factory off Brick Lane, East
End of London, 1978

197

Outside', establishing 'a radical class division across the entire globe, separating those protected by the sphere from those left vulnerable outside it'.[7]

The phrase 'migrant chic', therefore, is indeed a problematic one: it dilutes and obscures the extent of systemic misery and degradation experienced by most migrants and refugees by assimilating it into another spectacle – namely, the spectacle of fashion, which is characterised by ever-increasing acceleration, appropriation and transience. Yet it is also possible to interpret this apparent blunder in a different and more constructive manner: can 'migrant chic' not be seen as a call for us to confront the persistent division between the material production of fashion, to which the exploitation of cheapened migrant and refugee labour has always been central,[8] and the symbolic production of fashion, that is, the privileged domain of design, creativity and chic? After all, the so-called migrant crisis, when it comes to much of the urban garment industry, is *not* a crisis, but a key, endemic feature and facilitator of a 'particularly extreme form of flexibility', which is defined by low skill needs, high seasonal fluctuations and extensive subcontracting, and has remained at the heart of the obstinately volatile fashion production ever since the late-nineteenth-century period of growth to today.[9]

Beyond crisis
Thus, exploring the production of fashion allows us to interrogate the efficacy of the notion of 'crisis' – as well as of the labels 'migrant' and 'refugee'. Reflecting on the historically ingrained centrality of migrant and refugee labour to the production of clothing, on the other hand, enables us to challenge, and ultimately abolish, fashion's hierarchical division of labour as well as its tired and facile categories of 'inclusivity' and 'exclusivity'. Before asking who is excluded from, or who should be included within, fashion, we should first ask how the very terms of 'inclusion' and 'exclusion' are established, by whom, and according to what criteria. Who, in other words, has the power and privilege to articulate the terms of exclusion and inclusion, or of appropriation and appreciation, when millions of fashion objects themselves are being produced by immigrant and refugee workers in a globalised sweatshop? After all, *why* should it be unthinkable for migrants and refugees to associate themselves, and be associated, with the chic element?

In order to answer these questions, this essay aims to create a dialogue between analyses of recent immigration and refugee movements and those of the urban garment industry by first historicising the relationship between fashion production and the European refugee 'crisis', and then focusing on the plight of Syrian refugees working in the Turkish garment industry, including factories that produce clothing for European high street brands.[10] In doing so, this essay argues that it is important for us, namely, consumers, producers and researchers of fashion, to grasp how the critical, conceptual and intellectual capacities, aspirations, and strategic and tactical choices of migrant and refugee workers remain a threat to capital/borders[11] and thus are capable of reinventing fashion and relations of production in a way that facilitates the abolition of classes/borders and the expansion of the creative powers of *all* human beings in their relationship with fashion objects.[12]

Immigrants in the production of fashion: a reserve army of labour

Writing of the mechanisation of the clothing industry in the early 1860s, Karl Marx describes the sewing machine as 'the decisively revolutionary machine':

> *At last the critical point was reached. The basis of the old method, sheer brutality in the exploitation of the workpeople . . . no longer sufficed for the extending markets and for the still more rapidly extending competition of the capitalists. The hour struck for the advent of machinery.*[13]

But, as Annie Phizacklea convincingly argues, the introduction of the sewing machine in Britain in 1851 did not generate, in London, the move from home to factory production. Rather, the clothing industry's feasibility 'relied upon a cheap, unskilled reserve army of female and immigrant labour trapped in London's East End'.[14]

According to Phizacklea, the large-scale immigration, in 1881–6, of Russian and Polish Jewish refugees, who were fleeing the pogroms in their homelands, did not initiate but rather 'intensified' the system of sweating and subcontracting – an oppressive and malignant system that had already 'proliferated in the London clothing trade on the backs of largely female labour'. Confronted by racism and language barriers, the new refugees entered this system by finding work 'wherever they could or they made work for themselves in the highly competitive subcontracting system in clothing'. The fact that many of the immigrants had been tailors in their homelands was often not recognised by contemporary investigators of the East End clothing industry – Phizacklea reminds us that 'the ready-to-wear section of the clothing industry was traditionally Eastern European Jewish' and thus 'it was only to be expected that friends, relations, and co-ethnics would enter an industry where their compatriots had already created a niche' (figs 73–5).[15] Instead, Jewish immigrant workers were often racially stereotyped in order to explain the perceived primitiveness of the East End clothing trades, which had remained dependent upon the largely precarious sweatshop/workshop sector with its retinue of homeworkers, where conditions were mostly appalling. That is, there was no substantial shift, in the East End, to using capital-intensive technologies that would raise the productivity of labour in a regularised, and potentially more benign, setting: factory organisation. It is worth noting that by 1871, all of the 58 clothing factories in Britain were based in the provincial cities.[16]

Andrew Godley's important research on immigrant entrepreneurs demonstrates that the dominant, nineteenth-century view of clothing industry development was misleading for two related reasons: first, for its equation of factories with progress – that is, the false assumption that factory organisation was more efficient than workshop production. Godley shows that in 1907 workshops 'were still the dominant form of organisation in the clothing trades with 56 per cent

FIG. 74
Tailoring workshop, East End
of London, *c.*1900

FIG. 75
Sweatshop, East End of
London, *c.*1920s

of total employment. They were also 12 per cent more efficient than factories (in terms of net output per worker)' and East End Jewish workshops 'were able to out-compete factories everywhere but Leeds by 1911'. By 1935, the wholesale trade, that is, ready-made clothing, was 'the dominant source of output and employment in the industry with almost 40 per cent of net output' and 'even in the sectors which dominated the Leeds based industry it was the smaller-size firms which were most efficient'; London firms, likewise, were 'smaller than anywhere else, more efficient than anywhere else and these firms were increasingly concentrated in the East End'. Godley attributes the persistence, and high efficiency, of East End workshops to the fact that, despite the growing aggregate demand, the awaited demand for any specific model of a garment was very indeterminate. This highly unpredictable custom meant that firms had 'little incentive to invest in expensive machinery that would lead to high fixed costs'.[17] Small firms, in other words, were more conducive to the extraordinary flexibility required by volatile product demand, that is, by the dictates of fashion.

The perception of the clothing industry as a stubbornly backward and undeveloped sector was wrong, secondly, for its racialising construction of Jewish exceptionalism. Godley's research debunks the myth that the system of sweating was driven by Jewish immigrant workers' purported 'love of profit as distinct from any other form of money earning'[18] or by the so-called 'Jewish temperament [with] its desire to be independent'.[19] The persistence of sweating in the clothing industry, argues Godley, was caused by 'the nature of production of ready-made clothing, especially the high labour content. Whenever competition has pushed down garment prices, labour costs have always been the first to be put under pressure'. Besides, the limpness of cloth meant that 'the dexterity of the human hand in manoeuvring cloth through a sewing machine, especially the lighter fabrics,' has always been central to the production of clothing.[20]

This brief historical survey attests to what Nancy Green theorises as 'intermittent continuity' in the garment industry: seasonal, as well as intra-seasonal, fluctuations in demand and the resultant need for flexibility – that is, the ability to supply short runs of diversely styled garments at very short notice – often culminate in 'contracting within a context of cutthroat competition'.[21] Although the interventions of trade unions, human rights campaigners, global labour organisations, fashion retailers, investigative journalists, and labourers themselves lead, at times, to the amelioration of work conditions, the secondary sector of subcontracting continues to enable 'stubbornly recurrent pockets of evasion'. Thus, the question to be asked is whether such volatile flexibility can ever be managed without 'cutthroat competition, high turnover, and poor working conditions'.[22]

As recently as in August 2017, for example, the chief executives of Asos and New Look described the 'factories' in Leicester, a city in the East Midlands of England, as 'a ticking time bomb' due to 'unsafe conditions with fire escapes blocked up, workers exploited and paid far below minimum wage'.[23] It is revealing, but not surprising, that the Leicester garment trade, as has been noted by Debbie Coulter from the Ethical Trading Initiative, is 'booming primarily on the back of a growing band of start-up very low-cost Etailers and Cash and Carry merchandisers supplying market traders and cheap high street independent stores', who seem to have little regard for the workers, most of whom are either South Asian women with limited English or undocumented migrant workers.[24]

Thus, Green is right in pointing out that the Jewish tailor of the late nineteenth and early twentieth century, as a stock character, 'can only be but a metaphor' for successive generations of immigrants in the garment labour market. One might argue that both women and immigrants incline naturally towards homework and the informal labour market in order to gain quick access to a first job, where they can work among their own familial and regional networks and thus maintain a sense of community and tradition – Green quotes from a New York State labour investigator, who commented that 'the fertile soil of sweatshops is an immigrant community living in fear'. Yet it is also important, Green maintains, to consider the process of skill *acquisition*. In critically engaging with notions of innate or imported skill, Green argues that, for the bulk of the industry's labour force, skill signifies 'speed and accuracy': 'the repetitive tasks of the machine operator – 80 percent of the garment workers – are relatively easy to learn, and skill comes through practice.' In redefining skill as speed and accuracy, the industry provides those who have never sewn before in their lives with opportunities for 'easy entrance to the vast majority of operating jobs'. While acknowledging that 'garment work was chosen by vast numbers of women and immigrants because it fitted their needs' – seasonal fluctuations and the variety of workplaces do provide both women and immigrants new to the labour market with some room for manoeuvre and adaptation – Green concludes that, ultimately, what defines labour recruitment is industrial demand rather than labour supply, that is, the industry's ceaseless quest for cheapened labour.[25]

The key conclusions to be drawn from this history of immigrant presence in fashion production, which are equally relevant to understanding the plight of hundreds of thousands of Syrian refugees working in Turkish apparel 'factories', are threefold. First, an international reserve army of labour is necessary for the fluctuations in demand for labour generated not only by the particularly volatile nature of fashion production, but also, and more significantly, by the periodic cycle of prosperity and crisis, which is an integral component of capitalism.[26] In his 1845 book *The Condition of the Working Class in England*, Friedrich Engels tells us that 'the rapid extension of English industry could not have taken place if England had not possessed in the numerous and impoverished population of Ireland a reserve at command'.[27] Capitalism, in other words, operates through fluctuations and, therefore, must have a permanent reserve of workers, except in the brief periods of greatest prosperity – this reserve army, or surplus labouring population, 'embraces an immense multitude' during periods of crisis.[28] Marx argues that this 'relatively redundant population of labourers' that forms 'a disposable industrial reserve army' is a necessary product, and a condition of existence, of capitalistic accumulation, as it 'creates, for the changing needs of the self-expansion of capital, *a mass of human material always ready for exploitation*'.[29]

Second, what has been singled out as a 'refugee crisis' – wrongly, I will argue – should be seen as a consequence of wider, recurrent crises of overaccumulation that occur when surpluses of capital and labour exist side by side with seemingly no means to bring them together in a profitable way.[30] According to David Harvey, one way in which such surpluses may be absorbed is geographical expansion and spatial displacement through opening up 'new markets, new production capacities and new resource, social and labour possibilities elsewhere'.[31] Such crises of overaccumulation, however, have increasingly been paralleled by a rise in what Harvey calls 'accumulation by dispossession', that is, accumulation based upon predation, fraudulence and violence, leading, especially in impoverished countries, to the appropriation and devaluation of assets, dispossessing whole populations of their land and livelihood. Contemporary neo-liberal policies of deregulation, predatory actions of finance capital, privatisation of hitherto public spaces and resources, and the unfettered monopoly of power assumed by multinational capitalist corporations, all cause myriad forms of dispossession, including the displacement of millions of people from their homes, land and livelihood. As Ipsita Chatterjee poignantly reminds us, displacement is 'a fundamental transformation of the genetic code of a people, and thereby the ecology of the society' – once a mass of people are displaced and dispossessed, their displacement transforms them into 'refugees, migrants, and squatters akin to Marx's beggars and vagabonds', that is, into a disposable reserve army of labour.[32] What the notion of a 'refugee crisis' does is to obfuscate this deeply inherent relationship between imperialist capital accumulation by dispossession and the displacement of whole populations that creates an international reserve army of labour to be mobilised when capital needs them.[33] Such crisis talk also reinforces what De Genova aptly criticises as the 'depoliticising language of a "humanitarian crisis" with its root causes always attributed to troubles "elsewhere", usually in desperate and chaotic places ostensibly "outside" of Europe'.[34] Exonerating Europe from all responsibility for the (post)colonial root causes of chronic dispossession and displacement in 'other' places, this Eurocentric and imperialist language of crisis, in turn, legitimates increasingly violent practices of border enforcement and immigration policing by European border protection authorities.[35]

Third, the distinction between 'refugees' as compulsory migrants fleeing from war, persecution, or natural disaster on the one hand and 'migrants' as voluntary seekers of better life opportunities on the other should not always be taken for granted. Tom Vickers insightfully argues that the compulsion factor may also be relevant to migrant labour: 'In many cases, foreign investment-driven development of export-oriented agriculture and manufacturing in materially underdeveloped countries has displaced rural workers from the land and at times has led to

FIG. 76
Syrian refugee workers in
a workshop in Antakya,
Turkey, producing military
wear for the Syrian market,
2016

a restructuring of the labour force, by drawing more women into waged employment and creating rising unemployment among men.'[36] The dispossession caused by capitalist accumulation, in other words, means that for some people, 'voluntary' economic migration may be the only option for survival.

Furthermore, it is important to remember that refugees, just like migrants, may have capacities for recovery and resilience, as well as aspirations and life goals. In their publication *Commonwealth* (2009), Michael Hardt and Antonio Negri remind us that the poor, migrants, and precarious workers 'are often conceived as excluded, but really, though subordinated, they are completely within the global rhythms of bio-political production'.[37] Thus, the next section aims to discuss why, and how, we should try to excavate and understand what Hardt and Negri describe as 'the forms of life, languages, movements, or capacities for innovation' generated, in this case, by Syrian refugees working in the Turkish garment industry.

Syrian refugees in Turkish garment supply chains: a story of systemic violence
Since the Syrian civil war officially began on 15 March 2011, more than 5.6 million Syrians have fled the country as refugees, and over 6 million are internally displaced within Syria. The majority of Syria's 5.6 million refugees have fled, by land and sea, across borders to neighbouring countries where most of them live in urban areas, with around only 8 per cent accommodated in refugee camps.[38] Turkey hosts the largest number of registered Syrian refugees in the world: according to official government data, at the end of April 2018, there were 3,588,877 persons from Syria registered under temporary protection – a regime established to respond to the mass influx of individuals fleeing the ongoing war and conflict in Syria.[39]

Since 2015, there has been an increasing number of reports and investigations exposing the abuse and exploitation of Syrian refugees working in the Turkish garment industry (figs 76–8), including factories that produce clothing for European high street brands. When they visited Istanbul in July 2016, researchers from the Business & Human Rights Resource Centre, an international NGO that tracks the human rights impacts of over 6,500 companies in over 180 countries, observed discrimination, wages far below the minimum, and child labour. The workshops they saw 'typically had been between 10–20 workers' and they detected 'numerous examples of child labour and poor health & safety – including one factory on the first floor with a large hole in the wall'; they heard accounts of Syrians being paid well below the minimum wage, treated 'much more harshly for minor transgressions' compared to their Turkish fellow workers, and, in some cases, sacked after a few days' work 'without any pay for the hours worked'; they were also told that 'Syrian child labour was widely used in workshops and these children were typically aged between 11–14 (both boys and girls)'.[40] Elsewhere, Frederik Johannisson, an independent journalist and researcher, wrote about Shukri, a 12-year-old Syrian Kurd who works often 60 hours a week in a basement in an Istanbul suburb, 'supplying the 15 sewing machines producing clothing mainly destined for the

European market', and Leila, a 20-year-old Syrian woman, who works in an 'under the stairs' garment workshop in the coastal city of Mersin to earn 1.6 Turkish Lira (TL) (37p in 2016) per hour, which is drastically below the national minimum wage in Turkey.[41] A recent survey conducted by researchers from Istanbul University shows that Syrian women refugee workers in the textile sector are at the very bottom of the wage scale: their average monthly wage, which is approximately 776 TL (roughly £127 as of May 2018), is about half of what Turkish male workers earn and, also, is 489 TL less than the average of all workers (Turkish male and female, and Syrian male, workers included). Besides, the average monthly wage of the Syrian women refugee workers who participated in the survey is about half of the national minimum wage.[42]

The Labour Act of Turkey No. 4857 prohibits the employment of children under the age of 15 and limits the working hours of those under 18. In Turkey, child labour had been a long-standing problem, even before Syrian refugees arrived in the country.[43] However, as migration specialist Murat Erdoğan points out, Syrian child labour 'has become the norm', especially in seasonal, labour-intensive sectors such as textiles, since Syrian refugee children are seen as being 'easier to manipulate, less demanding and most definitely cheaper than anyone else (fig. 79). Children learn the language more easily, and they acquire the skills required for basic jobs much faster'.[44] In October 2016, when he visited Istanbul garment workshops to conduct an undercover investigation into allegations of exploitation of Syrian refugees and their children, BBC *Panorama* reporter Darragh MacIntyre described the situation as follows: 'I'd been told that child labour was endemic in Turkey. But I wasn't prepared for the reality of it. Or the scale of it. One basement workshop was almost entirely staffed with children, many of whom couldn't have been more than seven or eight years old, the very picture of Dickensian misery.'[45] In February 2017, journalist Burak Coşan reported that in the Küçükpazar neighbourhood of Istanbul's Fatih district, children aged between 10 and 14 years were working up to 12 hours a day; some of these children were seen 'carrying packages in the corridors bearing the logos of well-known brands' – one adult worker told Coşan that children's wages depended on 'their age and the job they do. Those who are ironing earn nearly 600 TL [per month]. Those running errands earn a maximum of 400 TL [per month]'.[46] Skill acquisition, in the case of Syrian refugee child workers, does not always lead to an increase in wages. In one case, a 16-year-old Syrian refugee worker told journalist Didem Tali that after working at the same shop for the past three years, and despite having learned everything he could, including operating all the machines and doing ironing, he was still earning 'a third to half of what Turkish people make', with his salary being the same as when he had started three years ago.[47] In another case, reported by journalist Patrick Kingsley, a 13-year-old Syrian refugee worker, who 'can perform most of the roles on the assembly line', including moulding leather into the shape of a shoe and threading its different parts together with the machine, was earning a daily wage of 'less than $10 – lower than the retail price of every pair of shoes' he makes.[48]

FIG. 77
A Syrian refugee boy working
in a Syrian-owned clothing
factory in Gaziantep, Turkey,
16 May 2016

FIG. 78
Syrian refugees working
in a Syrian-owned clothing
factory in Gaziantep, Turkey,
17 May 2016

What these reports and investigations reveal is an excruciatingly familiar story of accumulation by dispossession. Turkey's clothing industry, with a share of 3.4 per cent, is the eighth largest exporter in the world, and the third largest supplier to the EU (following China and Bangladesh).[49] In 2017, 71.4 per cent of the sector's exports have gone to EU countries, with Germany, Spain and the UK being the top three export nations respectively.[50] The Turkish textile and clothing industry, in other words, is one of the major players in the world market in terms of both production and exports, and continues to maintain and increase its competitiveness.[51] Yet Turkey's integration into the global production system has been characterised by the prevalent use of informal labour and, in particular, of women's informal work. According to Saniye Dedeoglu, the low level of foreign direct investment throughout the 1980s and 1990s was the reason why Turkey's international competitiveness, based on export-oriented and labour-intensive production, has led to the expansion of the informal sector. Small-scale, and sometimes family-run, garment workshops and home-based piecework are two important components of this largely unregulated sector, providing the labour-intensive garment industry with an abundant supply of cheapened labour. The industry 'operates from unregistered workplaces, where labour legislation and social security regulations are ignored'. One of the significant consequences of informalisation is that women's industrial work is usually not adequately recorded or recognised, and is thus rendered invisible. The workforce, observes Dedeoglu, 'is hired when orders have been placed and fired when orders stop coming in . . . Companies frequently do not pay the statutory social security contributions on behalf of their employees, or falsify records in order to pay less'.[52] Thus, workshop production and home-based work partake in a prevalent system of subcontracting, through which Turkish manufacturers reduce fixed costs; reach untapped resources of cheapened, disposable female and child labour; and achieve the flexibility necessary to cope with the erratic demands and aggressive purchasing practices of international retailers. This is how Turkey's garment industry established and maintained its competitiveness in the international market, to begin with.

Back in 2010, Nebahat Tokatli and others wrote about the ways in which Istanbul-based manufacturing supplier firms had been adapting to the new demands of international clothing retailers for increased speed, variety and fashionability – that is, to the pace of fast fashion driven by, and driving, hyper-obsolescence, high disposability and excessive consumerism. In order to deal with capacity- and specialty-related issues, as well as with the pressures of keeping prices competitively low, the clothing industry had relied, even before the era of fast fashion, on 'a cascade of operations' subcontracted to 'smaller workshops working at the edge of illegality'. The move to fast fashion with its ever-shorter lead times, unpredictable schedules and small-batch production runs, however, meant that Turkish manufacturer suppliers ended up having to do whatever was necessary to survive in a competitive global capitalist economy, where

FIG. 79
A Syrian refugee boy making
shoe parts at a Turkish-owned
workshop in Gaziantep,
Turkey, 16 May 2016

international retailers can shift their purchasing elsewhere in order to achieve lower costs and enhanced agility. In this context, it is especially those women who work in family-owned manufacturing workshops, or are engaged in home-based work, who shoulder the burden of the manufacturers' determination to meet the arduous demands of international retailers. Nevertheless, Tokatli and others also emphasised that competency acquisition provided some women, especially those from middle-class backgrounds, with opportunities for entrepreneurship and empowerment: 'It was the previously unavailable female labour hidden in residential neighbourhoods . . . that invigorated the subcontracting component – together with the creative minds, professional skills and entrepreneurial capabilities of educated, middle-class women'.[53]

As of 2018, however, there seems to be a widespread pessimistic perception among Turkish suppliers and factory owners that the *konfeksiyon* (ready-to-wear) industry has been undergoing a severe crisis due to the increased international competition between manufacturing countries, the shrinking of the market, and, more importantly, the fluctuating demands and cut-throat purchasing practices of international retailer brands. Industry experts claim that young Turkish workers are less and less drawn to working in garment factories not only because of long hours, low wages, strenuous working conditions and widespread lack of social security coverage, but also because of the expansion of the tertiary sector of the economy offering jobs seen as more comfortable and prestigious than garment production.[54] In this context of alleged ongoing crisis and increasingly frantic attempts to reduce costs and enhance flexibility, suppliers to national and international retailers – as well as, and especially, their mostly unauthorised sub-suppliers – alleviate the labour shortage problem and reinvigorate profits by drawing upon the cheapened and unregulated labour of Syrian refugee workers, which is perceived as throwing a new lifeline to the garment industry.[55] Recently, the Chairman and CEO of a major clothing company in Turkey has encapsulated the indispensable role played by Syrian refugee workers by saying: 'Had it not been for the Syrians, our shelves would have remained empty'.[56]

In this context, the question of improvement of working conditions, and the legalisation and formalisation of the labour force, through work permits and compliance monitoring and inspection schemes, is certainly not an insignificant one. However, despite the fact that work permits, since January 2016, have been made accessible for persons under Temporary Protection, providing legal access to employment for Syrians and other persons of concern living in Turkey, the number of Syrian nationals issued work permits in 2016 was just 13,290.[57] Only approximately 2,000 work permits were granted to workers in the industrial sectors, including the textile-apparel industry.[58] As Emre Korkmaz rightfully points out, this is significantly, and deceptively, low, given that 'approximately half of the Syrian refugees in Turkey are of working age'. The centrality of informal refugee labour to the garment industry stems not only from the sub-suppliers' need to reduce labour costs and meet rapid turnover and erratic deadlines. The flexibility of the informal sector, argues Korkmaz, also allows refugees and irregular migrants themselves to pursue 'survival strategies' based on their social networks and possibilities of entrepreneurship.[59]

Likewise, it is vital to hold international retailer brands accountable by asking them a) to monitor and audit not only the first-tier factories, that is, their official suppliers, but also the often undeclared second- and third-tier subcontractors, to which the first-tier factories outsource, and b) to modify their purchasing practices, so that the environment of abuse engendered by undeclared subcontracting and informal work arrangements can be eliminated. These are two of the useful recommendations made by Korkmaz and Samentha Goethals, whose fieldwork reveals how global buyers' unpredictable orders 'put significant stress on suppliers', leading the latter to outsource to smaller, undeclared subcontractors, as young buyers 'reportedly disregard price components of production, including labour costs, minimum wage, and health and safety, and tend to set unreasonably low prices'.[60]

What these recommendations do not address, however, is the historically recurrent incompatibility between fashion production on the one hand and factory organisation, formalisation and stricter regulation on the other. One should ask here an apparently cynical but still important question: if the constant growth in demand for consumer products is indispensable for capitalism to avert crises, then *why* should international retailer brands reduce the speed and intensity, which is what the question of changing buying practices ultimately boils down to? As insightfully argued by Andrew Brooks, the fact that late capitalism is particularly susceptible to crises implies that any radical attempt to modify the degree of surplus value extracted from labour would pull capitalism into deep recession. The surplus supply of labour at a global level means that 'crisis-ridden factories just close and reopen elsewhere'.[61] Thus, it is crucial to remember that the currently hegemonic discourse around social and sustainability compliance, corporate social responsibility, ethical supply chain audits and review of purchasing policies may actually be contributing to what Žižek calls 'extra-economic charity', which is needed by today's capitalism to maintain the cycle of social reproduction, as it is no longer capable of reproducing itself on its own.[62] Such extra-economic charity and benevolence obscures the extent of the systemic violence inherent in the very structure of capitalist social relations, reinforcing the myth of a 'responsible' or, even worse, 'moral' capitalism.[63]

Conclusion: beyond capital

What aspect of dispossession should we then focus on? And how can we challenge it? Speaking of the emergence of wholly new mechanisms of accumulation by dispossession, Harvey points out that 'the commodification of cultural forms, histories and intellectual creativity entails wholesale dispossessions', as capitalism 'internalises cannibalistic as well as predatory and fraudulent practices'.[64] The hierarchical division of labour between those who are given opportunities to use and develop their intellectual creativity in producing fashion as meaning and those who are expected to transform that meaning into actual, material fashion apparel – often under ruthlessly draining and wearisome conditions – dispossesses the latter of their skills, capacities and creativity. A significant segment of the Syrian refugee workers in garment supply chains, when they were living back in Syria, were engaged in jobs other than textiles and apparel production – jobs that require formal higher education and advanced skills. While this implies an enforced demotion into the garment sector out of desperation on the part of some refugee workers, a recently conducted survey also shows that 52 per cent of the Syrian refugee garment workers, when they were back in Syria, were actually involved in textiles- and clothing-related professions.[65] The degradation and obscuring of their skills, experience and knowledge is a consequence not only of the low-road labour practices endemic in the fashion industry. It is also the result of our own inability, as researchers speaking from within the privileged Inside, to relocate the discourse of fashion around the movements, competencies and creative aspirations of those workers who are allowed to produce fashion *as material object only* – and often under the most dismal, uninspiring and dehumanising conditions. The productivity, and *possibility* of creative powers, of the garment workers seems to be absent from the hegemonic fashion discourse, which is more about stimulating consumer desire through captivating brand images, trends and spectacles, and less about questions of labour, poverty and immigration and refugee movements. The capitalist, consumerist logic of transitory sign-value moving from one commodity to another, as Adam Briggs notes, 'ensures that the actual making of physical garments, and the conditions within which this occurs, along with the associated environmental impact, remain out of sight, unconsidered'.[66] A Syrian refugee worker employed on a daily basis, and without any social security coverage, in an 'under the stairs' garment workshop in the suburbs of Istanbul conveys this sense of utter invisibility and dispossession in the following words: 'Machines have all the rights. If one breaks, they will fix it straight away, because they benefit from the machine. But if anything happens to a Syrian, they will throw him away like a piece of cloth'.[67]

A piece of cloth, however, is never – and ideally should never be – a piece of cloth only. We are all viscerally, intellectually and aesthetically connected to our garments. As Brooks suggests, the fashion industry might provide 'potential for a collective sense of common responsibility to be forged on account of the shared intimacy associated with garments which are made, worn and re-worn around the world by diverse people'.[68] Therefore, fashion production *on all its levels* should be a creative process by enabling the flourishing of innovative, intellectual and conceptual faculties of *all* workers in their relationship, and intimacy, with fashion objects. The hierarchical division of labour at the heart of fashion production – between the mostly Eurocentric symbolic, cultural and discursive production on the one hand and the peripheralised material production on the other – makes it a tremendous challenge for us to find ways to carry out Hardt and Negri's important project: translating the productivity and possibility of the poor into power.[69] Reducing the sheer amount of speed, precariousness, drudgery and exploitation in the sweatshop regime through systemic and spatial interventions is extremely difficult in the absence of a fundamental political transformation that would lead garment workers to achieve the collective ownership of their own means of production.[70] This is exactly the reason why we should develop, in the meantime, engaged and innovative methodologies that would facilitate us in creating mutually transformative conversations with garment workers – conversations that would hybridise the discourse and practice of fashion by putting centre stage workers' perceptions and experiences of, and tastes and skills in, fashion *in its entirety*, including its hitherto privileged creative, aesthetic and immaterial aspects. This requires us, above all, to challenge the widespread assumption that garment work in a sweatshop environment requires no previous knowledge or skills.

The specific significance of immigrant and refugee workers stems from the fact that their dispossession reveals some of the ways in which fashion, and indeed capitalism, has survived crises by regenerating the flexibility necessary to handle the magnitude and fickleness of consumer demand. Their mostly unacknowledged centrality to fashion production exposes the limitations of the hegemonic fashion discourse. Thus, the extent to which they are capable of affecting the conditions surrounding fashion production should be analysed.[71] But also, and more importantly, we should bear in mind that immigrant and refugee workers are not only workers – they are also, and inevitably, immigrants and refugees. Their often agonising journeys unmask the porousness, and hence the constructedness and artificiality, of geographical and ideological borders. Their multi-layered and shifting identities as both immigrants/refugees and workers unveil the very limitations of 'work' as well as of the worker's identity. Drawing on the work of philosopher and politician Mario Tronti, Hardt and Negri remind us of the importance, for workers, of struggling against work, against themselves, against the identity that defines them as workers. 'The primary object of class struggle', they argue, 'is not to kill capitalists but to demolish the social structures and institutions that maintain their privilege and authority, abolishing too, thereby, the conditions of proletarian subordination'. They elucidate that the refusal of work, and the abolition of the worker, does not signify the end of production; rather, it means 'the invention, beyond capital, of as yet unimagined relations of production that allow and facilitate an expansion of our creative powers'.[72] One of the ways to explore the possibilities of self-transformation beyond the capitalist structures and institutions of worker subordination – and beyond the identity of the worker – will be to facilitate immigrant and refugee workers in repossessing not only their skills and competencies but also their broader intimacy with fashion as meaning. Another way will be to work together towards creating autonomous, non-hierarchical and hybridised spaces of liberation where we can mix symbolic and material production, art and craftspersonship, utility and chic, and leisure and creativity. After all, there is no reason why the 'migrant chic' should be an unimaginable, unseemly idea – as long as immigrant and refugee garment workers *themselves* partake in its production.

Acknowledgements
I am grateful, first and foremost, to Dr Djurdja Bartlett for encouraging me to produce this article. Next, I would like to thank Dr Sophie Oliver and anonymous peer review readers for their astute recommendations. My interest in, and knowledge of, the garment industry was nurtured by 'The Production of Fashion' lectures delivered by Adam Briggs at London College of Fashion. I wish to thank him for his support and encouragement. I also thank Veysel Eşsiz from the Refugee Rights Turkey for providing me with the statistical information relating to Syrian refugees in Turkey.

Notes

Preface

1   See, for example, Anna Cafoll, 2018, 'The Whistleblower: Chris Wylie on fashion, culture wars & the alt-right', *Dazed*, 29 March; http://www.dazeddigital.com/politics/article/39542/1/the-whistleblower-chris-wylie-cambridge-analytica-fashion-and-politics (accessed 31 March 2018); Alice Hines, 2018, 'The Whistleblower's New Clothes', *Vestoj*, 29 March; http://vestoj.com/the-whistleblowers-new-clothes/ (accessed 31 March 2018).

2   Carole Cadwalladr, 2018, '"I made Steve Bannon's psychological warfare tool": meet the data war whistleblower', *Observer*, 18 March; https://www.theguardian.com/news/2018/mar/17/data-war-whistleblower-christopher-wylie-faceook-nix-bannon-trump (accessed 31 March 2018).

3   Ibid.

4   Cafoll 2018.

5   Claudia Croft, 2018, 'The Prada Perspective', British *Vogue*, March, pp. 300–7, p. 306.

6   Elizabeth Wilson, 1982, *Mirror Writing* (London: Virago), p. 122.

7   Elizabeth Wilson donated the outfit to the Victoria and Albert Museum, London; it was on display at the Museum's exhibition titled *Street Style*, curated by Amy de la Haye, in 1994. Wilson discussed this outfit and the cultural climate of the time with the author (19 June 2018).

8   Elizabeth Wilson, 1985, *Adorned in Dreams: Fashion and Modernity* (London: Virago); Christopher Breward and Caroline Evans (eds), 2005, *Fashion and Modernity* (Oxford: Berg Publishers).

9   Karl Marx and Friedrich Engels, 2010 [1848], Manifesto of the Communist Party, in *Marx & Engels, Collected Works*, 1845–48 (London: Lawrence & Wishart), vol. 6, p. 488.

10 Karl Marx, 1976 [1867], *Capital: A Critique of Political Economy* (Harmondsworth, UK: Penguin), p. 609. Marx reports that, due to the extension of the railway system throughout the country, 'purchasers now come up from Glasgow, Manchester, and Edinburgh once every fortnight or so to the wholesale city warehouses … and give small orders requiring immediate execution, instead of buying from stock as they used to do'.

11 Ibid., p. 608.

1 Can Fashion Be Defended?

1   Entry on Thursday, 3 March 1864, from Jules Michelet, 1976, *Journal* [1861–7] (Paris: Gallimard), vol. 3, p. 243.

2   Entry on Thursday, 3 March 1864, from Edmond and Jules de Goncourt, 1956, *Journal. Mémoires de la vie littéraire, 1864–1878* (Paris: Pasquelle & Flammarion), vol. 2, p. 25.

3   After Napoleon III's rise to power, Michelet lost his professorship at the Collège de France, when he refused to take the oaths to the empire. Equally, one of Michelet's guests, Étienne Arago, a French writer, politician and co-founder of the newspaper *Le Figaro*, spent ten years in exile in the mid-nineteenth century due to his opposition to Napoleon III.

4   Having opened his salon in Paris in 1858, the Englishman Charles Frederick Worth was already well known for dressing European royalty, with the French Empress Eugénie as his most prestigious client.

5   François Boucher, 1952, 'Geopolitique du costume', *L'Amour de l'art*, 1st trimester.

6   For an overview, see Djurdja Bartlett, 2010, 'Introduction to Dress and Fashion in East Europe, Russia and the Caucasus', in D. Bartlett (ed.), *Berg Encyclopedia of World Dress and Fashion* (Oxford & New York: Berg Publishers), vol. 9, pp. 3–14.

7   The Hungarian Royal Opera gala was presented, richly illustrated, in society magazines: *Theatre Life* (*Szinházi élet*), 1938, no. 16, pp. 13–23, and *The Company* (*A Társaság*), 10 April, no. 14.

8   In general, throughout the twentieth century, ethnic dress and fashion remained the competing sartorial phenomena, depending on the political and cultural agendas of various social groups and their representatives.

9   For an overview of the phenomenon of socialist fashion, see Djurdja Bartlett, 2010, *FashionEast: The Spectre that Haunted Socialism* (Cambridge, MA: MIT Press).

10 Michel de Certeau, 1988, *The Practice of Everyday Life* (Berkeley: University of California Press), pp. 35–8.

11 Fredric Jameson, 2002, *A Singular Modernity: Essay on the Ontology of the Present* (London: Verso Books), p. 12; for the concept of an uneven modernity, see Marshall Berman, 1982, *All That Is Solid Melts into Air: The Experience of Modernity* (New York: Simon and Schuster).

12 At the beginning of 2018, the western media reported widely on these events, which inevitably led to a prison sentence for those who dared to challenge the official dress code. See, for example, Najmeh Bozorgmehr and Monavar Khalaj, 2018, 'Iranian women lift headscarves in protest as discontent rises', *Financial Times*, 30 January; www.ft.com/content/8570afb2-059a-11e8-

9650-9c0ad2d7c5b5 (accessed 14 December 2018); Thomas Erdbrink, 2018, 'Compulsory Veils? Half of Iranians Say "No" to Pillar of Revolution', *New York Times*, 4 February; www. nytimes.com/2018/02/04/world/middleeast/iran-hijab-veils.html (accessed 14 December 2018).

13 Here I draw on Judith Butler's concept of performativity in her work of 1990, *Gender Trouble* (New York: Routledge).

14 Quoted in Agata Pyzik and Michał Murawski, 2018, 'Vogue Poland', *Calvert Journal*, 15 February; www.calvertjournal. com/features/show/9656/vogue-poland-jurgen-teller (accessed 9 June 2018).

15 Ibid.

16 For an overview of the first seven years of Russian *Vogue*, see Djurdja Bartlett, 2006, 'In Russia, at Last and Forever: The First Seven Years of Russian *Vogue*', in *Fashion Theory: The Journal of Dress Body & Culture*, nos 1–2, pp. 175–203.

17 Pyzik and Murawski 2018. The Law and Justice Party, founded in 2001 by Lech and Jarosław Kaczyński, has acted both in opposition and power; it has been ruling the country since 2015.

18 Boris Groys, 2014, *On the New* (London: Verso Books), p. 49. Groys is not talking about dress, but fashion more generally.

19 Eric Hobsbawm, 1995, *The Age of Extremes: The Short Twentieth Century, 1914–91* (London: Abacus), p. 178.

20 Vanessa Friedman, 2013, 'Lunch with the FT: Franca Sozzani', *Financial Times*, Life and Arts section, 31 May, p. 3.

21 Cited in Julia Segreti, 2017, 'Missoni talks politics with pink cat-eared hats at Milan show', *Reuters.com*, 25 February; www. reuters.com/article/us-fashion-milan-missoni-idUSKBN1640KX (accessed 24 July 2018).

22 Ibid.

23 See Janelle Okwodu, 2017, 'The Women's March Pussyhat Takes Milan Fashion Week', *Vogue.com*, 25 February; www.vogue.com/article/milan-fashion-week-ready-to-wear-fall-2017-missoni-pussyhats (accessed 24 July 2018).

24 L.S. Hilton, 2018, 'It's not a contradiction to be politically serious and take pleasure in fashion', *The Sunday Times*, Style supplement, 29 April, pp. 28–33, p. 32.

25 Ibid., p. 28.

26 Quoted in Jo Ellison, 2017, 'How Woke Are You?', *Financial Times*, Life and Arts section, 30 September, p. 18.

27 Karl Marx, 1976 [1867], *Capital: A Critique of Political Economy* (Harmondsworth, UK: Penguin), vol. 1, p. 165.

28 Ibid. In the English translation, 'phantasmagoric' is substituted by 'fantastic'.

29 Peter Stallybrass, 1998, 'Marx's Coat', in Patricia Spyer (ed.), *Border Fetishisms: Material Objects in Unstable Spaces* (London: Routledge), p. 202.

30 Ibid., pp. 186–7.

31 Georg Simmel, 1997 [1889], 'On the Psychology of Money', in David Frisby and Mike Featherstone (eds), *Simmel on Culture* (London: Sage Publishing), p. 237.

32 Walter Benjamin, 1999 [1935], 'Paris, the Capital of the Nineteenth Century', in W. Benjamin, *The Arcades Project* (Cambridge, MA: The Belknap Press of Harvard University Press), pp. 4–26.

33 Rita Felski, 1995, *The Gender of Modernity* (Cambridge, MA: Harvard University Press), p. 61.

34 Ibid., p. 62.

35 Impressionist and post-Impressionist painters such as Manet, Degas and Seurat depicted a new kind of 'consumer': clerks and shopgirls. For an overview, see T.J. Clark, 1984, *The Painting of Modern Life: Paris in the Art of Manet and His Followers* (Princeton: Princeton University Press). For an overview of the working class participating in 'the pleasures of decadence', see Thomas Crow, 1983, 'Modernism and Mass Culture', in Benjamin H.D. Buchloh et al. (eds), *Modernism and Modernity* (Halifax: Nova Scotia College of Art and Design).

36 Kathleen Canning, 2013, 'Claiming Citizenship: Suffrage and Subjectivity in Germany after the First World War', in K. Canning, Kerstin Barndt and Kristin McGuire (eds), *Weimar Publics/Weimar Subjects: rethinking the political culture of Germany in the 1920s* (New York: Berghahn Books), pp. 131–2. For an excellent account of the relationship between women, modernity and the big city, see Elizabeth Wilson, 1985, *Adorned in Dreams: Fashion and Modernity* (London: Virago).

37 For example, in 1932–3, the French magazine *VU* published the Working Women series in six instalments. All were written by liberal journalist Emmanuel Berl, and a number of them were photographed by Germaine Krull. A prominent French journalist and editor, Lucien Vogel, established *VU* in 1928, and was involved in its publication until 1936. Vogel mixed his professional interest in fashion and the arts with his left-leaning political views.

38 *UHU* was started by the leading German publishing house Ullstein in 1924, which was run as a family business until the Nazis stripped them of its ownership in 1934. A well-known photographer, Karl Schenker, shot the story 'Living by the Typewriter' (*UHU*, no. 10, July 1932). Focusing on fashion and advertising, Yva (real name Else Neulander Simon) was a prolific commercial photographer in the 1920s and early 1930s, until she was taken to a concentration camp, where she died. Of 20 photo stories published in *UHU* between 1930 and 1933, nine were taken by Yva (for details see Marion Beckers and Elisabeth Moortgat, 2001, *Yva: Photography, 1925–1938*, exh. cat., Berlin).

39 Boris Groys, 2010, 'The Obligation to Self-Design' in B. Groys, *Going Public* (Berlin & New York: Sternberg Press, p. 23.

40 Marianne Pollak, 1929, 'The Devil Dresses' (Der Kleiderteufel), in *The Discontented* (*Die Unzufriedene*), 26 October, no. 43, p. 3. Published in Vienna between 1923 and 1934 by the Austrian Socialist party (SDAP), *The Discontented* was a popular women's weekly that addressed various issues in women's everyday life, unlike the party organ *Woman* (*Die Frau*), which strictly covered official policies.

41 Anonymous, 1930, 'Women, The Stone Issues' (Frauen, die steine Fragen), *The Cuckoo* (*Der Kuckuck*), 4 May, no. 18, p. 3. *The Cuckoo* was the Austrian Socialist Party's illustrated picture magazine, published from 1929 to 1934.

42 For an overview, see, for example, Helmut Gruber, 1991, *Red Vienna: Experiment in Working-Class Culture 1919–1934* (New York: Oxford University Press); Julia Sneeringer, 2002, *Winning Women's Votes: Propaganda and Politics in Weimar Germany* (Chapel Hill & London: University of North Carolina).

43 The French Communist Party started *Views* (*Regards*) in 1932. It was published until 1939, and revived following the end of the Second World War.

44 Nancy Armstrong, 2002, *Fiction in the Age of Photography: the Legacy of British Realism* (Cambridge, MA: Harvard University Press), p. 121.

45 Sabine Hake, 1987, 'Girls and Crisis: the Other Side of Diversion', *New German Critique*, Winter, no. 40, p. 158.

46 Miriam Hansen Bratu, 1999, 'The Mass Production of the Senses: Classical Cinema as Vernacular Modernism' in *Modernism/Modernity*, April, no. 2, p. 72.

47 Patrice Petro, 1989, *Joyless Streets: Women and Melodramatic Representation in Weimar Germany* (Princeton: Princeton University Press), p. 71.

48 Lesley Stern, 2001, 'Paths That Wind through the Thicket of Things', in *Critical Inquiry*, 'Things' special issue, Autumn, vol. 28, no. 1, pp. 320–1.

49 Siegfried Kracauer, 1995 [1927], 'The Little Shopgirls go to the Movies', in S. Kracauer, *The Mass Ornament: Weimar Essays* (Cambridge, MA: Harvard University Press), pp. 291–304.

50 Ibid., p. 303.

51 Karl Marx, 1979 [1852] 'The Eighteenth Brumaire of Louis Bonaparte', in *Marx & Engels: Collected Works 1851–1853* (London: Lawrence & Wishart), vol. 11, p. 149.

52 Ibid. Louis-Napoleon Bonaparte, a nephew of Emperor Napoleon Bonaparte, was elected President of France in 1848 but grabbed power by means of a *coup d'état* in December 1851. A year later, he declared himself Emperor Napoleon III, head of the Second French Empire.

53 Barbara Vinken, 2005, *Fashion Zeitgeist: Trends and Cycles in the Fashion System* (Oxford: Berg Publishers), p. 17.

54 According to GlobalData Retail, Primark had around 7 per cent of the British clothing sector in 2018, rising from 4 per cent in the previous year (quoted in the *Observer*, 1 July 2018, p. 53). The UK-based assets of the Weston family, which include Primark and Selfridges, are worth £4.492bn, according to the 2018 Sunday Times Rich List (quoted in *The Sunday Times*, Style Magazine, 6 May 2018, pp. 34–5).

55 Igor Kopytoff, 1986, 'The cultural biography of things: commoditization as process,' in Arjun Appadurai (ed.), *The Social Life of Things: Commodities in Cultural Perspective* (Cambridge: Cambridge University Press), p. 68.

56 Ibid., p. 89.

57 Bruno Latour, 2000, 'The Berlin Key or how to do words with things', in Paul Graves-Brown (ed.), *Matter, Materiality and Modern Culture* (London: Routledge), p. 10.

58 However, not even ethnic dress has been immune to change. While change was slow and insignificant in isolated mountainous regions with their deprived villages, it took place more rapidly in those regions that, although rural, were on the established trade routes, which brought some villages into contact with new commercial and cultural influences. For an overview, see Dorothy Noyes and Regina Bendix, 1998, 'Introduction: In Modern Dress: Costuming the European Social Body, 17th–20th Centuries', in the *Journal of American Folklore*, vol. 111, no. 440, pp. 107–14.

59 Joanne Garde-Hansen and Kristyn Gorton, 2013, *Emotion Online: Theorizing Affect on the Internet* (Basingstoke & New York: Palgrave Macmillan), p. 41.

60 Gosha Rubchinskiy held his first fashion show in Moscow in 2008, but his international fashion career only took off following his partnership with the Japanese fashion company Comme des Garçons in 2012. In the years 2017–18, Rubchinskiy collaborated with Adidas, taking his fashion shows to the Russian cities hosting the 2018 World Cup: Kaliningrad, St Petersburg and Yekaterinburg. In April 2018, Rubchinskiy announced via Instagram that he would stop presenting fashion shows and would launch a new project, still backed by Comme des Garçons. From the beginning, Rubchinskiy has cultivated an image of a multidisciplinary creative, engaging not only with fashion but also with photography, video and film.

61 Emma Hope Allwood, 2017, 'Gosha on why he returned to Russia and his image of youth', *Dazeddigital*, 13 January; www.dazeddigital.com/fashion/article/34307/1/gosha-rubchinskiy-returns-to-russia-youth (accessed 6 April 2017).

62 The etymology of the word *gopnik* is unclear. It was already a derogatory term in socialist times.

63 Steve Slater, 2015, 'Gosha Rubchinskiy tells the truth of youth', *i-D.vice.com*, 8 October; i-d.vice.com/en_uk/article/vbex4x/gosha-rubchinskiy-tells-the-truth-of-youth (accessed 13 October 2017).

64 Apart from Adidas and Burberry, the all-important headwear was designed by leading milliner Stephen Jones. Both Jones and Burberry's then-creative director Christopher Bailey were sitting in the front row for the show, which took place in St Petersburg.

65 In 2005, the Oxford English Dictionary defined 'chav' as 'a young working-class person who dresses in casual sports clothing' (cited in Owen Jones, 2011, *Chavs: The Demonization of the Working Class* [London: Verso Books], p. 8). The references to 'chavs' and Burberry are scattered throughout Owen Jones's book. On Burberry and 'chavs', see Andrew O'Hagan, 2005, 'Burberry versus the Chavs', *Daily Telegraph*, 27 October; Claire Bothwell, 2005, 'Burberry versus The Chavs', *The Money Programme*, BBC Two, 28 October.

66 Covering Rubchinskiy's collection for Spring/Summer 2018, the magazine *i-D* produced the documentary film *Inside Gosha Rubchinskiy Post-Soviet Generation*, and posted it online on 31 July 2017; www.youtube.com/watch?v=zZLVXgHxqVl (accessed 30 September 2017). In the first two months, the film had 330,327 views.

67 Morwenna Ferrier, 2016, 'The man who made Russian fashion cool', *The Guardian*, 12 October; www.theguardian.com/fashion/2016/oct/12/russian-fashion-gosha-rubchinskiy-post-soviet-designer-menswear (accessed 3 October 2017).

68 Georgian-born Demna Gvasalia started the brand Vetements with his brother Guram and a group of collaborators in Paris in 2014, after working for the fashion house Maison Martin Margiela from 2010. The collection for Autumn/Winter 2015–16 put Vetements on the fashion map. In October 2015, Gvasalia was appointed a creative director of the prestigious Parisian fashion house Balenciaga, and his Autumn/Winter 2016–17 collection was his first show for the house. In 2015, Gvasalia was shortlisted for the 2015 LVMH prize, the following year he was awarded the British Fashion Awards for both Vetements and Balenciaga, while in 2017 he received the CFDA International Award for Balenciaga.

69 Ulrich Lehmann, 2000, *Tigersprung: Fashion in Modernity* (Cambridge, MA: MIT Press), p. xx.

70 While they have occasionally been considered together, Rubchinskiy and Gvasalia are very different, both in their aesthetic and their customer base. The obvious link, however, has been the extremely talented stylist Lotta Volkova, who has collaborated with both designers. Born in Vladivostok and belonging to the same generation, Volkova has styled Gvasalia's Vetements and Balenciaga shows, as well as a large number of fashion editorials presenting Rubchinskiy, Vetements and Balenciaga's fashions in cutting-edge magazines such as *Re-Edition*, *032c* and *Dazed*. In these she has shown a strong predilection for Soviet iconography, yet also addresses contemporary issues such as gender fluidity.

71 For an overview, see Elizabeth Waters, 1989, 'Restructuring the "Woman Question": Perestroika and Prostitution', *Feminist Review*, Autumn, no. 33, pp. 3–19.

72 Without being quite sure about Gvasalia's inspirations, fashion critics noted his 'fetishistic vision', 'the thrill of fetishism', 'fashion fetishism', and 'wayward sexiness'. For references to fetishism in relation to this collection, see, for example, Suzy Menkes's review of the Balenciaga Spring/Summer 2017 collection, 'Fetishizing the Past', *Vogue.co.uk*, 2 October; www.vogue.co.uk/article/suzy-menkes-review-balenciaga-spring-summer-2017-paris-fashion-week (accessed 6 April 2017); see also Sarah Mower's review of the same collection at *Vogue.com*, 2 October 2016; http://www.vogue.com/fashion-shows/spring-2017-ready-to-wear/balenciaga (accessed 6 April 2017).

73 Jacques Derrida, 1994, *Spectres of Marx: The State of the Debt, the Work of Mourning and the New International* (New York & London: Routledge). Derrida's volume, initially presented at the conference 'Whither Marxism' in 1993 (University of California, Riverside), was a reaction to the political situation caused by the fall of the Berlin Wall in 1989 and the demise of communism, and specifically to Francis Fukuyama's 1992 book *The End of History and the Last Man* (New York: The Free Press/Macmillan).

74 Derrida 1994, p. 219.

75 Stallybrass 1998.

76 As described in Sarah Mower, 2018, 'Spring 2019 Ready-to-wear: Vetements', *Vogue.com*, 1 July; www.vogue.com/fashion-shows/spring-2019-ready-to-wear/vetements (accessed 18 August 2018); Vanessa Friedman, 2018, 'The Revenge of Vetements', *New York Times*, 2 July.

77 Cited in Mower 2018.

78 Friedman 2018.

79 Llewellyn Negrin, 2015, 'The Contemporary Significance of "Pauperist" Style', in *Theory, Culture & Society*, vol. 32, nos 7–8, pp. 203–4.

80 Commenting on the various expressions of Soviet nostalgia, Alexievich states: 'On the eve of the 1917 Revolution, Alexander Grin wrote: "And the future seems to have stopped standing in its proper place." Now, a hundred years later, the future is, once again, not where it ought to be. Our time comes to us second-hand'. See Svetlana Alexievich, 2016, *Second-hand Time* (London: Fitzcarraldo Editions), p. 34.

80 Derrida 1994, pp. 45–6.

82 Caroline Evans, 2003, *Fashion at the Edge: Spectacle, Modernity and Deathliness* (New Haven, CT & London: Yale University Press), pp. 37–8.

83 Suzy Menkes, 2017, '#SuzyCouture Vetements: Subversive Street Style', *Vogue.co.uk*, 24 January; www.vogue.co.uk/article/suzy-menkes-review-vetements-menswear-autumnwinter-2017 (accessed 31 October 2017).

84 Bruce Robbins, 1998, 'Actually Existing Cosmopolitanism', in Pheng Cheah and B. Robbins (eds), *Cosmopolitics: Thinking and Feeling beyond the Nation* (Minneapolis: University of Minnesota Press), p. 3.

85 Sheldon I. Pollock, Homi K. Bhabha, Carol Appadurai Breckenridge and Dipesh Chakrabarty, 2000, 'Cosmopolitanisms: Introduction', in *Public Culture*, 'Cosmopolitanisms' special issue, Fall, vol. 12, no. 3, p. 588.

86 André Leon Talley, 2018, 'The historic blackness of Tyler Mitchell and Beyoncé's *Vogue* cover', *Washington Post*, 10 August; www.washingtonpost.com/opinions/the-historic-blackness-of-tyler-mitchell-and-beyonces-vogue-cover/2018/08/10/7d0a6078-9cbe-11e8-843b-36e177f3081c_story.html?utm_term=.48e05951c946 (accessed 13 August 2018).

87 www.vogue.com/article/beyonce-behind-the-scenes-vogue-cover-shoot-video (accessed 15 August 2018).

88 Cited in Chioma Nnadi, 2018, 'Meet Tyler Mitchell, the Photographer Who Shot Beyoncé for *Vogue*'s September Issue', *Vogue.com*, 6 August; www.vogue.com/article/tyler-mitchell-beyonce-photographer-vogue-september-issue (accessed 29 August 2018).

89 'Beyoncé in Her Own Words: Her Life, Her Body, Her Heritage', American *Vogue*, 6 August 2018; www.vogue.com/article/beyonce-september-issue-2018 (accessed 13 August 2018).

90 For example, while the blurb on the cover of American *Vogue* in March 2013 proclaims 'Queen B! Beyoncé Rules the World', her straight hair and curves, visible but controlled either by Photoshop or Spandex underwear, show that this world is exclusively white. Two years later, on American *Vogue*'s September 2015 cover, Beyoncé's hair is not Afro-styled, but rather is wet and falling free around her face. At this point, her hair could be straightened or left to dry in its naturally curly state.

91 'Beyoncé in Her Own Words', 6 August 2018.

92 Daphne A. Brooks, 2016, 'Black, Proud and Saying It Loud', *Observer*, 13 March, pp. 18–21, p. 18.

93 Brooks 2016, pp. 18–21, pp. 20–1.

94 Richard Powell, 2009, *Cutting a Figure: Fashioning Black Portraiture* (Chicago: University of Chicago Press), p. xv.

95 Monica Miller, 2009, *Slaves to Fashion: Black Dandyism and the Styling of Black Diasporic Identity* (Durham, NC: Duke University Press), p. 25.

96 Cited in Cathy Horyn, 2008, 'Conspicuous by Their Presence', *New York Times*, 19 June 2008. Even before this all-black issue, Meisel promoted black models in his work. On this occasion, he was given almost 100 pages for his editorial. Naomi Campbell was supposed to feature in four of them, but finally appeared on 20 pages. She also appears on the fold-out cover, along with Liya Kebede, Sessilee Lopez and Jourdan Dunn. Horyn's article

offers additional information on this all-black issue.

97 bell hooks, 1995, 'In Our Glory: Photography and Black Life', in bell hooks, *Art on My Mind: Visual Politics* (New York: New Press), pp. 54-64, p. 63.

98 Cited in Tate VanderPoel-Smith, 2018, Interview with Tyler Mitchell, 24 April; www.this-generation.com/interviews/tyler-mitchell (accessed 12 January 2019).

99 Edward Enninful, 2018, Editor's Letter, British *Vogue*, August, p. 33.

100 Cited in Decca Aitkenhead, 2018, 'Oprah's Next Act', British *Vogue*, August, pp. 116–21, p. 116.

101 Powell 2009, p. xvi.

102 Sara Ahmed, 2004, 'Affective Economies', in *Social Text*, Summer, vol. 22, no. 2, p. 119.

103 Lynn Hirschberg, 2010, 'The Art of Reality', *W* magazine, November, pp. 108–15; p. 115.

104 Susan Bordo, 1986, 'The Cartesian Masculinization of Thought', *Signs*, Spring, vol. 11, no. 3, p. 451.

105 Ibid., p. 454.

106 Meredith Jones, 2016, 'Je Suis Kim', in *Critical Studies in Fashion & Beauty*, December, vol. 7, no. 2, p. 132.

107 Ibid.

108 Garde-Hansen and Gorton 2013, p. 34.

109 José Van Dijck, 2013, *The Culture of Connectivity: A Critical History of Social Media* (New York: Oxford University Press), p. 6.

110 Nicholas Mirzoeff, 2015, *How to See the World* (London: Pelican), p. 22.

111 Andrew Marr, 2016, 'The Invention of Marxism's Mr Cool', *The Sunday Times*, 27 November 2016, p. 19. Dressed in a boring grey suit, Erich Honecker was the most powerful East German politician in the period 1976–89.

112 For the genesis of the so-called Mao suit, see Verity Wilson, 2002, 'Dressing for Leadership in China: Wives and Husbands in an Age of Revolutions (1911–1976)', in *Gender and History*, November, vol. 14, no. 3, pp. 608–28.

113 In China, Mao suits differed in colour and accessories, marking the political and social status of their wearers. For an overview, see Tina May Chen, 2001, 'Dressing for the Party: Clothing, Citizenship, and Gender-formation in Mao's China', in *Fashion Theory*, vol. 5, no. 2.

114 For an overview, see François Hourmant, 2018, *Les années Mao en France: avant, pendant et après mai 68* (Paris: Odile Jacob).

115 In the late 1960s, the full truth about Mao's Cultural Revolution and its millions of innocent victims was not yet known in the West. For an overview of the Cultural Revolution, see Frank Dikötter, 2016, *The Cultural Revolution: A People's History 1962–1976* (London: Bloomsbury).

116 Valerie Steele and John S. Major, 1999, *China Chic: East Meets West* (New Haven, CT: Yale University Press), p. 88.

117 Dalí requested full control of that issue, and was even allowed to intervene in the paid advertisements. This was stated in the regular column 'Point of View' (Le Point de vue), which, on this occasion, was renamed 'Dalí's Point of View' (Le Point de vue de Dalí), French *Vogue*, December 1971, p. 159.

118 Hebe Dorsey, 1971, 'The Vogué and Salvador Dalí', *International Herald Tribune*, 10 December, p. 7. Dalí added the accent to *Vogue*'s title, so as to differentiate even further the issue he guest-edited. As well as the portrait of Veruschka as Chairman Mao, a merged portrait of Marilyn Monroe and Mao appeared on the cover of this issue.

119 See Joan Rivière, 1986 [1929], 'Womanliness as a Masquerade', in Victor Burgin, James Donald and Cora Kaplan (eds), *Formations of Fantasy* (London: Methuen), pp. 35–44.

120 Hito Steyerl, 2012, 'The Spam of the Earth: Withdrawal from Representation', in H. Steyerl, *The Wretched of the Screen* (Berlin: Sternberg Press), p. 172.

121 Paul Vale, 2013, 'Turkey Uprising: Ceyda Sungur, "Woman In Red", Becomes Iconic Image For Activists', *Huffington Post UK*, 6 June; www.huffingtonpost.co.uk/2013/06/05/turkey-uprising-ceyda-sungur_n_3388712.html?utm_hp_ref=tw (accessed 29 May 2018).

122 See for example, Ahdaf Soueif, 2011, 'Image of Unknown Woman beaten by Egypt's military echoes around world', *The Guardian*, 18 December; www.theguardian.com/commentisfree/2011/dec/18/egypt-military-beating-female-protester-tahrir-square (accessed 14 December 2018); Dina Zayed, 2011, 'Attack on Egyptian women protesters sparks uproar', *Reuters.com*, 21 December; www.reuters.com/article/us-egypt-protests-women/attack-on-egyptian-women-protesters-spark-uproar-idUSTRE7BK1BX20111221 (accessed 14 December 2018).

123 In December 2011, during the Egyptian uprising, the artist and scholar Bahia Shehab stood on the streets of Cairo with a spray-can in her hand, objecting to the Egyptian authorities by delivering the message 'No: a Thousand Times No' on walls across the city. This 'No to Stripping the People' graffiti belongs to that series. The footprint reads 'Long live a peaceful revolution.'

124 Mona Abaza, 2014, 'Gender Representation in Graffiti Post-25 January', in Hyldig Dal, *Cairo,* *Images of Transition* (Bielefeld: Transcript Verlag), p. 250; cited in Agata Lisiak, 2014, 'The Ballerina and the Blue Bra: Femininity in Recent Revolutionary Iconography', *View: Theories and Practices of Visual Culture* (*Widok. Teorie I praktyki kultury wizuainej*), 5, p. 12; pismowidok.org/index.php/one/article/view/162/290 (accessed 9 June 2018). See also Lisiak for discussing the role of femininity in the Occupy movement and the Arab Spring in 2011.

125 Elisa Adami, 2016, 'How Do You Watch a Revolution? Notes from the 21st Century', *Journal of Visual Culture*, vol. 15, no. 1, pp. 69–84, p. 70.

126 Hito Steyerl, 2009, 'In Defense of the Poor Image' in *e-flux journal*, November, no. 10, p. 7; www.e-flux.com/journal/in-defense-of-the-poor-image (accessed 2 April 2018).

127 Dorinne Kondo, 1997, *About Face: Performing Race in Fashion and Theater* (New York: Routledge), p. 105.

2 Fashion: An Oriental Tyranny

1 The 'Oriental' was neither tied to a precise region, nor to a precise religion (e.g. Islam). It was conceived as the opposite of the West. See Andrea Polaschegg, 2005, *Der andere Orientalismus: Regeln deutsch-morgenländischer Imagination im 19. Jahrhundert* (Berlin: de Gruyter).

2 See Friedrich Creuzer, 1837–43, *Symbolik und Mythologie der alten Völker, besonders der Griechen*, 4 vols (Leipzig/Darmstadt: Carl Wilhelm Leske); Edgar Quinet, 1841, 'De la renaissance orientale', in *Revue de Deux Mondes* 28, pp. 112–30.

3 Barbara Vinken, 2013, *Angezogen – Das Geheimnis der Mode*

(Stuttgart: Klett-Cotta),
pp. 113–42.

4   See Edward Said, 1978,
    Orientalism (New York: Pantheon
    Books). See also Barbara
    Vinken (ed.), 2015, *Translatio
    Babylonis. Unsere orientalische
    Moderne* (Paderborn: Fink).

5   Manuel Borutta, 2010,
    *Antikatholizismus: Deutschland
    und Italien im Zeitalter der
    europäischen Kulturkämpfe*
    (Göttingen: Vandenhoeck und
    Rupprecht Verlag).

6   Emile Zola, 1917 [1893–8],
    Les Trois Villes, 3 vols (Paris:
    Bibliothèque Charpentier).

7   See for the philosophical texts
    that ground this discourse,
    Barbara Vinken, 2016, *Die
    Blumen der Mode – Klassische
    und Neue Texte zur Philosophie
    der Mode* (Stuttgart:
    Klett-Cotta).

8   For a development of this
    discourse under communism,
    see Djurdja Bartlett, 2010,
    *FashionEast – The Spectre that
    Haunted Socialism* (Cambridge,
    MA: MIT Press).

9   See Barbara Vinken, 1995,
    'Republic, Rhetoric, and
    Sexual Difference', in Anselm
    Haverkamp (ed.), *Deconstruction
    is/in America* (New York &
    London: New York University
    Press), pp. 181–99.

10 Jean-Jacques Rousseau, 1968
    [1758], *Politics and the Arts:
    Letter to M. D'Alembert on the
    Theatre*, trans. Allan Bloom
    (Ithaca: Cornell University
    Press), p. 100.

11 Jean-Jacques Rousseau, 1961
    [1761], *Julie, ou La Nouvelle
    Héloïse* II, Œuvres complètes,
    Letter 21 (Paris: Gallimard),
    pp. 267–8.

12 Rousseau 1968, p. 101.

13 See Friedrich Nietzsche, 1913
    [1878], *Human, All Too Human:
    A Book for Free Spirits*, Part II,
    trans. Paul V. Cohn (New York:
    The MacMillan Company).

14 See Barbara Vinken, 2005,
    *Fashion Zeitgeist. Trends and
    Cycles in the Fashion System*
    (Oxford: Berg Publishers).

15 See Nietzsche 1913, p. 305.

16 Friedrich Nietzsche, 1954
    [1878], *Menschliches,
    Allzumenschliches* II, in Karl
    Schlechta (ed.), *Werke in drei
    Bänden* (München: Hanser),
    p. 962, trans. by the author.

17 See Nietzsche 1913.

18 For the return of myth in
    naturalism see Barbara Vinken,
    2015, 'Nana. Venus à rebours.
    Das Paris des II. Empire als
    Wiederkehr Roms/Babylons',
    in B. Vinken (ed.), *Translatio
    Babylonis* (Paderborn: Fink),
    pp. 201–20.

19 See Emile Zola, 1971 [1883],
    Au Bonheur des dames
    (Paris: Garnier-Flammarion),
    p. 171; Barbara Vinken, 1995,
    'Temples of Delight: Consuming
    Consumption in Emile Zola's
    "Au bonheur des dames"', in
    Margaret Cohen and Christopher
    Prendergast (eds), *Spectacles
    of Realism: Body, Gender,
    Genre*, Cultural Politics, vol. 10
    (Minneapolis: Minnesota Press),
    pp. 247–68.

20 Zola 1971, p. 437, trans.
    by the author.

21 See Ernest Renan, 1864–74,
    Mission de Phénicie (Paris:
    Imprimerie Impériale), pp.
    284–300; here p. 297, 'Le fleuve
    Adonis sort d'une caverne
    située dans le pan coupé à pic
    de la montagne, à une hauter
    de deux ou trois metres [...] De
    nombreuses sources jaillissent
    en outre de tous les côtés,
    en particulier des assises du
    temple. Ces eaux réunies se
    précipitent par une nouvelle
    cascade dans un bassin
    circulaire, qui paraît aussi avoir
    été agrandi ou rectifié de main
    d'homme.'

22 From 'Samson Agonistes', in
    John Milton (1671), *Paradise
    Regained; A Poem in IV books;
    To Which is Added Samson
    Agonistes*, II ed. (London: John
    Starkey at the Mitre in Fleet
    Street, near Temple Bar).

23 See Thorstein Veblen, 1912
    [1899], *The Theory of the
    Leisure Class: An Economic
    Study of Institutions* (New York:
    Macmillan & Co), title of chapter
    four, p. 68.

24 See Veblen 1912, pp. 178, 182.

25 See Veblen 1912, p. 175.

26 See Veblen 1912, p. 149.

27 See Veblen 1912, pp. 179–80.

28 See Veblen 1912, p. 180.

29 Simone de Beauvoir, 2009
    [1949], *The Second Sex*, vol. II,
    trans. Constance Borde and
    Sheila Malovany-Chevallier
    (New York: Random House),
    pp. 649–51.

30 See Veblen 1912, pp. 183–4.

31 Adolf Loos, 1982, *Spoken into
    the Void: Collected Essays,
    1897–1900* (Cambridge,
    MA: MIT Press), p. 99.

32 See Loos 1982, p. 99.

33 Ibid.

34 Loos 1982, p. 102.

35 Ibid.

36 Ibid.

37 See Werner Sombart, 1992
    [1913], *Liebe, Luxus und
    Kapitalismus. Über die
    Entstehung der modernen
    Welt aus dem Geist der
    Verschwendung* (Berlin: Klaus
    Wagenbach Verlag), p. 121.

38 See Sombart 1992, p. 127.

39 Pierre Bourdieu, 1984 [1975],
    'Haute Couture et Haute Culture',
    in *Questions de sociologie* (Paris:
    Éditions de Minuit), pp. 196–206,
    p. 204.

40 See Bourdieu 1984, p. 205.

41 Bourdieu 1984, p. 204.

3   Wang Guangmei's Crimes of Fashion

1   CCP Central Committee,
    'Resolution on certain questions
    in the history of our party since
    the founding of the People's
    Republic of China', 27 June
    1981; www.marxists.org/
    subject/china/documents/cpc/
    history/01.htm (accessed
    15 April 2017).

2   Frank Dikötter, 2016, *The
    Cultural Revolution: A People's
    History, 1962–1976* (London:
    Bloomsbury), p. x.

3   Dikötter 2016, p. xi. 'Mao
    Zedong Thought' (Mao Zedong
    sixiang) refers to the ideological
    principles and dictats on
    Marxism-Leninism and the
    Chinese revolution, developed
    by Mao and consequently
    enshrined in the Chinese
    Communist Party's constitution
    – even to this day.

4   Roderick MacFarquhar
    and Michael Schoenhals,
    2006, *Mao's Last Revolution*
    (Cambridge, MA: Harvard
    University Press), p. 90.
    'Bombard the headquarters'
    (Paoda siling bu) refers to a
    proclamation written by Mao
    in August 1966 that criticised
    Party elements for obstructing
    revolutionary progress, and
    in so doing, encouraged the
    revolutionary masses to take the
    Cultural Revolution to the Party
    itself (hence, 'headquarters').

5   'Capitalist roader' was a
    common Maoist accusation
    used against those who, even
    if they were themselves not
    actually capitalist (or bourgeois),
    promoted or permitted
    capitalistic interests, and thus
    allowed China and its revolution
    to return to the capitalist road.

6   Odd Arne Westad, 2010, 'The
    Great Transformation: China
    in the Long 1970s', in Niall
    Ferguson et al. (eds), *The Shock
    of the Global: The 1970s in
    Perspective* (Cambridge,
    MA: Harvard University Press),
    pp. 70–1.

7   Dikötter 2016, p. xiv.

8 Jonathan Spence, 1990, *The Search for Modern China* (New York: W.W. Norton & Co.), pp. 612–13.

9 CCP Central Committee, 'Decision of the Central Committee of the Chinese Communist Party Concerning the Great Proletarian Cultural Revolution (Adopted on August 8, 1966)': www.marxists.org/subject/china/peking-review/1966/PR1966-33g.htm (accessed 15 April 2017).

10 See Ji-li Jiang, 2007, *Red Scarf Girl: A Memoir of the Cultural Revolution* (New York: Harper Collins), pp. 29–31. In general, while the Cultural Revolution's radical politics put new pressures on fashion, the intersection of politics and fashion had already been a recurrent historical theme for China. See especially Antonia Finnane, 2007, *Changing Clothes in China: Fashion, History, Nation* (London: Hurst); Tina Mai Chen, 2001, 'Dressing for the Party: Clothing, Citizenship, and Gender-formation in Mao's China', *Fashion Theory*, vol. 5, no. 2, pp. 143–71; Valerie Steele and John S. Major, 1999, 'Fashion Revolution: The Maoist Uniform', in V. Steele and J.S. Major (eds), *China Chic: East meets West* (New Haven, CT: Yale University Press), pp. 55–67.

11 Verity Wilson, 1999, 'Dress and the Cultural Revolution', in Valerie Steele and John S. Major (eds), *China Chic: East meets West* (New Haven, CT: Yale University Press), p. 174. This view was typical of western observers like US Congressman Lester Wolff, who saw the sartorial landscape as a 'system of oneness'. See 'Impressions on a trip to China', 25 May 1976, CIA-RDP79M00467A000400020015-0.

12 Wilson 1999, pp. 174–5; Antonia Finnane, 1999, 'Military Culture and Chinese Dress', in Valerie Steele and John S. Major (eds), *China Chic: East meets West* (New Haven, CT: Yale University Press), pp. 119–31.

13 Jianhua Zhao, 2013, *The Chinese Fashion Industry: An Ethnographic Approach* (London: Bloomsbury), p. 49.

14 Juanjuan Wu, 2009, *Chinese Fashion: From Mao to Now* (New York: Berg Publishers), p. 2.

15 Ibid.

16 Ibid.

17 Ibid., p. 5.

18 Wilson 1999, p. 174.

19 Dikötter 2016, pp. 99–100.

20 Peidong Sun, 2016, 'The Collar Revolution: Everyday Clothing in Guangdong as Resistance in the Cultural Revolution', in Patricia M. Thornton, Peidong Sun and Chris Berry (eds), *Red Shadows: Memories and Legacies of the Chinese Cultural Revolution*, The China Quarterly Special Issues: New Series, no. 12 (Cambridge: Cambridge University Press), pp. 178–9.

21 Ibid., pp. 180, 182–5.

22 For the prosecution of Wang Guangmei, see also Finnane 2007.

23 Jung Chang and Jon Halliday, 2007, *Mao: The Unknown Story* (London: Vintage), p. 641.

24 See Yuwu Song, 2013, 'Wang Guangmei (1921–2006)' in Yuwu Song (ed.), *Biographical Dictionary of the People's Republic of China* (Jefferson, NC: McFarland & Company), p. 301.

25 Spence 1990, p. 596. The Hundred Flowers (1956–9) refers to the brief liberalisation of socio-political expression (and dissent) amongst many Chinese intellectuals, encouraged by Mao's idea to 'let a hundred flowers bloom; [and] a hundred schools of thought contend', so as to encourage the internal reform of the revolution. However, the criticism of the Chinese Communist Party that emerged from this liberalisation was not anticipated, and the Party quickly turned around with a violent, intensive campaign to repress all opposition and criticism. The Great Leap Forward (1958–61) was the name given to Mao's grandiose campaign to turn China from an agrarian economy to a modern, industrialised state in a short period of time. With plans for rapid industrialisation and large-scale agricultural collectivisation, based more on Maoist ideology than rational economic planning, the Great Leap inflicted serious damage on the Chinese economy, and the structural upheaval caused to the agrarian economy resulted in a famine that left over 40 million dead.

26 Dikötter 2016, p. 24.

27 MacFarquhar and Schoenhals 2006, p. 10.

28 Chang and Halliday 2007, pp. 600, 641.

29 Spence 1990, p. 593.

30 Zhisui Li, 1996, *The Private Life of Chairman Mao* (London: Arrow), p. 400.

31 Spence 1990, p. 593.

32 CCP Central Committee, 'Circular of the Central Committee of the Communist Party of China on the Great Proletarian Cultural Revolution', 16 May 1966; www.marxists.org/subject/china/documents/cpc/cc_gpcr.htm (accessed 15 April 2017).

33 CCP Central Committee, 'Decision of the Central Committee of the Chinese Communist Party Concerning the Great Proletarian Cultural Revolution (Adopted on August 8, 1966)'; www.marxists.org/subject/china/peking-review/1966/PR1966-33g.htm (accessed 15 April 2017).

34 Chang and Halliday 2007, pp. 642–5; 'The President's Daily Brief', 10 April 1967, CIA-RDP79T00936A005100170001-2, p. 24. From the *CIA Freedom of Information Act Electronic Reading Room* (*CIA FOIA*).

35 A 'struggle session' (pidou hui) involved an accused person being forced, in front of a crowd, either to self-criticise and confess his/her crimes or to be confronted by his/her accusers. It was often utilised as a direct way of carrying out 'class struggle' by the Chinese Communists in the Maoist era.

36 The transcript was published in *Thrice Interrogating Big Pickpocket Wang Guangmei (Denunciation Materials)* (*Sanshen dapashou Wang Guangmei [pipan cailiao]*). This translation is from 'Interrogation Record: Wang Guangmei', in Michael Schoenhals (ed.), 1996, *China's Cultural Revolution, 1966–1969: Not A Dinner Party* (London: M.E. Sharpe), pp. 101–16. The Qinghua students' self-identification as the Jinggangshan Regiment speaks to the reification of military culture and identity at the time. 'Jinggangshan' (Well Ridge Mountain) was the legendary birthplace of the PLA, and by taking this name they were making a semiotical claim to revolutionary solidarity with the military.

37 'Interrogation Record: Wang Guangmei', p. 103. The 'Three-Anti Element' was anti-CCP, anti-Mao Zedong Thought and anti-socialist.

38 'Interrogation Record: Wang Guangmei', p. 103.

39 Ibid.

40 Ibid., pp. 105–6.

41 These 'Ghostbusters' were also members of the Jinggangshan Regiment.

42 'Interrogation Record: Wang Guangmei', p. 115.

43 The 'jet plane' pose was a form of physical torture where victims were made to stand with bent knees and arms pulled backwards. It was particularly popular with the Red Guards and used during 'struggle sessions' to force victims to confess in front of large crowds.

44 'Interrogation Record: Wang Guangmei', p. 106.

45 Invented in the mid-1920s, the *qipao* combined the shape of contemporary western fashions with Chinese-style details, such as the side fastening and high collar. It became a form of Chinese national dress during the Republican period (1925–49), and continued to be worn into the 1950s and early 1960s.

46 Finnane 2007, p. 227.

47 Chang and Halliday 2007, pp. 644–5.

48 Ibid., p. 645.

49 Li 1996, p. 175.

50 CIA Directorate of Intelligence, 'The role of the Red Guards and Revolutionary Rebels in Mao's Cultural Revolution', November 1968, POLO 24, p. 66; CIA East Asia – Pacific Division, Office of Current Intelligence, 'Chinese Affairs', 7 July 1975, CIA-RDP79T00865A001300 120001-5, p. 15. Both from the *CIA Freedom of Information Act Electronic Reading Room (CIA FOIA)*.

51 Kuai Dafu, 2013, 'The whole story of the Qinghua struggle against Wang Guangmei' (Qinghua pidou wang guangmei shimo), *China Through the Ages (Yanhuang chunqiu)*, no. 3; www.yhcqw.com/html/qlj/2013/31/8JJ7.html (accessed 15 April 2017).

52 'Mao Zedong's public criticism of Wang Guangmei and decision on the "23 Articles"' (Mao Zedong gongkai piping Wang Guangmei qinding 'er'shisan tiao'). From 'Cultural Revolution online' (Wengewang), a digital repository for historical documents, photographs,

and other archival material related to the Cultural Revolution: www.wengewang.org (accessed 15 April 2017).

53 See 'Announcement regarding struggling against the big pickpocket Wang Guangmei on 10 April' (Guanyu siyue shiri jiudou dapashou Wang Guangmei de tongzhi 1967.04.05), *Jinggangshan*, no. 31, 6 April 1967. From 'Cultural Revolution online' (Wengewang): www.wengewang.org (accessed 15 April 2017).

54 See note 36.

55 'The President's Daily Brief', 10 April 1967, CIA-RDP79T00936A005100170001-2, p. 24, from the *CIA Freedom of Information Act Electronic Reading Room (CIA FOIA)*.

56 'Anecdotes about Liu Shaoqi and Wang Guangmei – before the 1966 Pakistan visit' (Liu Shaoqi, Wang Guangmei yishilu – yijiu liuliu nian chufang Bajisitan zhiqian), *Railway Red Flag (Tiedao hongqi)*, no. 6–7, 21 May 1967. From 'Cultural Revolution online' (Wengewang): www.wengewang.org (accessed 15 April 2017).

57 'Wang Guangmei's true colours' (Wang Guangmei jiujing shi shenme huose), *Fight the Black Wave (Zhenheilang)*, 16 January 1967. From 'Cultural Revolution online' (Wengewang): www.wengewang.org (accessed 15 April 2017). 'Fox spirit' (Huli jing), originally from *The Journey to the West*, one of the Four Great Classical Novels of Chinese literature, published in the sixteenth century, refers to a particular type of demoness who took the form of a seductive women, i.e. evil vixen.

58 Finnane 2007, p. 227.

59 'Concentrate hatred at the dagger's tip – Revolutionary student representative Comrade Zhu Deyi's speech, 1967.04.10'

(Ba chouhen ningji zai cidao jianshang 1967.04.10 – geming xuesheng daibiao Zhu Deyi tongzhi fayan), *Jinggangshan*, no. 33–4, 11 April 1967. From 'Cultural Revolution online' (Wengewang): www.wengewang.org (accessed 15 April 2017).

60 Elizabeth J. Perry, 2002, 'Moving the masses: Emotion work in the Chinese revolution', *Mobilization*, vol. 7, no. 2, pp. 122–3.

4 Style Activism: The Everyday Activist Wardrobe

1 See Carol Tulloch, 2016a, *The Birth of Cool: Style Narratives of the African Diaspora* (London, Oxford, New York, New Delhi, Sydney: Bloomsbury), pp. 1–8.

2 These include *A Riot of Our Own*, exhibition, Chelsea Space, London, 2008, curated by Carol Tulloch; Carol Tulloch, 2014, '"A Riot of Our Own": A Reflection on Agency', in *Open Arts Journal*, 4; openartsjournal .org/issue- 3/2014s12ct/; Mark Sealy and Carol Tulloch (eds), 2015, *Syd Shelton: Rock Against Racism* (London: Autograph), p. 11; Carol Tulloch, 'Unexpected Directions, Necessary Observations: Making Sense of the World Through Making', Keynote Lecture, *Decorating Dissidence: Modernism, Feminism and the Arts*, Conference, Queen Mary University of London, 3–4 November 2017.

3 I would like to thank Syd Shelton for supplying all his images as sponsorship in kind for this article.

4 Carol Tulloch, 2015, Preface, in Mark Sealy and Carol Tulloch (eds), *Syd Shelton: Rock Against Racism* (London: Autograph), p. 11.

5 Ibid.

6 Tulloch 2016a, pp. 199–200.

7 Penny Sparke, 2016, Introduction, in Penny Sparke

and Fiona Fisher (eds), *The Routledge Companion to Design Studies* (London & New York: Routledge), p. 13.

8 Guy Julier, 2015, 'Introduction: Material Preference and Design Activism', in *Design and Culture*, vol. 5:2, p. 146. The origins of design activism are credited to Victor Papanek; see Alison Clarke, 2015, '"Actions Speak Louder": Victor Papanek and the Legacy of Design Activism', in *Design and Culture*, vol. 5:2, pp. 151–68.

9 As acknowledged by the conference *Decorating Dissidence: Modernism, Feminism and the Arts*, at Queen Mary University of London, 2017.

10 Tanisha C. Ford, 2015, *Liberated Threads: Black Women, Style and the Global Politics of Soul* (Chapel Hill: University of North Carolina Press) p. 3.

11 See Carol Tulloch, 2016b, a book review of *Liberated Threads* by Tanisha C. Ford (2015), in *International Journal of Fashion Studies*, vol. 4:1, pp. 137–9.

12 Jo Wreford, 2016, 'Forty Years and Counting' in *Reminiscences of RAR: Rocking Against Racism* (London: Redwords), p. 241.

13 The term 'style activism' has also been used to reflect an engagement with style, rather than fashion. See Derek Wynne and Justin O'Connor, 1998, 'Consumption and the Postmodern City', in *Urban Studies*, vol. 35, no. 5/6, May, pp. 841–64.

14 https://www.theguardian.com/uk-news/2018/dec/02/revealed-the-stark-evidence-of-everyday-racial-bias-in-britain (accessed 3 December 2018).

15 Ford 2015, p. 101.

16 Bobby Seale, 2007, Foreword, *Black Panther: The Revolutionary Art of Emory Douglas* (New York: Rizzoli), p. 13.

17 *Oxford Dictionary of English.*

18 Michelle Bogre, 2012, *Photography as Activism: Images for Social Change* (New York & London: Focal Press), p. 2.

19 Tulloch 2015, p. 11.

20 Bogre 2012, pp. xii–9.

21 Bogre 2012, p. xii.

22 Victor Burgin (ed.), 1988 [1982], *Thinking Photography* (London: Macmillan Publishers), p. 2.

23 Liz Wells, 2000, *Photography: A Critical Introduction* (London & New York: Routledge), p. 4.

24 Burgin 1988, p. 2.

25 Erina Duganne, 2010, *The Self in Black and White: Race and Subjectivity in Postwar American Photography* (Lebanon, NH: University Press of New England), p. 6.

26 Duganne 2010, pp. 6–7.

27 See David Dabydeen, John Gilmore and Cecily Jones (eds), 2007, *The Oxford Companion to Black British History* (Oxford & New York: Oxford University Press), pp. 377–8; www.independent.co.uk/arts-entertainment/music/features/loved-the-music-hated-the-bigots-7138621.html; www.theguardian.com/politics/2008/feb/24/race (accessed 2 December 2018).

28 Wreford 2016, pp. 240–3. Interestingly, Jo Wreford's personal account of the emergence of the letter, and why, explains that it took place around a pine table that she views as the materialisation and absorption of an anti-racist act.

29 Letters section, *Sounds*, 28 August 1976, p. 33. The Rock Against Racism letter came under the heading 'Enoch Clapton?'. Interestingly, there are slightly different versions of the letter in terms of the signature. For example, the one that appeared in *Melody Maker, Mailbag*, p. 13, also published on 28 August 1976, had Peter Bruno as the sole signatory – he won an LP for his contribution. While the letter in *New Musical Express*, 11 September 1976, p. 50, had no signatories.

30 David Widgery, 1986, *Beating Time: Riot 'n' Race 'n' Rock 'n' Roll* (London: Chatto & Windus), pp. 11–18.

31 Widgery 1986, p. 40.

32 Carol Tulloch, 2014, '"A Riot of Our Own": A Reflection on Agency', in *Open Arts Journal*, 3 (Summer), pp. 25–59; openartsjournal.org/issue-3/2014s12ct/ (accessed 9 April 2018).

33 Barbara Ehrenreich, 2007, *Dancing in the Streets: A History of Collective Joy* (London: Granta), p. 221.

34 Ehrenreich 2007, p. 260.

35 Syd Shelton, 2008, 'Syd Shelton', in *A Riot of Our Own* (London: Chelsea Space), unpaginated.

36 Paul Ricoeur, 1994, *Oneself as Another*, trans. Kathleen Blamey (Chicago & London: University of Chicago Press), p. 107.

37 Sarat Maharaj, 2012, Keynote Lecture, *Social Fabric Symposium*, Iniva, London, 10 March, unpublished paper. See also Tulloch 2014, p. 44.

38 *Oxford Dictionary of English.* See also Tulloch 2014, p. 44.

39 Carol Tulloch, 2012, 'Rock Against Racism: In Black and White', in Carol Tulloch (ed.), *A Riot of Our Own: Photographs by Syd Shelton 1976, 1981, Galerija Makina, Croatia, 11–23 September 2012* (London: TrAIN), p. 14.

40 Paul Gilroy, 2015, 'Rebel Souls: Dance-floor Justice and the Temporary Undoing of Britain's Babylon', in Mark Sealy and Carol Tulloch (eds), *Syd Shelton: Rock Against Racism* (London: Autograph), pp. 23–4.

41 This crowd had gathered on New Cross Road, opposite Pagnell Street, Lewisham, London, as this area provided a good assembly point. New Cross Road was much wider at this junction. Syd Shelton in conversation with Carol Tulloch, 3 December 2018.

42 Tulloch 2016a, pp. 43–5.

43 Ben Highmore, 2018, 'Mundane Tastes: Ubiquitous Objects and the Historical Sensorium', in Malcolm Quinn et al. (eds), *The Persistence of Taste: Art, Museums and Everyday Life After Bourdieu* (London & New York: Routledge), pp. 275–85.

44 Tulloch 2016a, pp. 43–5.

45 William Stott, 1986, *Documentary Expression in 1930s America* (Chicago & London: University of Chicago Press), p. 11.

46 Syd Shelton in conversation with Carol Tulloch, 3 December 2018.

47 Sara Schneckloth, 2008, 'Marking Time, Figuring Space: Gesture and the Embodied Moment', in *Journal of Visual Culture*, vol. 7, no. 3, p. 280.

48 Schneckloth 2008, p. 287.

49 Ibid., referencing Carrie Noland, 2008, 'Miming Signing', in Carrie Noland and Sally Ann Ness (eds), *Migrations of Gesture* (Minneapolis: University of Minnesota Press).

50 *John Berger: The Art of Looking*, BBC 4, Ma.ja.de. Film-Produktion, 6 November 2016.

51 Norman Mailer, 2009 [1974], *The Faith of Graffiti* (London: Harper Collins), p. 31.

52 Widgery 1986, p. 122.

53 Paul Alkebulan, 2007, *Survival Pending Revolution: The History of the Black Panther Party* (Tuscaloosa: University of Alabama Press), p. 113. The other weddings were that of Charles Bursey and Shelley Sanders on 1 May, which took place in Oakland at the same church that officiated the Graham and Douglas ceremony; in Kansas City Phyllis Story and Phillip Ortega were married on 16 May; and at Berkeley Free Church the wedding of Ray 'Masai' Hewitt and Shirley Neely took place, on 19 August. St Augustine's and the Berkeley Free Church both took an active role in the civil rights activities of their communities. See: www.staugepiscopal.org/about-us/history and www.oac.cdlib.org/findaid/ark:/13030/tf7489n8kh/ (accessed 23 July 2018).

54 Ford 2015, p. 107.

55 Avril Lansdell, 1986, *Wedding Fashions 1860–1980* (Princes Risborough: Shire Publications), p. 87.

56 Edwina Ehrman, 2014, *The Wedding Dress* (London: V&A Publishing), p. 145; Lansdell 1986, pp. 87–91.

57 Ehrman 2014, pp. 145–6.

58 Ehrman 2014, p. 151.

59 Bobby Seale, 2006, Foreword, Michael Famighetti (ed.), *The Black Panthers: Photographs by Stephen Shames* (New York: Aperture), p. 11.

60 Krista Thompson, 2015, *Shine: The Visual Economy of Light in African Diasporic Aesthetic Practice* (Durham, NC: Duke University Press), p. 236.

61 Colette Gaiter states that, according to FBI records, 'estimates of the *Black Panther* peak circulation range from 139,000 to 400,000, it had its highest circulation in 1970 and 1971'. See Colette Gaiter, 2007, 'What Revolution Looks Like: The Work of Black Panther Artist Emory Douglas', in Sam Durant (ed.), *Black Panther: The Revolutionary Art of Emory Douglas* (New York: Rizzoli), p. 96. BPP historian Billy X. Jennings believed that 'The BPP newspaper became the No. 1 Black weekly newspaper in the country from 1968 to 1971, selling over 300,000 copies each week'; sfbayview.com/2015/05/remembering-the-black-

panther-party-newspaper-april-25-1967-september-1980/ (accessed 4 June 2018).

62 Gaiter 2007, p. 94.

63 Ibid.

64 Vanessa Brown, 2015, *Cool Shades: The History and Meaning of Sunglasses* (London, New Delhi, New York & Sydney: Bloomsbury), pp. 1–2.

65 Brown 2015, pp. 112–13.

66 'A Wedding of Revolutionaries', in *The Black Panther*, 23 August 1969, p. 13; see also Eldridge Cleaver, 1968, *Soul On Ice* (New York: Dell Publishing), p. 205.

67 Alkebulan 2007, p. 113.

68 Marie Corbin, 1978, *The Couple* (Harmondsworth, UK: Penguin), p. 13.

69 Corbin 1978, p. 13.

70 Corbin 1978, p. 27.

71 Katrina Rolley, 1992, 'Love, Desire and the Pursuit of the Whole: Dress and the Lesbian Couple', in J. Ash and E. Wilson (eds), *Chic Thrills: A Fashion Reader* (London: Pandora Press), p. 33.

72 Maria Tamboukou, 2010, *Nomadic Narratives, Visual Forces: Gwen John's Letters and Paintings* (New York: Peter Lang Publishing), p. 18.

73 Carol Tulloch, 2018, 'The Glamorous "Diasporic Intimacy" of Habitus: Taste, Migration and the Practice of Settlement', in Malcolm Quinn, David Beech, Michael Lehnert, Carol Tulloch and Stephen Wilson, *The Persistence of Taste: Art, Museums and Everyday life After Bourdieu* (London & New York: Routledge), p. 263.

74 See Pierre Bourdieu, 1992, *Distinction: A Social Critique of the Judgement of Taste* (London: Routledge), pp. 169–225; Carol Tulloch, 2018, 'Taste, the home and everyday life', in Malcolm Quinn, David Beech, Michael Lehnert, Carol Tulloch and Stephen Wilson (eds),

The Persistence of Taste: Art, Museums and Everyday life After Bourdieu (London & New York: Routledge), pp. 253–5.

75 Tulloch 2018, pp. 264–72.

76 Karl Maton, 2008, 'Haitus', in Michael Grenfell (ed.), *Pierre Bourdieu: Key Concepts* (London & New York: Routledge), p. 49.

77 Tulloch 2018, p. 253.

78 Maurice Merleau-Ponty, 1962, *Phenomenology of Perception* (London and New York: Routledge), pp. 30–59.

5 Bombshell: Fashion in the Age of Terrorism

1 I am aware, however, that exponentially more people suffer from terrorist activity in Africa and the Middle East.

2 'The Terror Wars have been internalised. Terror becomes an organizing principle of society – a culture of terror based on the fear of the other.' See Henry Giroux, 2016, *America at War with Itself* (San Francisco: City Lights Books), p. 90. See also Henry Giroux, 2006, *Beyond the Spectacle of Terrorism* (New York: Routledge).

3 Jean Baudrillard, 2012, *The Spirit of Terrorism*, trans. Chris Turner (London: Verso Books), p. 81. Originally published in 2002 as *La Violence du mondial* (Paris: Editions Gallilée).

4 See Jacques Derrida, 'Autoimmunity: Real and Symbolic Suicides', in Giovanna Borradori (ed.), 2003, *Philosophy in a Time of Terror: Dialogues with Jürgen Habermas and Jacques Derrida* (Chicago: University of Chicago Press), pp. 85–136.

5 Lauren Sheffield, 2016, 'The Complete History of the Naked Dress', *Harper's Bazaar*, 14 July; www.harpersbazaar.com.sg/fashion/the-complete-history-of-the-naked-dress-2/

(accessed 28 March 2018). Countless fashion writers cite this dress as the first. Also www.elle.com.au/fashion/the-most-scandalous-dresses-of-all-time-10545 (accessed 28 March 2018). The dress and its effect are also described in Donald Spoto, 1993, *Marilyn Monroe: The Biography* (New York: Harper Collins), p. 512.

6 Personal telephone interview with Edward Meyer, Vice President of Exhibitions, Ripley's Believe It or Not Museum, 8 March 2018.

7 All quoted in Dewayne Bevil, 2017, 'Ripley's Shows Off Multi-Million-Dollar Marilyn Monroe Dress,' *Orlando Sentinel*, 8 November; www.orlandosentinel.com/travel/attractions/theme-park-rangers-blog/os-bz-ripley-marilyn-monroe-dress-20171108-story.html (accessed 28 March 2018). Nolan is Executive Director of Julien's Auction House.

8 This directive apparently came from Caroline Kennedy. Jennifer Swann, 2015, 'Fifty-two Years Later, People are Still Obsessed with Jackie O's Pink Chanel Suit', *Vice.com*, 23 November; www.vice.com/en_us/article/avyyqp/people-are-still-obsessed-with-jackie-os-pink-chanel-suit-52-years-later-511 (accessed 28 March 2018).

9 Quoted in Cathy Horyn, 2013, 'Jacqueline Kennedy's Smart Pink Suit, Preserved in Memory and Kept Out of View', *New York Times*, 14 November; www.nytimes.com/2013/11/15/fashion/jacqueline-kennedys-smart-pink-suit-preserved-in-memory-and-kept-out-of-view.html (accessed 28 March 2018).

10 Julia Kristeva, 1982, *Powers of Horror*, trans. Leon Roudiez (New York: Columbia University Press),

p. 4. Originally published in 1980 as *Pouvoirs de l'horreur* (Paris: Editions du Seuil).

11 Even in 1962, rumours about Monroe's relationship with Kennedy abounded, which only intensified after Monroe's famous appearance in this dress. Jacqueline Kennedy did not attend the birthday gala.

12 Quoted in J. Randy Taraborrelli, 2010, *The Secret Life of Marilyn Monroe* (New York: Grand Central Publishing), p. 433.

13 While some earlier biographers, such as Donald Spoto, minimised JFK's relationship with Monroe, others such as Christopher Andersen describe a protracted affair between the two. See Donald Spoto, 1993, *Marilyn Monroe: The Biography* (New York: Harper Collins), p. 486 and ff. Christopher Andersen's 2013 book, *These Few Precious Days: The Final Year of Jack and Jackie* (New York: Gallery Books), confirms that the two conducted a two-and-a-half-year affair, with the full knowledge of Jacqueline Kennedy.

14 Quoted in Minh-ha T. Pham, 2011, 'The Right to Fashion in the Age of Terrorism,' *Signs*, vol. 36, no. 2 (Winter), pp. 385–410.

15 Ibid., p. 387.

16 Anon., 2015, 'France in Mourning: Fashion World Vows Defiance Against Terrorism,' *Women's Wear Daily*, 15 November; wwd.com/business-news/financial/france-mourning-fashion-world-vows-defiance-against-terrorism-paris-attacks-10279328/ (accessed 28 March 2018).

17 Anon., 2015, 'Lettre ouverte d'une Musulmane à Daech,' *Huffington Post France*, 15 November; www.huffingtonpost.fr/may/lettre-ouverte-dune-musulmane-a-daech_b_8569944.html (accessed 28 March 2018).

18 Jean Baudrillard, 2012, *The Spirit of Terrorism*, trans. Chris Turner (London: Verso Books), p. 10.

19 W.J.T. Mitchell, 2005, 'The Unspeakable and the Unimaginable: Word and Image in a Time of Terror,' *ELH*, 72:2, pp. 291–308.

20 It is worth noting that the Islamic terrorists who perpetrated the June 2017 attack on London Bridge successfully held the police at bay by wearing fake suicide vests, fashioned out of water bottles duct-taped to ordinary belts. Here, even the codes of what might be called 'conventional terrorist garments' had been scrambled. See Yonette Joseph, 2017, 'London Bridge Attack: The Implements of Terror,' *New York Times*, 11 June; www.nytimes. com/2017/06/11/world/europe/ london-bridge-attack-knives- fake-suicide-vests-van.html (accessed 26 March 2018).

21 Images from Meisel's 'State of Emergency' photo shoot are available online at: trendland. com/state-of-emergency- by-steven-meisel/.

22 Ida Minerva Tarbell, 2011 [1939], *All in the Day's Work: An Autobiography* (Urbana & Chicago: University of Illinois Press), p. 211.

23 Walter Benjamin, 1999 [1935], *The Arcades Project*, trans. Howard Eiland and Kevin McLaughlin (Cambridge, MA: Harvard University Press), p. 79.

24 Quoted on artist's website: ivanaspinelli.net/global-pin-up/ (accessed 28 March 2018). Originally published in Franco Speroni, 2006, 'Global Pin- up Bazaar,' *Extrart.it* (site now defunct; available at: ivanaspinelli.net/global-pin-up/ [accessed 28 March 2018]).

25 In 2017, the German parliament approved a partial ban on face coverings such as the burqa and the niqab.

26 The burkini, created in 2004 by Australian designer Aheda Zanetti, has no particular religious significance and was intended mainly to provide a modest alternative to typical swimwear. 'It's just a garment to suit a modest person … [I]t's not symbolizing Islam,' says Zanetti. Quoted in Dominique Musbergen, 2016, 'Burkini-wearing Woman Gets Chased Off French Beach', *Huffington Post*, 19 September; www.huffingtonpost.com/entry/ burkini-french-beach-us_ 57df960be4b04a1497b53f0e? section=& (accessed 28 March 2018).

27 Quoted in Amanda Taub, 2016, 'France's "Burkini" Bans Are About More Than Religion or Clothing', *New York Times*, 18 August. See also Max Bearak, 2016, 'France's Burkini Bans Lead to Cries of Hypocrisy and Sexism', *Washington Post*, 24 August; www.washingtonpost. com/news/worldviews/ wp/2016/08/24/frances- burkini-bans-lead-to-cries-of- hypocrisy-and-sexism/?utm_ term=.aa31564681c1 (accessed 28 March 2018).

28 Quoted in Erin McLaughlin, Radina Gigova and Laila Ben Allal, 2016, 'Burkini Ban Protest', *CNN.com*, 25 August; edition. cnn.com/2016/08/25/europe/ burkini-ban-protest-london- french-embassy/ (accessed 28 March 2018).

29 The attempt to justify restrictions on Muslim women's dress in the name of French secularism, or even feminism, hark back of course to the longstanding volatile debate about veiling. For an excellent overview and brilliant interpretation of this debate see Joan Scott, 2007, *The Politics of the Veil* (Princeton: Princeton University Press).

30 Ben Quinn, 2016, 'French Police make Woman Remove Clothing on Nice Beach Following Burkini Ban', *The Guardian*, 24 August; www.theguardian. com/world/2016/aug/24/ french-police-make-woman- remove-burkini-on-nice-beach (accessed 28 March 2018).

31 Quoted in Romaissaa Benzizoune, 2016, 'At the Beach in My Burkini', *New York Times*, 26 August; www.nytimes.com/ 2016/08/28/opinion/sunday/at- the-beach-in-my-burkini.html (accessed 28 March 2018).

32 Quoted in Anon., 2016, 'Interdiction des burkinis: la justice conforte l'arrêté de la mairie de Cannes', *Le Monde*, 13 August; www.lemonde.fr/ societe/article/2016/08/13/ le-tribunal-administratif- valide-l-arrete-municipal- bannissant-le-burkini-a- cannes_4982397_3224. html#2h4PGyIS62ZFSHYU.99 (accessed 28 March 2018).

33 Quoted in Anon., 2016, 'France Corsica Brawl: Mayor Bans Burkinis Amid Tensions', *BBC. com*, 15 August; www.bbc.com/ news/world-europe- 37082637 (accessed 28 March 2018).

34 Anon., 2016, 'Nicolas Sarkozy: La République a trop reculé,' *Le Figaro*, 24 August; www. lefigaro.fr/politique/2016/08/24/ 01002-20160824ARTFIG00249- nicolas-sarkozy-la-republique- a-trop-recule.php (accessed 15 April 2018).

35 A spokesperson for the CCIF called the burkini ban evidence of 'a hysterical political Islamophobia that pits citizens against one another'. Quoted in Angelique Chrisafis, 2016, 'French PM supports local bans on burkinis', *The Guardian*, 17 August; www.theguardian.com/ world/2016/aug/17/french-pm- supports-local-bans-burkinis (accessed 28 March 2018).

36 This form of preventive explosion can be understood as a symbolic or metaphoric version of the airport security practice of blowing up abandoned suitcases: in both cases, controlled explosions represent attempts to forestall bigger, more serious ones.

37 Quoted in Alissa J. Rubin, 2016, 'Fighting for the Soul of France, More Towns Ban a Bathing Suit: The Burkini', *New York Times*, 17 August; www.nytimes. com/2016/08/18/world/europe/ fighting-for-the-soul-of-france- more-towns-ban-a-bathing- suit-the-burkini.html (accessed 28 March 2018).

38 On Bardot's symbolic importance to France and her selection as the first 'celebrity' Marianne, see Ginette Vincendeau, 2000, *Stars and Stardom in French Cinema* (London & New York: Continuum), p. 36.

39 Hugo Martin, 2014, 'Full Body Scanners Pulled from Airports Get Use in Prisons', *Los Angeles Times*, 25 May; www.latimes. com/business/la-fi-fullbody- scanners-airports-prisons- 20140523-story.html (accessed 28 March 2018).

40 In 2013, bowing to complaints about privacy concerns, the United States pulled the X-ray scanners, replacing them in many places with millimeter wave scanners, which produce more generic, less graphic, bodily outlines. Dara Continenza, 2015, 'Can the TSA See You Naked?', *Smartertravel.com*, 18 February; www.smartertravel. com/ 2015/02/18/can-the-tsa- see-you-naked/ (accessed 28 March 2018).

41 See David Kravets, 2012, 'Homeland Security Concedes Airport Body Scanner Vulnerabilities', *Wired*, 7 May; www.wired.com/2012/05/

body-scanner-vulnerabilities/ (accessed 28 March 2018). See also Anon., 2013, 'At Last! Controversial Naked Image Body Scanners to be Removed from US Airports', *Daily Mail*, 13 January; www.dailymail. co.uk/news/article-2264568/ Federal-government-remove-controversial-naked-image-body-scanners-airports-passengers-privacy-concerns. html (accessed 28 March 2018).

42 See Kravets 2012.

43 I see this techno-surveillance culture as being in line with mandatory ultrasound laws in the case of abortions (some American states require women to view uterine ultrasounds before proceeding with the procedure), for example, wherein we find the general expectation that women's bodies be rendered transparent, their flesh dissolved technologically into a window through which the state may peer.

44 See Amy de la Haye, 2012, *A to Z of Style* (New York: Harry Abrams).

45 Vanessa Friedman, 2015, 'The Met Gala: A Red Carpet Review', *New York Times*, 6 May; www. nytimes.com/2015/05/06/ fashion/the-met-gala-a-red-carpet-review.html (accessed 28 March 2018).

46 Quoted in Faran Krentcil, 2017, 'Kendall Jenner Wore 85,000 Crystals Held Together by a Piece of String to the Met Gala', *Elle*, 1 May; www.elle.com/ fashion/celebrity-style/news/ a44952/kendall-jenner-naked-dress/ (accessed 28 March 2018).

47 In Alex Gilvarry's 2012 novel, *From the Memoirs of a Non-Enemy Combatant* (New York: Penguin), a fashion designer – entangled in a terrorist plot – designs a mesh, see-through, crystal-embellished 'haute couture burqa', a garment ironically

combining the perceived provocation of modest Islamic dress (the fear of 'otherness', the fear of what lies beneath) and the erotic, 'bombshell' provocation of conventional western 'naked dresses'.

48 Leslie Camhi, 2017, 'The Great Bust-Up,' American *Vogue*, vol. 207, no. 5 (May), pp. 202–3, 228–9.

6 Insurgent Trend: The Popularity of the Keffiyeh

1 The keffiyeh is a headdress traditionally worn by Arab men in arid regions. Made in cotton or a wool/cotton mix, the square piece of fabric is secured to the head by an agal. The keffiyeh has a number of variants, including the 'hatta', a similar headdress or veil traditionally worn by women, but in a very different way. Early examples were of plain fabric but the dog-tooth pattern became popular after the 1930s with some regional variance in colour.

2 Daniel Miller, 1998, 'Why some things matter', *Material Cultures* (Chicago: University of Chicago Press), p. 6.

3 Sophie Woodward and Tom Fisher, 2014, 'Fashioning through materials: material culture, materiality and processes of materialization', *Critical Studies in Fashion and Beauty*, vol. 5, no. 1, p. 16.

4 Samih K. Farsoun, 2004, *Culture and Customs of the Palestinians* (Connecticut: Greenwood Press), p. 52.

5 Farsoun 2004, pp. 52–3.

6 Rosemary Sayigh, 1979, *Palestinians: From Peasants to Revolutionaries* (London: Zed Books), pp. 44–5.

7 Ted Swedenburg, 2003, *Memories of Revolt: The 1936–1939 Rebellion and*

the Palestinian National Past (Fayetteville: Arkansas University Press), p. 32.

8 Swedenburg 2003, p. 32.

9 'Troops Comb Jerusalem', *Belfast Newsletter*, 20 October 1938, p. 7.

10 Robin H. Martin, 2007, *Palestine Betrayed: A British Palestine Policeman's Memoirs, 1936–1948* (Ringwood, UK: Seglawi Press), p. 43.

11 Raymond F. Betts, 1998, *Decolonization*, 2nd ed. (London: Routledge), p. 55.

12 Ted Swedenburg, 1991, 'Popular Memory and the Palestinian National Past', in Jay O'Brien and William Roseberry (eds), *Golden Ages, Dark Ages: Imagining the Past in Anthropology and History* (Berkeley: University of California Press), p. 163.

13 Image found in Sarah Graham-Brown, 1988, *Images of Women: The Portrayal of Women in Photography of the Middle East 1860–1950* (London: Quartet Books), p. 233. She in turn found the photograph published in *The Arab Women and the Palestine Question* (proceedings of a conference of Eastern women), Cairo, 15–18 October 1938. Also mentioned by Ted Swedenburg in Swedenburg 2003.

14 Raj Desai and Harry Eckstein, 1990, 'Insurgency: The Transformation of Peasant Rebellion', *World Politics*, vol. 42, no. 4, pp. 441–65.

15 Sherry Lowrance, 2012, 'Nationalism without Nation: State-building in early twentieth-century Palestine', *Middle East Critique*, vol. 21, no. 1, pp. 81–99.

16 UN Resolution 181, 29 November 1947.

17 Swedenburg 2003, p. 182.

18 Ted Swedenburg, 1990, 'The Palestinian Peasant as National Signifier', *Anthropological Quarterly*, vol. 63, no. 1, p. 20.

19 *For the Land – Palestine*, 1981, poster designed by Ismail Shammout (1930–2006). Fatah (Palestinian National Liberation Movement) Collection: American University of Beirut / The Palestine Poster Project Archives; www.palestineposterproject. org/poster/for-the-land-palestine.

20 *Time*, 13 December 1968, front cover.

21 Farsoun 2004, p. 53.

22 It has only been through the work done by artists, activists and filmmakers that images and film footage have re-emerged to show what Arab rebels of both genders wore in the past. See Rona Sela's books and her 2017 documentary film *Looted and Hidden: Palestinian Archives in Israel*.

23 Stuart Hall and Tony Jefferson (eds), 1976, *Resistance through Rituals: Youth Subcultures in Post-War Britain* (London: Routledge).

24 Dick Hebdige, 1979, *Subculture: The Meaning of Style* (London: Routledge).

25 Caroline Evans, 1997, 'Dreams That Only Money Can Buy … Or, The Shy Tribe in Flight from Discourse', *Fashion Theory*, vol. 1, no. 2, pp. 169–88.

26 Jaafar Alloul, 2016, 'Signs of Visual Resistance in Palestine: Unsettling the Settler-Colonial Matrix, *Middle East Critique*, vol. 25, no. 1, pp. 41–2.

27 Ignor Kopytoff, 1986, 'The cultural biography of things: commoditization as process', in Arjun Appadurai, *The Social Life of Things: Commodities in Cultural Perspective* (Cambridge: Cambridge University Press), p. 90.

28 Kibum Kim, 'Where Some See Fashion, Others See Politics', *New York Times*, 11 February 2007.

29 Matt Davies and Simon Philpott, 2012, 'Militarization and Popular

Culture', in Kostas Gouliamos and Christos Kassimeris (eds), *The Marketing of War in the Age of Neo-Militarism* (London: Routledge), pp. 42–59.

30 Charlie Porter, 2001, 'What a riot', *The Guardian*, 6 July.

31 Nick Rees-Roberts, 2015, 'Raf Simons and Interdisciplinary Fashion from Post-Punk to Neo-Modern', *Fashion Theory*, 19:1, p. 20.

32 Nashwa Salem, 2008, 'Transnational Resistance or Cultural Exotica? Interrogating the Multicultural Accommodation of the Kufiya', *Borderlands*, vol. 7, no. 3, pp. 7–10.

33 Rachel Shabi, 2008, 'On trend? Check', *The Guardian*, 1 November.

34 Jessica Steinberg, 2015, 'When the keffiyeh turned Couture', *Times of Israel*, 22 October.

35 Vera Eccarius-Kelly, 2010, 'Nationalism, Ethnic Rap and the Kurdish Diaspora', *Peace Review*, vol. 22, no. 4, p. 425.

36 Jan Nederveen Pieterse, 1995, 'Aesthetics of Power: Time and Body Politics', in Annelise Moors et al. (eds) *Discourse and Palestine: Power, Text and Context* (Amsterdam: Spinhuis), p. 67.

37 'From Hebron, Palestinian scarf resists ... Chinese competition', *YNet Magazine*, 25 April 2015; Silvia Boarini, 2015, 'The last keffiyeh factory in Palestine', *Middle East Eye*, 23 July.

38 Nadine Dahan, 2017, 'Topshop pulls "keffiyeh playsuit" after row about cultural theft', *Middle East Eye*, 6 April.

8 Dressing the Opposition

1 Michael Deacon, 2015, 'God Save the Queen, but Lord help scruffy Jeremy Corbyn', *Daily Telegraph*, 15 September 2015; www.telegraph.co.uk/news/

politics/Jeremy_Corbyn/11867374/ God-Save-the-Queen-but-Lord-help-scruffy-Jeremy-Corbyn. html (accessed 15 May 2018).

2 Anthony Sullivan, 2015, 'Fashion', in Daniel T. Cook and Michael J. Ryan (eds), *The Wiley Blackwell Encyclopedia of Consumption and Consumer Studies* (Chichester: Wiley Blackwell).

3 Joanne Entwistle, 2000, *The Fashioned Body: Fashion, Dress and Modern Social Theory* (Cambridge: Polity Press), p. 40.

4 Carol Tulloch, 2010, 'Style – Fashion – Dress: From Black to Post-Black', *Fashion Theory*, vol. 14, no. 3, pp. 273–303.

5 George Orwell, 2001 [1937], *The Road To Wigan Pier* (London: Penguin), p. 157.

6 For more on this see Anthony Sullivan, 2016, 'Marx: Fashion and Capitalism', in Agnès Rocamora and Anneke Smelik (eds), *Thinking Through Fashion: The Key Theorists* (London: I.B. Tauris).

7 Entwistle 2000, p. 106.

8 J.C. Flügel, 1950 [1930], *The Psychology of Clothes* (London: Hogarth Press), p. 23.

9 Valerie Steele, 1985, 'The Social and Political Significance of Macaroni Fashion', *Costume*, vol. 19, no. 1, pp. 1–51.

10 Christopher Breward, 2016, *The Suit: Form, Function and Style* (London: Reaktion Books), Kindle ed., 1047.

11 Anne Hollander, 1994, *Sex and Suits: The Evolution of Modern Dress* (New York: Kodansha), p. 3.

12 Christopher Breward, 1999, *The Hidden Consumer: Masculinities, Fashion and City Life 1860–1914* (Manchester: Manchester University Press).

13 Breward 2016, Kindle ed., 1047.

14 Breward 1999.

15 Hollander 1994, p. 22.

16 Michel Foucault, 1984 [1978], *The History of Sexuality: An Introduction* (London: Peregrine Publishing), p. 95.

17 For more on this see Jane Tynan, 2016, 'Michael Foucault: Fashioning the Body Politic', in Agnès Rocamora and Anneke Smelik (eds), *Thinking Through Fashion: The Key Theorists* (London: I.B. Tauris).

18 Breward 2016, Kindle ed., 1031.

19 Breward 2016, Kindle ed., 1222.

20 Peter McNeil, 2018, *Pretty Gentlemen: Macaroni Men and the Eighteenth-Century Fashion World* (New Haven, CT & London: Yale University Press), p. 151.

21 McNeil 2018, p. 92.

22 McNeil 2018, p. 95.

23 George Otto Trevelyan, 1880, *The Early History of Charles James Fox* (London: Longmans, Green and Co.), p. 64, in McNeil 2018, p. 93.

24 Anon., 1807, *The Life of The Right Honorable Charles James Fox, Late Principal Secretary of State for Foreign Affairs* [etc.] (London: Albion Press), p. 18, in McNeil 2018, p. 94.

25 As Brooks argues, British protectionism and trade policy blocked Indian industrialisation in a process repeated across the colonised world. See Andrew Brooks, 2015, *Clothing Poverty: The Hidden World of Fast Fashion and Second-hand Clothes* (London: Zed Books).

26 Breward 2016, Kindle ed., 829.

27 J.B. Paoletti, 1985, 'Ridicule and Role Models as Factors in American Men's Fashion Change 1880–1910', *Costume*, 19 (1), pp. 121–34 in Breward 2016, Kindle ed., 253.

28 Breward 2016, Kindle ed., 845.

29 Breward 2016, Kindle ed., 1221.

30 See, for example, McKenzie Wark, 1991, 'Fashioning the Future: Fashion, Clothing, and the Manufacturing of Post-Fordist Culture', *Cultural Studies*, vol. 5, no. 1, pp. 61–76.

31 For more on power dressing, and Molloy's role in this, see Joanne Entwistle, 2007, '"Power Dressing" and the Construction

of The Career Woman', in Malcolm Barnard (ed.), *Fashion Theory: A Reader* (London: Routledge).

32 Breward 2016, Kindle ed., 1318.

33 Francis Fukuyama, 1992, *The End of History and the Last Man* (London: Penguin).

34 Michael Roberts, 2009, *The Great Recession: profit cycles, economic crisis, a Marxist view*, Internet Archive; archive.org/ details/TheGreatRecession. ProfitCyclesEconomicCrisis AMarxistView (accessed 30 April 2018).

35 David Harvey, 2005, *A Brief History of Neoliberalism* (Oxford: Oxford University Press), p. 19.

36 Ashifa Kassam, 2014, '"Yes he can!" How Spanish indignado Pablo Iglesias aims to use a wave of protest to build "a decent country"', *The Guardian*, 5 July 2014; www.theguardian. com/world/2014/jul/06/pablo-iglesias-indignado-podemos-spain (accessed 30 April 2018).

37 In the 2014 Euro elections Podemos came from nowhere to win 1.2 million votes. See Andy Brown, 2016, 'Reassessing Podemos', *International Socialism*, no. 150; isj.org.uk/reassessing-podemos/ (accessed 30 April 2018).

38 For more on oppositional dress as anti-fashion see Elizabeth Wilson, 2003 [1985], *Adorned in Dreams: Fashion and Modernity* (London: I.B. Tauris), pp. 179–206.

39 Breward 2016, Kindle ed., 1857.

40 For an accessible introduction to Gramsci's ideas, and his theorisation of how political leadership or hegemony can be contested and won beyond the narrow conventional political sphere, see Steve Jones, 2006, *Antonio Gramsci* (London: Routledge).

41 Manel Barriere, Andy Durgan and Sam Robson, 2015, 'The Challenge of Podemos', *International Socialism*, no. 145;

isj.org.uk/the-challenge-of-podemos/ (accessed 30 April 2018).

42 For more on the post-Chávez crisis in Venezuela see 'How Venezuela's crisis developed and worsened', BBC News, 21 May 2018; www.bbc.co.uk/news/world-latin-america-36319877 (accessed 5 June 2018).

43 Chantal Mouffe interview transcript, translated by David Broder, available at www.versobooks.com/blogs/3341-chantal-mouffe-we-urgently-need-to-promote-a-left-populism (accessed 3 June 2018).

44 Ernesto Laclau and Chantal Mouffe, 1985, Hegemony and Socialist Strategy (London: Verso Books).

45 Although he has now been accused of betraying Podemos's principles over a €600,000 house, purchased with his partner Irene Montero. See Sam Jones, 2018, 'Spain's Podemos leader to face party vote over luxury house purchase', The Guardian, 20 May 2018; www.theguardian.com/world/2018/may/20/spain-podemos-leader-pablo-iglesias-no-confidence-vote-anti-austerity-principles-house-purchase (accessed 5 June 2018).

46 Brown 2016, p. 110.

47 For more on the issues raised by celebrity and politics see Jessica Evans and David Hesmondhalgh (eds), 2005, Understanding Media, Understanding Celebrity (Oxford: Oxford University Press).

48 Nicos Poulantzas, 1978, State, Power, Socialism (London: New Left Books).

49 Lucy Rogers and Nassos Stylianou, 2015, 'How bad are things for the people of Greece?', BBC News, 16 July 2015; www.bbc.co.uk/news/world-europe-33507802 (accessed 30 April 2018).

50 'Greece paralysed by first general strike for months',

BBC News, 27 November 2014; www.bbc.co.uk/news/world-europe-30223547 (accessed 15 May 2018).

51 Despite the party's initial programme rejecting austerity, Tsipras called a referendum in July 2015 on whether or not to undertake a further round of public spending cuts to secure a bail-out from the Troika. The overwhelming 'Oxi', or 'No', vote was ignored.

52 Vanessa Friedman, 2015, 'The Wardrobe of Politics of Greece's New Prime Minister', New York Times, 4 February 2015; www.nytimes.com/2015/02/05/fashion/the-wardrobe-politics-of-greeces-new-prime-minister.html (accessed 30 April 2018).

53 Farid Chenoune, 1993, A History of Men's Fashion (Paris: Flammarion).

54 Friedman 2015.

55 Jean Baudrillard, 1998 [1970], The Consumer Society (London: Sage Publishing), p. 87.

56 Yanis Varoufakis, 2015, 'How I became an Erratic Marxist', The Guardian, 18 February; www.theguardian.com/news/2015/feb/18/yanis-varoufakis-how-i-became-an-erratic-marxist (accessed 30 April 2018).

57 Yanis Varoufakis, 2013, Talking to My Daughter About the Economy: A Brief History of Capitalism (London: Bodley Head), p. 124.

58 Imogen Fox, 2015, 'Greek finance minister Yanis Varoufakis goes casual at number 10', The Guardian, 2 February; www.theguardian.com/fashion/fashion-blog/2015/feb/02/greek-finance-minister-yanis-varoufakis-on-how-not-to-dress-for-a-meeting (accessed 15 May 2018).

59 Ambrose Evans-Pritchard, 2015, 'Greece's rock-star finance minister Yanis Varoufakis defies ECB's drachma threats', Daily Telegraph, 3 February;

www.telegraph.co.uk/finance/economics/11388263/Greeces-rock-star-finance-minister-Yanis-Varoufakis-defies-ECBs-drachma-threats.html (accessed 30 April 2018).

60 Foucault 1984 [1978], p. 95.

61 Breward 2016, Kindle ed., 287.

62 Corbyn helped found the Stop the War Coalition, which organised Britain's biggest peacetime demonstration against Tony Blair's decision to invade Iraq in 2003 alongside the United States.

63 'Scruffy Jeremy Corbyn winds up Tories in 1984', BBC Newsnight, 18 August 2015; www.youtube.com/watch?v=wZsYvkTw4Rg (accessed 5 June 2018).

64 Boris Johnson, 2017, 'Don't feel sorry for that mutton-headed old mugwump Jeremy Corbyn – he poses an enormous threat to our country if he gets into No 10', The Sun, 26 April.

65 Deacon 2015.

66 The Times, 19 April 2017.

67 Mark L. Thomas, 2017, 'After the surge: Corbyn and the road ahead', International Socialism, no. 156, p. 115.

68 Dealing effectively with damaging accusations of anti-Semitism in the Labour Party, orienting Labour electorally given the divisive 'Brexit' referendum vote, and facing a Parliamentary Party and political establishment hostile to his left wing politics were/are amongst his many challenges.

69 See, for example, Joshua Chaffin, 2018, 'Can Jeremy Corbyn restore Labour's working class vote?', Financial Times, 3 June; www.ft.com/content/5822e600-5f55-11e8-ad91-e01af256df68 (accessed 5 June 2018).

70 Harry Wallop, 2014, 'Why a hairdresser is so important in the salons of power', Daily Telegraph, 7 January; www.

telegraph.co.uk/news/politics/david-cameron/10555890/Why-a-hairdresser-is-so-important-in-the-salons-of-power.html (accessed 30 April 2018).

71 John Crace, 2016, 'David Cameron lets his mask slip with "do up your tie" jibe at Corbyn', The Guardian, 24 February; https://www.theguardian.com/politics/2016/feb/24/cameron-strays-from-the-script-with-corbyn-do-up-your-tie-jibe (accessed 18 June 2018).

72 Jon Stone, 2017, 'Jeremy Corbyn says he will break political rules to overturn the "rigged system"', The Independent, 20 April; www.independent.co.uk/news/uk/politics/jeremy-corbyn-snap-general-election-speech-overturn-rigged-system-break-rules-cosy-cartel-a7691676.html (accessed 20 June 2018).

73 Dick Pels, 2003, 'Aesthetic Representation and Political Style: Re-Balancing Identity and Difference in Media Democracy', in D. Pels and John Corner (eds), Media and the Restyling of Politics: Consumerism, Celebrity and Cynicism (London: Sage Publishing), p. 58.

74 Walter Benjamin, 1992, Illuminations, ed. Hannah Arendt (London: Fontana).

75 Pels 2003, p. 58.

76 Joshua Meyrowitz, 1985, No Sense of Place: The Impact of Electronic Media on Social Behaviour (New York & Oxford: Oxford University Press).

77 Pels 2003, p. 58.

78 Ibid.

79 Ibid.

80 Pels 2003, p. 59.

81 John Crace, 2017, I Maybot: The Rise and Fall (London: Guardian Books/Faber and Faber).

82 Karl Marx, 1993 [1857], Grundrisse (London: Penguin).

83 Thomas Hobbes, 2017, 'Shock General Election result shows

the importance of authenticity and youth targeting', *Marketing Week*, 9 June; www.marketingweek.com/2017/06/09/general-election-aftermath-labour-conservatives-corbyn (accessed 30 April 2018).

84 Liam Young, 2018, *Rise: How Jeremy Corbyn Inspired the Young to Create a New Socialism* (London: Simon and Schuster), Kindle ed., 925.

85 Roland Barthes, 1990 [1983], *The Fashion System* (Berkeley: University of California Press).

86 For a clear overview of both the productivity and logocentric limitations of Barthes's work on fashion see Part Two of Paul Jobling, 1999, *Fashion Spreads: Word and Image in Fashion Photography since 1980* (Oxford: Berg Publishers).

87 Following disappointing results in the June 2016 elections the two men fell out over whether to take Podemos further left or towards the centre. For more on this see Guy Hedgecoe, 2017, 'Podemos leaders battle for party's soul in search of winning formula', *The Irish Times*, 12 January; www.irishtimes.com/news/world/europe/podemos-leaders-battle-for-party-s-soul-in-search-of-winning-formula-1.2933076 (accessed 5 June 2018).

88 Robert Shrimsley, 2018, 'Conservative predictions of Jeremy Corbyn's decline are premature', *Financial Times*, 11 June; www.ft.com/content/56b5ba20-6cb3-11e8-92d3-6c13e5c92914 (accessed 13 June 2018).

9 Three Pairs of Khaki Trousers

1 For this essay, I received funding from National Research Foundation through the Archive and Public Culture Research Initiative, University of Cape Town.

2 In a further sense of removal, I have taken these three objects out of the archival framing of the museum to further interrogate their critical potential, thus the objects are twice removed.

3 See Carolyn Hamilton, 2011, 'Backstory, Biography, and the Life of the James Stuart Archive', in *History in Africa*, African Studies Association, vol. 38, pp. 319–41, p. 327.

4 Apartheid was a radical system of segregation, discrimination and oppression based on the grounds of race that existed in South Africa between 1948 and 1994.

5 Khusu was identified as 'Basutho' and worked as a chef in a hotel in Cape Town.

6 Tribal or ethnic categorisations have had damaging impacts on questions of identity politics, land-rights and heritage practices and concepts of material culture. See Carolyn Hamilton and Nessa Leibhammer (eds), 2017, *Tribing and Untribing the Archive: Identity and the Material Record in Southern KwaZulu-Natal in the Late Independent and Colonial Period* (Pietermaritzburg: University of KwaZulu Natal Press).

7 See Robyn-Leigh Cedras, 2016, *In the Halls of History: The Making and Unmaking of the Life-Casts at the Ethnography Galleries of the Iziko South African Museum*, M.Phil Thesis, University of Cape Town.

8 Accession number SACHM82/406.

9 Lelong Immelman donated a selection of her father's clothing to the museum that included this pair of trousers, a safari suit, shirts, a vest, ties, socks and a pair of jogging shorts.

10 Sweet-Orr & Lybro opened in 1931 in Elsies River, Cape Town, manufacturing workwear trousers and overalls that included the international brand Lybro.

11 Beaded artefacts in all forms entered ethnographic collections from the late nineteenth century. See Anitra Nettleton, 2014, 'Women, Beadwork and Bodies: The Making and Marking of Migrant Liminality in South Africa, 1850–1950', in *African Studies*, vol. 73 (3), pp. 314–64, and John M. MacKenzie, 2009, 'Museums and Empire: Making and Marking of Migrant Liminality in South Africa, 1850–1950', in African Studies, vol. 73 (3), pp. 314–64, and John M. MacKenzie, 2009, *Museums and Empire: Natural History, Human Cultures and Colonial Identities* (Manchester: Manchester University Press). All four pairs of 'Xhosa' trousers were purchased from the South African beadwork collector and dealer Stephen Long.

12 Accession number SAM14394.

13 Sandra Klopper and Fiona Rankin-Smith, 2010, 'Migrant Workers, Production, and Fashion', in Joanne B. Eicher and Doran H. Ross (eds), *Encyclopedia of World Dress and Fashion Vol 1: Africa* (London: Berg Publishers), p. 530.

14 Nettleton 2014, pp. 351–2.

15 Material culture objects in ethnographic collections are largely registered in museums without details of makers and particularly of wearers, and the 'unknown' moniker is a common feature not only in South African museums but globally too.

11 'Thrown Away Like a Piece of Cloth'

1 Catie L'Heureux, 2016, 'Anna Wintour Is Sorry for Calling Yeezy "Migrant Chic"', *The Cut*, 15 April; www.thecut.com/2016/04/anna-wintour-apologizes-kanye-migrant-chic.html (accessed 6 May 2018).

2 The United Nations High Commissioner for Refugees (UNHCR) highlights the importance of making a clear distinction between the terms 'refugee' and 'migrant': refugees 'are persons fleeing armed conflict or persecution', whereas migrants 'choose to move not because of a direct threat of persecution or death, but mainly to improve their lives by finding work, or in some cases for education, family reunion, or other reasons.' According to the UNHCR, the majority of people arriving in Italy and Greece 'especially have been from countries mired in war or which otherwise are considered to be "refugee-producing" and for whom international protection is needed.' See Adrian Edwards, 2016, 'UNHCR viewpoint: "Refugee" or "migrant" – Which is right?', UNHCR website, 11 July; www.unhcr.org/uk/news/latest/2016/7/55df0e556/unhcr-viewpoint-refugee-migrant-right.html (accessed 7 May 2018).

3 Alexander Betts and Paul Collier, 2017, *Refuge: Transforming a Broken Refugee System* (New York: Oxford University Press), p. 2.

4 Betts and Collier 2017, p. 3.

5 Nicholas De Genova, 2013, 'Spectacles of migrant "illegality": the scene of exclusion, the obscene of inclusion', *Ethnic and Racial Studies*, vol. 36, no. 7, pp. 1180–98; doi: 10.1080/01419870.2013.783710 (accessed 6 May 2018).

6 Nicholas De Genova, 2016, 'The "Crisis" of the European Border Regime: Towards a Marxist Theory of Borders', *International Socialism*, vol. 150, p. 50. Emphasis in original.

7 Slavoj Žižek, 2016, *Against the Double Blackmail: Refugees, Terror and Other Troubles with the Neighbours* (London: Penguin), p. 6.

8 For an explanation of the term 'cheapened labour', see Cynthia Enloe, 2004, *The Curious Feminist: Searching for Women in a New Age of Empire* (Berkeley: University of California Press), p. 60.

9 Nancy Green, 1997, *Ready-to-Wear and Ready-to-Work: A Century of Industry and Immigrants in Paris and New York* (Durham, NC & London: Duke University Press), p. 139.

10 Danielle McMullan, 2016, 'What's changed for Syrian refugees in Turkish garment supply chains? 6 months on: A second survey & analysis of company action to address exploitation & abuse', *Business & Human Rights Resource Centre*, October; www.business-humanrights.org/sites/default/files/documents/Syrian%20Refugees%20In%20Turkey%20PUBLIC.PDF (accessed 25 May 2018).

11 Harry Braverman, 1998 [1974], *Labour and Monopoly Capital: The Degradation of Work in the Twentieth Century* (New York: Monthly Review Press), p. 96.

12 Michael Hardt and Antonio Negri, 2009, *Commonwealth* (Cambridge, MA: The Belknap Press of Harvard University Press), p. 333.

13 Karl Marx, 1990 [1867], *Capital. A Critical Analysis of Capitalist Production, London 1887* (Berlin: Dietz Verlag), p. 412. For a thorough discussion of the relevance of Marx's conceptual framework to fashion, see

Anthony Sullivan, 2016, 'Karl Marx: Fashion and Capitalism', in Agnès Rocamora and Anneke Smelik (eds), *Thinking through Fashion: A Guide to Key Theorists* (London & New York: I.B. Tauris), pp. 28–45.

14 Annie Phizacklea, 1990, *Unpacking the Fashion Industry: Gender, Racism, and Class in Production* (London & New York: Routledge), p. 23.

15 Phizacklea 1990, pp. 25–6, 111.

16 Andrew Godley, 1996, 'Immigrant Entrepreneurs and the Emergence of London's East End as an Industrial District', *London Journal*, vol. 21, no. 1, p. 38.

17 Godley 1996, pp. 39–42.

18 Beatrice Potter, 1903, 'The Tailoring Trade' and 'The Jewish Community (East London)', in Charles Booth (ed.), *Life and Labour of the People in London*, 1st series, vol. 4, ch. III, pp. 60–1, quoted in Godley 1996, p. 39.

19 D. Munby, *Industry and Planning in Stepney* (Oxford: Oxford University Press), p. 168, quoted in Andrew Godley, 1997, 'Introduction: The Development of the Clothing Industry: Technology and Fashion', *Textile History*, vol. 28, no. 1, p. 7.

20 Godley 1997, p. 7.

21 Green 1997, p. 159.

22 Green 1997, p. 150.

23 Ashley Armstrong, 2017, 'Leicester factories "ticking time bomb" as Asos and New Look join lobbying forces', *Telegraph*, 19 August; www.telegraph.co.uk/business/2017/08/19/leicester-factories-ticking-time-bomb-asos-new-look-join-lobbying/ (accessed 12 May 2018).

24 Jane Moyo, 2017, 'Media investigation into the Leicester garment trade: ETI response', Ethical Trading Initiative website, 23 January; www.ethicaltrade.org/blog/media-investigation-leicester-garment-trade-eti-response (accessed 12 May 2018).

25 Green 1997, pp. 170–87.

26 The term 'reserve army', before it was theorised by Karl Marx in Chapter 25, Section 3 of the first volume of *Capital* (see Marx 1990 [1867], p. 545), had been used by Friedrich Engels. For an evaluation of the importance of Engels's recognition of a reserve army as a permanently essential part of capitalism, see Eric Hobsbawm, 2011, *How to Change the World: Tales of Marx and Marxism* (New Haven, CT & London: Yale University Press), p. 94.

27 Friedrich Engels, 2010 [1845], *The Condition of the Working Class in England in 1844* (New York: Cambridge University Press), p. 90.

28 Engels 2010 [1845], p. 85.

29 Marx 1990 [1867], p. 547. Emphasis added.

30 David Harvey, 2017, *The Ways of the World* (London: Profile Books), p. 245.

31 Harvey 2017, p. 246.

32 Ipsita Chatterjee, 2014, *Displacement, Revolution, and the New Urban Condition: Theories and Case Studies* (New Delhi: Sage Publishing), pp. 57–8.

33 Tom Vickers, 2012, *Refugees, Capitalism and the British State: Implications for Social Workers, Volunteers and Activists* (London & New York: Routledge), p. 7.

34 De Genova 2016, p. 43.

35 De Genova 2016, p. 37.

36 Vickers 2012, p. 12.

37 Hardt and Negri 2009, p. xi.

38 UNHCR (United Nations Refugee Agency), 'Syria Regional Refugee Response'; data2.unhcr.org/en/situations/syria (last modified 10 May 2018).

39 Göç İdaresi Genel Müdürlüğü (Directorate General of Migration Management), 'Yıllara Göre Geçici Koruma Kapsamındaki Suriyeliler' (Syrians within the Scope of Temporary Protection by Years);

http://www.goc.gov.tr/icerik6/gecici-koruma_363_378_4713_icerik (last modified 26 April 2018).

40 McMullan 2016.

41 Frederik Johannisson, 2016, 'Hidden child labour: how Syrian refugees in Turkey are supplying Europe with fast fashion', *The Guardian*, 29 January; www.theguardian.com/sustainable-business/2016/jan/29/hidden-child-labour-syrian-refugees-turkey-supplying-europe-fast-fashion (accessed 25 May 2018). In 2016, the net minimum wage in Turkey was 1,300.99 Turkish Liras (approx. £301 as of January 2016) per month. As of 2018, the net minimum wage is 1,603.12 (approx. £260 as of May 2018) per month.

42 Ertan Erol et al., 2017, *Suriyeli Sığınmacıların Türkiye'de Emek Piyasasına Dahil Olma Süreçleri ve Etkileri: İstanbul Tekstil Sektörü Örneği* (İstanbul: Birleşik Metal-İş Yayınları); www.academia.edu/34930885/Suriyeli_G%C3%B6%C3%A7men_Eme%C4%9Fi_%C4%B0stanbul_Tekstil_Sekt%C3%B6r%C3%BC_Ara%C5%9Ft%C4%B1rmas% (accessed 25 May 2018).

43 See Serdar M. Değirmencioğlu et al., 2010, 'Extreme forms of child labour in Turkey', in Gary Craig (ed.), *Child Slavery Now: A Contemporary Reader* (Bristol: The Policy Press), pp. 215–27.

44 Didem Tali, 2016, 'As refugees pour in, child labour booms in Turkey', *Aljazeera America*, 4 January; america.aljazeera.com/articles/2016/1/4/as-refugees-pour-in-child-labor-booms-in-turkey.html (accessed 26 May 2018).

45 Darragh MacIntyre, 2016, 'The kids who have to sew to survive', BBC *News*, 23 October; www.bbc.co.uk/news/business-37693173 (accessed 30 May 2018).

231

46 Burak Coşan, 2017, 'Foreign child workers exploited in sweatshops in Istanbul's Küçükpazar', *Hürriyet Daily News*, 20 February; www.hurriyetdailynews.com/foreign-child-workers-exploited-in-sweatshops-in-istanbuls-kucukpazar-109944 (accessed 30 May 2018).

47 Tali 2016.

48 Patrick Kingsley, 2016, 'From war to sweatshop for Syria's child refugees', *The Guardian*, 6 May; www.theguardian.com/world/2016/may/06/war-to-sweatshop-for-child-refugees (accessed 25 May 2018).

49 Ministry of Economy, Republic of Turkey, 2018, 'Clothing Industry'; www.economy.gov.tr/portal/content/conn/UCM/uuid/dDocName:EK-257464 (accessed 2 June 2018).

50 ITKIB Apparel R&D Department, 2018, 'General Outlook to Turkish Apparel Sector in 2017', January; www.ihkib.org.tr/fp-icerik/ia/d/2018/01/29/general-outlook-to-turkish-apparel-sector-in-2017-201801291605550383-6367D.pdf (accessed 2 June 2018).

51 Ministry of Economy, Republic of Turkey, 2018.

52 Saniye Dedeoglu, 2008, *Women Workers in Turkey: Global Industrial Production in Istanbul* (London & New York: Tauris Academic Studies), pp. 50–60.

53 Nebahat Tokatli et al., 2011, 'The Clothing Industry in Istanbul in the Era of Globalisation and Fast Fashion', *Urban Studies*, vol. 48, no. 6, pp. 1206–12.

54 Didem Danış, 2016, 'Konfeksiyon Sektöründe Küresel Bağlantılar: Göçmen İşçiler, Sendikalar ve Küresel Çalışma Örgütleri' (Global Dealings in Apparel Manufacturing: Migrant Workers, Trade Unions and Global Labour Initiatives),

Alternatif Politika, vol. 8, no. 3, pp. 571–4.

55 Dasha Afanasieva, 2016, 'In Turkish sweatshops, Syrian children sew to survive', *Reuters Investigates*, 26 July; www.reuters.com/investigates/special-report/europe-migrants-turkey-children/ (accessed 16 June 2018). See also Tali 2016.

56 Şehriban Kıraç, 2017, 'Suriyeliler olmasaydı raflar boş kalırdı', *Cumhuriyet*, 12 December; www.cumhuriyet.com.tr/haber/ekonomi/885029/Suriyeliler_olmasaydi_raflar_bos_kalirdi.html (accessed 16 June 2018).

57 Çalışma ve Sosyal Güvenlik Bakanlığı (The Ministry of Labour and Social Security), 2016, 'Yabancıların Çalışma İzinleri' (Work Permits of Foreigners); www.csgb.gov.tr/media/7315/yabancilarin-%C3%A7ali%C5%9Fma-%C4%B0z%C4%B0nler%C4%B0-2016.pdf (accessed 24 June 2018).

58 Emre E. Korkmaz, 2017, 'How do Syrian refugee workers challenge supply chain management in the Turkish garment industry?', Working paper published by the International Migration Institute (IMI), University of Oxford, 9 March, p. 5; www.imi.ox.ac.uk/publications/how-do-syrian-refugee-workers-challenge-supply-chain-management-in-the-turkish-garment-industry (accessed 24 June 2018).

59 Korkmaz 2017, p. 8.

60 Samentha Goethals and Emre E. Korkmaz, 2017, 'What's changed for Syrian refugees in Turkish garment supply chains? A survey & analysis of company action to address exploitation & abuse', *Business & Human Rights Resource Centre*, November, p. 13; www.business-humanrights.org/sites/default/files/

Syrian%20Refugess%20in%20Turkey_Public%5B2%5D.pdf (accessed 25 May 2018).

61 Andrew Brooks, 2015, *Clothing Poverty: The Hidden World of Fast Fashion and Second-Hand Clothes* (London: Zed Books), pp. 247–9.

62 Slavoj Žižek, 2008, *Violence* (London: Profile Books), p. 20.

63 Žižek 2008, p. 8.

64 Harvey 2017, p. 260.

65 Erol et al. 2017.

66 Adam Briggs, 2013, '"Capitalism's Favourite Child": The Production of Fashion', in Stella Bruzzi and Pamela Church Gibson (eds), *Fashion Cultures Revisited: Theories, Explorations and Analysis* (London & New York: Routledge), p. 194.

67 Darragh MacIntyre, 2016, 'Undercover: The Refugees Who Make Our Clothes', BBC One *Panorama*, 24 October.

68 Brooks 2015, p. 245.

69 Hardt and Negri 2009, p. xi.

70 Brooks 2015, p. 250. I borrow the term 'sweatshop regime' from Alessandra Mezzadri, 2017, *The Sweatshop Regime: Labouring Bodies, Exploitation, and Garments Made in India* (New York: Cambridge University Press).

71 Tokatli 2011, p. 1212.

72 Hardt and Negri 2009, pp. 332–3.

Contributors

Djurdja Bartlett is Reader in Histories and Cultures of Fashion at the London College of Fashion, University of the Arts London (UAL), where she directs Transnational Fashion Hub. She is also member of the research centre for Transnational Art, Identity and Nation (TrAIN, UAL).

Serkan Delice is Lecturer and Research Coordinator in Cultural and Historical Studies at the London College of Fashion, UAL.

Rhonda Garelick is Professor of Art, Design, History and Theory and Associate Dean of Fashion at Parsons School of Design, New School University, New York.

Erica de Greef is Senior Curator of Fashion at Zeitz MOCAA, Cape Town.

Jin Li Lim is a historian of modern China and an adjunct lecturer in Cultural and Contextual Studies at LASALLE College of the Arts, Singapore.

Gabi Scardi is an art critic, curator and writer.

Anthony Sullivan is Senior Lecturer in Cultural and Historical Studies at the London College of Fashion, UAL.

Carol Tulloch, writer and curator, is Professor of Dress, Diaspora and Transnationalism at UAL, based at Chelsea College of Arts, She is also a member of TrAIN, UAL, and an Honorary Senior Research Fellow at the Victoria and Albert Museum, London.

Jane Tynan is Senior Lecturer in Cultural and Historical Studies at Central Saint Martins, UAL.

Barbara Vinken is Professor of French and Comparative Literature at Ludwig-Maximilians-Universität, Munich.

Image Credits

Yale University Press would like to thank the copyright holders for granting permission to reproduce works illustrated in this publication.

Every effort has been made to contact the holders of copyright material, and any omissions will be corrected in future editions if the publisher is notified in writing.

Credits for images are given below (page numbers refer to captions, as applicable).

Front cover Courtesy of Missoni
Page 2 See page 50, fig. 21
Pages 4–5 (Left to right)
see page 50, fig. 20; page 81, fig. 36; page 146 (no fig.); page 211, fig. 79
Page 7 See page 154 (no fig.)
Page 9 Fig. 1 Dan Kitwood/ Getty Images News
Page 11 Fig. 2 © Victoria and Albert Museum, museum no. T.945-1994, Given by Elizabeth Wilson
Page 17 Fig. 3 Wiki Commons, Public Domain
Page 19 Fig. 4 Courtesy of Szabo Ervin Library, Budapest
Page 20 Fig. 5 Courtesy of Russian State Library, Moscow
Fig. 6 Courtesy of Russian State Library, Moscow
Page 21 Fig. 7 Courtesy of Donghua University Library, Shanghai
Page 22 Fig. 8 Courtesy of *Vogue Polska*
Page 25 Fig. 9 Victor Boyko/Getty Images Entertainment
Page 29 Fig. 11 Courtesy of Musée de l'Histoire vivante, Paris
Page 34 Fig. 12 Courtesy of Papaya Dog/M.Tomash/INRUSSIA
Page 35 Figs 13 & 14 Kay-Paris Fernandes/Getty Images Entertainment
Page 39 Fig. 15 Courtesy of VETEMENTS
Page 41 Fig. 16 Courtesy of Ana and Danko Steiner
Page 44 Fig. 17 Robert Beck/Getty Images/Sports Illustrated Collection
Page 47 Fig. 18 Courtesy of Tyler Mitchell/Art Partner, New York
Page 48 Fig. 19 Courtesy of Mary

Boone Gallery, New York
Page 50 Fig. 20 Wiki Commons, Public Domain (see also page 4) Fig. 21 Courtesy of Alex Chatelain (see also page 2)
Page 52 Fig. 22 Courtesy of Norman Parkinson Archive/Iconic Images
Page 55 Fig. 23 Courtesy of Osman Örsal
Page 56 Fig. 24 Courtesy of the artist, Bahia Shehab
Page 57 Fig. 25: Reuters (see also back cover)
Page 61 Fig. 26 Metropolitan Museum of Art, New York, acc. no. 32.25.12-c, Rogers Fund 1932
Page 63 Fig. 27 Metropolitan Museum of Art, New York, acc. no. 32.25.12-c, Rogers Fund 1932
Page 64 Fig. 28 Victoria and Albert Museum, London, museum no. T.57 to B-1962, Given by Mrs B. M. Bohener
Page 68 Fig. 29 Metropolitan Museum of Art, New York, acc. no. C.1.69.14.12a, b, Gift of Mary Pierrepont Beckwith 1969
Page 73 Fig. 30 Li Zhensheng/ Contact Press Images
Page 75 Fig. 31 Li Zhensheng/ Contact Press Images
Page 77 Fig. 32 *Zhongguo huabao* (*China Pictorial*)
Fig. 33 *Zhongguo huabao* (*China Pictorial*)
Fig. 34 *Zhongguo huabao* (*China Pictorial*)
Page 78 Fig. 35 Private Collection
Page 81 Fig. 36 Yang Kelin, ed., *Wenhua da gaming bowu guan* (*Museum of the Cultural Revolution*) (Hong Kong: Dongfang chubanshe, 1995) (see also page 5)
Page 82 Fig. 37 *Zhongguo huabao* (*China Pictorial*)
Page 83 Fig. 38 *Zhongguo huabao* (*China Pictorial*)
Page 85 Fig. 39 © Syd Shelton
Page 87 Fig. 40 David Fenton/ Getty Images
Page 90 Fig. 41 © Syd Shelton
Page 91 Fig. 42 © Syd Shelton
Fig. 43 © Syd Shelton
Page 94 Fig. 44 © Syd Shelton
Page 95 Fig. 45 © Syd Shelton

Page 105 Fig. 47 John F. Kennedy Archives, Boston
Page 109 Fig. 48 Associated Press/ Shutterstock
Page 114 Fig. 49 Courtesy of the artist, Sharif Waked
Page 116 Fig. 50 Courtesy of the artist, Ivana Spinelli
Page 118 Fig. 51 Bettmann Archive/ Getty Images
Page 120 Fig. 52 David McNew/ Getty Images News
Page 121 Fig. 53 John Shearer/ Getty Images Entertainment
Fig. 54 Theo Wargo/Getty Images Entertainment
Fig. 55 Larry Busacca/Getty Images Entertainment
Page 125 Fig. 56 Library of Congress, Washington D.C.
Page 128 Fig. 57 Getty Images/Hulton Archive
Page 130 Fig. 58 Getty Images
Page 131 Fig. 59 Getty Images
Page 132 Fig. 60 Courtesy of P R Consulting, Paris/Raf Simons
Fig. 61 Dominique Charriau/WireImage/Getty Images
Page 134 Fig. 62 Cynthia Johnson/ The LIFE Images Collection/Getty Images
Page 136 Fig. 63 Joe Klamar/Agence France-Presse/Getty Images
Page 137 Fig. 64 Edward Berthelot/ Getty Images
Page 142 Above and right © The Nancy Spero and Leon Golub Foundation for the Arts/Licensed by VAGA, New York
Page 144 Courtesy of the artist, Köken Ergun
Page 146 Courtesy of the artist, Artur Żmijewski, and Galerie Peter Kilchmann, Zurich (see also page 5)
Page 148 Courtesy of the artist, Sharif Waked
Page 150 Courtesy of the artist, Sharif Waked
Page 152 Courtesy of the artist, Rineke Dijkstra, and Marian Goodman Gallery, New York, London, Paris
Page 153 Courtesy of the artist, Rineke Dijkstra, and Marian Goodman Gallery, New York, London, Paris

Page 154 Courtesy of the artist, Do Ho Suh, and Lehmann Maupin, New York and Hong Kong (see also page 7)
Page 156 Courtesy of the artist, Yoshua Okón, and Mor Charpentier Gallery, Paris
Page 158 Above and right Courtesy of the artist, Mella Jaarsma
Page 160 Courtesy of the artist, Kader Attia; installation view taken during *Streamlines. Welthandel und Migration*, exhib., Deichtorhallen, Halle für aktuelle Kunst, Hamburg, 04.12.2015–12.03.2016
Page 167 Fig. 65 Javier Sorano/ Getty Images
Page 171 Fig. 66 Anadolu Agency/ Getty Images
Page 173 Fig. 67 Bloomberg/ Getty Images
Page 174 Fig. 68 Bloomberg/ Getty Images
Fig. 69 Anadolu Agency/Getty Images
Page 175 Fig. 70 Rob Scott Photography
Page 176 Fig. 71 Press Association Images
Page 177 Fig. 72 Press Association Images
Page 180 Courtesy of Iziko Museums of South Africa
Right © Andrew Juries, 2017
Page 182 © Andrew Juries, 2017
Page 184 © Andrew Juries, 2017
Page 186 © Andrew Juries, 2017
Page. 188 © Andrew Juries, 2017
Page 189 © Andrew Juries, 2017
Page 190 © Andrew Juries, 2017
Page 194 © Andrew Juries, 2017
Page 197 Fig. 73 Homer Sykes Archive/Alamy Stock Photo
Page 200 Fig. 74 Heritage Images/ Getty Images
Fig. 75 Heritage Images/Getty Images
Page 205 Fig. 76 SOPA Images Limited/Alamy Stock Photo
Page 208 Fig. 77 Chris McGrath/ Getty Images
Page 209 Fig. 78 Chris McGrath/ Getty Images
Page 211 Fig. 79 Chris McGrath/ Getty Images (see also page 79)
Back cover See page 57, fig. 25

Index

First published by Yale
University Press 2019
302 Temple Street, P.O. Box
209040, New Haven CT
06520-9040

47 Bedford Square,
London WC1B 3DP
yalebooks.com /
yalebooks.co.uk

Text © 2019 The Authors

All rights reserved. This
book may not be reproduced
or transmitted in any form
or by any means, electronic
or mechanical, including
photocopy, recording or any
other information storage
and retrieval system (beyond
that copying permitted by
Sections 107 and 108 of the
US Copyright Law and except
by reviewers for the public
press), without prior permission
in writing from the publisher.

ISBN 978-0-300-238860 HB
Library of Congress Control
Number: 2019939700

10 9 8 7 6 5 4 3 2 1
2023 2022 2021 2020 2019

Designer: Kathrin Jacobsen
Copy-editor: Denny Hemming

Printed in Hong Kong

Front cover: Missoni, 'Pussy'
hats, Autumn/Winter 2017–18
Photographer Victor Boyko

page 2: Model Veruschka
as Chairman Mao,
French *Vogue*, guest editor
Salvador Dalí, December 1971
Photographer Alex Chatelain

page 7: Do Ho Suh, *Uni-Form/s:
Self-Portrait/s: My 39 Years*,
2006. Fabric, fibreglass resin,
stainless steel, casters,
169 x 254 x 56 cm

Back cover: The stripping and
beating of a veiled woman
during a demonstration in
Cairo's Tahrir Square,
17 December 2011

FSC MIX
Paper from
responsible sources
www.fsc.org FSC® C014688